PELICAN BOOKS

A550

THE TRIPLE THINKERS

EDMUND WILSON

THE TRIPLE THINKERS

Twelve Essays on Literary Subjects

BY

EDMUND WILSON

*

What is the artist if he is not a triple thinker?
Flaubert to Louise Colet

PENGUIN BOOKS

Penguin Books Ltd, Harmondsworth, Middlesex
AUSTRALIA: Penguin Books Pty Ltd, 762 Whitehorse Road,
Mitcham, Victoria

—

First published by John Lehmann 1952
Published in Pelican Books 1962

—

Made and printed in Great Britain
by C. Nicholls & Company Ltd
Set in Monotype Baskerville

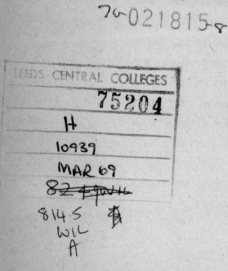

Contents

Acknowledgements

Acknowledgements are due to the *Atlantic Monthly*, the *Hound & Horn*, the *New Republic*, the *New Yorker*, and *Partisan Review*, in whose pages some of this material first appeared. *The Historical Interpretation of Literature* has been published by the Princeton University Press in a volume called *The Intent of the Critic*.

Foreword

THIS volume contains nine of the ten essays published under the same title in 1938, with three new ones: *Morose Ben Jonson, 'Mr Rolfe'*, and *The Historical Interpretation of Literature*. The old essays have been revised – in some cases, completely rewritten. I have never changed seriously the substance of what I wrote in the first edition, but I have sometimes allowed myself references to books which had not then been published – as when I have given Joyce's *Work in Progress* its eventual title of *Finnegans Wake* or mentioned Auden's preface to the new edition of Henry James's *The American Scene*. When I have wanted to note a new event or to add a new idea, I have put it in a postscript or a footnote.

I may take this occasion to comment on certain criticisms that have been made of these essays and of those in *The Wound and the Bow*. It has sometimes been complained in connexion with my studies of Dickens and Housman that, because I have had little to say about the humour of the former or the poetry of the latter, I must entirely have failed to appreciate the genius of my subjects. Now, my purpose has always been to try to contribute something new: I have aimed either to present some writer who was not well enough known or, in the case of a familiar writer, to call attention to some neglected aspect of his work or his career. I did not feel that there was anything fresh to say about either the humour of *Pickwick* or the pathos of the *Shropshire Lad*. I thought that I could assume that they were already well known to anyone with enough interest in literature to read a volume of literary criticism. But the classical scholarship of Housman in its bearing on his poetry and his personality and the social and moral criticism embodied in Dickens' later novels have not had justice done them. On the other hand, in the case of a writer like Pushkin or John Jay Chapman, I had to introduce him to a public who knew almost nothing about him, so I have started from the beginning and described his most obvious qualities.

Another objection is perhaps more valid. I have occasionally been accused of conveying too favourable an impression of certain rather imperfect works – notably, Dickens' later novels and Flaubert's *L'Éducation sentimentale* – by retelling them in such a way as to conjure out of sight their demerits. Well, it is true that it is pleasantly possible to go through a book that one has read before, skimming over the boring parts or disregarding some fundamental weakness, and that one can sometimes in this way arrive at the book that the author *intended* to write but did not quite fill in or rise to, and enjoy it as one could not do otherwise. When I reread *Our Mutual Friend*, for example, probably the weakest of Dickens' social novels, it is true that I leapt over the love scenes and the less successful grotesques, and got for the first time a good view of the general structure of the novel and the purport of its complicated parable, in such a way as is not always easy with even the best of Dickens, who so energetically plays on our interest with first one, then another, of his entertaining groups that we may miss the plan and the point. And so with *L'Éducation sentimentale*, if one can manage to displace one's attention from the hero, Frédéric Moreau, so that one is no longer bothered by his two-dimensional flatness and his lack of human development, one can survey for the first time the big canvas which Flaubert has animated, but to the historical and esthetic values of which – it is a real and grave fault – Frédéric tends to act as a non-conductor.

When I was writing about James, however, I did not review in this selective way the three long later novels that I had read first twenty years before; and it may be that, if I had done so, I should have given a somewhat different account. In looking into them again just now, I seemed sometimes to catch sight of qualities which I had not appreciated in my college days – at an age when James's lack of real 'love interest' is likely to prejudice one against him – and to which I feared I might not have done justice. But there is really no way of considering a book independently of one's special sensations in reading it on a particular occasion. In this as in everything else one must allow for a certain relativity. In a sense, one can never read the book that the author originally wrote, and one can never read the same book twice.

Mr More and the Mithraic Bull*

I MET Mr Paul Elmer More several times, but had an extended conversation with him only once. I wrote down a record of it at the time and give it here, as I wrote it then, embedded in a Princeton week-end.

I was taken to Mr More's house by Dean Gauss, who was one of his closest friends at Princeton. Dean Gauss, on this Saturday afternoon, had a special reason for wanting to consult him.

At that time – this visit took place in the December of 1929 – compulsory chapel had been partially abolished at Princeton, but it had been found desirable to make the students attend half the chapel services on Sundays in order to keep them in town over the week-ends. Those students who professed unorthodox views – and who were often, as it turned out, the same ones that wanted to spend Saturday night in Philadelphia or New York – were obliged to attend non-sectarian religious discussions which took place on Sunday evenings and were conducted by members of the faculty in rotation.

That month it had been Dean Gauss's turn, and he had begun on his first evening by attempting to find out how much the students knew about or were interested in religion. It had turned out that, though several boys believed in Heaven, nobody believed in the Devil; and when he had chalked up a list of theological words beginning with *infralapsarian* and *supralapsarian* and ending with *theism* and *deism*, it had been obvious that nobody knew anything about any of them. In dismissing the class, he had invited them to hand in questions which might stimulate discussion; and the sole response to this had been a letter written in Latin by a

* Written on the occasion of Paul Elmer More's death, 9 March 1937.

9

freshman and expressing a desire to learn something about Mithraism. Dean Gauss had decided to brush up on the subject by calling on Mr More, who had the history of religions at his fingertips.

Mr More had at that time just built himself a new house in the new residential section of Princeton near the Graduate School, and we approached it along a rainy new-laid pavement. The sitting-room, where we waited a few moments, was comfortable but rather sombre. With its walls densely lined with books, it was pre-eminently the room of a scholar – though there were a few carefully chosen articles of ornament: two small panes of Dutch stained glass, for example, which Mr More had brought back from Europe and had had inlaid in the glass of a large window at the further end of the room.

But Mr More did not make us wait long: he appeared almost at once, brisk enough, and greeted us with an alertness and an evident pleasure at having people come to see him, very attractive in a man of sixty-five. He was short and had picked up some of the plumpness that goes with a sedentary occupation. He had a Roman nose, a pale grey eye, and an iron lock of hair on his forehead – in general, a peculiar iron-grey aspect. There was in his face much strength and some nobility, but a curious absence of colour.

Affably he attended to the tea and began talking about T. S. Eliot, whom he had suggested inviting to Princeton to lecture. I was surprised to see how much he admired Eliot. He told us, in reply to our questions, that Eliot was 'tall and thin, quite strikingly good-looking', and that he, More, had gone to Eliot's house in London and had met people there. He explained to us that Eliot's grandfather had been chancellor of Washington University in St Louis at the time when he, More, had been a student there, so that he had already known the poet's family. And as he went on, I came to realize that it was for him a matter of deep gratification to have made the acquaintance of another writer of high intellectual distinction who had come like More himself out of that old Middle-Western world, who had the freedom of that literary life of Europe from which More's provincialism had largely shut him out, and who had been kind enough to bring More into contact with it – a man who, with all his brilliant reputation, his position as a god of the young, was yet a scholar and a serious critic, preoccupied with problems of morality, and striving, although by a different route, just as More himself was, to find his way back to the Christian religion.

We talked about Eliot's influence among the students, and More demurred over Eliot's poety. I asked him whether he didn't admire *The Waste Land*. 'Well, one can see', he conceded, 'that it's written by a man of parts.' But it seemed to be *The Hippopotamus* which presented the most serious difficulties. 'I must say that it reads aloud very well,' he confessed; but he couldn't understand what Eliot meant by it. I suggested that it was a satire on the Church. 'But', Mr More protested, 'I can't understand how Eliot reconciles that with his present position.' I reminded him that Eliot had written the poem a good many years before; but Mr More only shook his head and repeated that he could not reconcile those two things. Nor could he follow Eliot's enthusiasm for Baudelaire: 'It seems to me that he finds in Baudelaire . . . things that aren't there.' I admitted that there might be something in that, but asked him why he could not admire Baudelaire. 'Why,' he replied – he had an abrupt hesitation, as over the difficulty of dealing urbanely with a subject about which he felt so strongly, with an author of whom he so greatly disapproved, and upon whom, if he had been writing an essay, he would certainly have visited his stinging indignation – 'I'm old-fashioned about Baudelaire. I recognize his power – and his significance in his time – but as a guide to life – !' He stopped, and neither Gauss nor I tried to debate the matter further.

It was the moment of the great controversy over Humanism, and we tried to draw him out on this subject. I had been hearing from a friend at Harvard of the belief of the fanatical Babbitt that his doctrine was gradually but surely taking possession of all the ablest minds of the time, and of the legend, circulated among his students, that the old man had a great map in his study and stuck a thumb-tack into it at every point where a Humanist centre was supposed to have sprung up. But Mr More was much more sensible and less pretentious. When Gauss asked him whether he felt it was true that a great tide of Humanism was rising: 'Well,' he replied, 'I'd rather say that it was having a great splurge just now, but it's partly based on misunderstanding.' Yet he spoke with evident satisfaction of an article on Stuart P. Sherman which Seward Collins had recently published in the *Bookman*. Sherman had been the favourite disciple who had turned renegade to the Humanist band – the split had come when Sherman praised Whitman – and Seward Collins had now repudiated Sherman. 'It seems', remarked Mr More, 'as if something like a conversion had taken place there.'

Gauss and More discussed their first acquaintance. The Dean in those now remote days had been an eager young journalist and poet, just back from the Paris of the nineties, with long yellow hair and a flowing Latin Quarter tie, and he had written a furious letter of protest to More over a review of some French life of Sainte-Beuve which the latter had published in the Nation. 'It wasn't a slating, was it?' said More, almost chuckling at the memory of past ferocity. 'It was just a bit – contemptuous.' He had answered Gauss's letter and received a second letter equally violent. Then he had invited Gauss to lunch and had found him, he said, quite amiable and mild. One of the great sources of More's strength, I realized, lay in the fact that he always knew precisely what he thought and was always ready to face anybody down, uncompromisingly and promptly. I looked at Gauss: his golden locks were gone and had left a prodigiously high domed bald forehead. With his fine profile of a blond South German Dante, in his Princetonian soft shirt and tweed golf suit, he sat today, lying back in his chair, the great expounder of French romanticism, hobnobbing with the great anti-romantic. So much subtler a mind than More, with so much wider a range of imaginative sympathy, and correspondingly so much less fixed in his opinions, he looked out coolly through his eyeglasses without rims on those prejudices and principles of More's which years ago had aroused his indignation. The amenities and responsibilities of Princeton had dimmed the flamboyance of his romanticism. But Paul Elmer More, still just as positive, still nearly as narrow as then, sat attentively forward in his chair, still ready to face anybody down.

Dean Gauss now remembered Mithra and asked for light from Mr More on the subject. Mr More, who had the pride of learning, replied with immediate gusto: 'Why, I don't suppose I know any more about Mithraism than you do, Christian!' – At this moment there came into the room a sister of Mr More's, who lived with him. She was a pleasant old lady, with none of her brother's asperity – dressed in black and very deaf. She had just been going through her bureau-drawers, she said – 'And it's so hard to know what to throw away! It's really not worth the trouble trying to sort things!' Mr More admitted rather perfunctorily and speaking loudly in order to make her hear, that this did constitute a perplexing problem, and quickly brought the conversation back to Mithra.

'Well,' he demanded in a brisk businesslike manner, pouring his sister a cup of tea, 'what d'ye want to know about Mithraism, Christian?' His voice, nasal, clear, and Middle-Western, had a suggestion, not unattractive, of the homely plain-spoken manner of the old successful American merchant or banker. 'The Mithraic bee', began Gauss, 'was a symbol of immortality –' 'I've never heard of that,' Mr More caught him up. 'Where'd you find that?' 'I can't remember where,' replied Gauss. 'That's what I wanted to ask you. I read it years ago in some book and I can't remember now what it was. I thought you might know.' But Mr More did not know: he mentioned all the books he had read that dealt with Mithraism and said that there was nothing in any of them about it. What he knew, it was plain, he knew: he needed to consult no index. 'I suppose', Dean Gauss pursued, 'that the bee came to stand for immortality through the belief that bees were bred spontaneously in the carcasses of dead animals. It was really the carrion-fly. Virgil talks about it in the *Georgics*.' 'The "out of the strong came forth sweetness" of the Bible,' put in Mr More. 'Yes,' said Gauss. 'Clovis was a Mithraist –' 'That I didn't know,' said Mr More. 'Yes, Clovis was a Mithraist,' the Dean pursued, 'and his emblem before his conversion was the bee.' 'Is that a guess?' demanded Mr More. 'No,' said the Dean. 'I read it all somewhere, but I can't remember where.' Clovis's bee, which Mr More had never heard of and as to which, failing definite authority, he was not prepared to indulge in speculation, seemed to have made him a shade impatient. He delivered, however, a short lecture on what he did know about Mithraic myths; and it was amazing how much he knew and how accurately he was able to retail it. He traced Mithra, the God of Light, from the Vedic hymns into Persian mythology, and from the Orient into Greece, indicating his various transformations with confidence, lucidity, and logic, but with a curious effect of his having retained them as ideas without their passing through the picture-making imagination. And yet the Mithra he described was alive, devoid of mystery, form, or colour though he was. It reminded me of a book called *Error's Chains*, which I had used to look at in my grandfather's library and which had had many illustrations of the heathen gods, old line drawings done from paintings and statues. – Miss More was sitting beside me on the couch and could not hear the general conversation, so we talked separately from time to time while the discussion of Mithraism proceeded. 'You might just as well take it all out and burn it up!' she declared, still thinking of her bureau-drawers. 'When it's been accumulating as long as that, it's not worth the trouble to go through it and pick things out to save!'

At this point Mr Frank Jewett Mather arrived. He was a cheerful little man in a checked vest and spats, with the pocky pointed moustache of an old beau and the rosiness of a child. And he turned out to know a lot about Mithraism. He told us that it had had a great success with the Roman soldiers because it had promised them a sure immortality, and that it had developed in the third century into a serious competitor to Christianity. – Mr More's sister suddenly got up: 'I'm going to burn up all that old stuff!' she announced, with the air of one who has finally arrived at a thoroughly satisfactory resolution – and she said good-bye and went upstairs. – Mr Mather explained in detail the symbolism of Mithraic art. There was a Mithraic bull in the Museum, he said, which he had bought and brought back from Europe and which was one of the best things the Museum had. 'I didn't know that,' said Gauss with interest. 'I must go over and see it.' 'It's the best Mithraic bull on this side,' said Mather. 'The only really first-rate one.' It was a marble relief of the Sun-God holding a bull by the horns; there was a dog which was leaping at the throat of the bull and a snake which was attacking his testicles; the snake and the dog were Evil and Darkness. 'Let's go over and see it!' the Dean proposed to me.

Mr More now reverted to the days of the *Nation*. He told us that Oswald Garrison Villard had sometimes disapproved of what he wrote but had always had somebody else speak to him about it. Mr More seemed frankly delighted at this evidence that Villard had found him formidable. 'Afraid the "inner check" wouldn't work!' Frank Mather impishly put in. But Mr More possessed no technique to deal with people who made jokes about Humanism and did not deign to reply to this. 'Who originated the term "inner check"? Was it you or Babbitt?' asked Mather. 'I was the first to use it,' said More. 'In the *Shelburne Essays*. But Babbitt has made much more of it than I have.' And he added, after a moment's pause: 'I think the phrase occurs once in Emerson.'

In the course of the conversation that followed, Mr

Mather ventured to remark that he didn't see how Humanism was going to get us very far by going back to the Council of Chalcedon. Mr More was then nearing the completion of his series of volumes on Greek philosophy and Christianity. A man of true spiritual vocation, unable to remain a simple rationalist but prevented by a Protestant education and an obstinate hardheaded common sense from finding a basis in the mysticism of Rome, he had devoted long and diligent years to establishing an historical tradition which would justify his peculiar point of view. At that time he had just published the volume which brought the line of development to its climax with the promulgation at Chalcedon in the fifth century of the dogma of the Incarnation – a doctrine which, in laying down the dual nature of Christ, in representing him as both human and divine, had seemed to Mr More to make it possible for him to preserve the philosophy of Plato, so attractive to his intellectual and aesthetic side, and at the same time not to cut himself loose from the supernatural authority of religion. So he made no reply to this gibe – but presently, with a touch of severity, accused Mather of being 'a half-way Platonist like Santayana'. He seemed to me that day very clear-cut against the background of the college community. He was himself not really typical of the American academic world: he was an independent scholar, who had denounced in the most vigorous language the lack of sincerity and the incompetence of the colleges. He stood out, not merely through his distinction of learning, his Greek and Sanskrit and Hebrew and Persian and the rest, but by reason of his unremitting seriousness, his stubborn insistence on the importance of maintaining in one's relation to literature a position which should be realistic in the sense that it would never lose contact with moral problems as he himself understood them, his refusal to allow himself to be seduced by purely aesthetic or intellectual satisfactions. Gauss told him about a student at one of the Sunday-night meetings who had put himself down as a 'synthetic hedonist'; More smiled, but said, 'I wonder what he meant.'

We discussed an exhibition of modern art then on view in New York. Gauss thought Seurat essentially classical, but Mather insisted that he was decadent; Seurat's figures, he said, seemed to be perfectly realized, but actually they were hanging in the air, like the characters of Proust or Henry James, with no real connexion with anything. And this led us to contemporary writing. Mr More, who in a recent essay had allowed his intolerance of his contemporaries to go to lengths of positive ill temper in characterizing as 'an explosion in a cesspool' Dos Passos's *Manhattan Transfer*, conceded now, with an evident desire to be fair, that he 'recognized the element of protest in Dos Passos and Joyce'. I said that, though there was protest in Dos Passos, I did not believe there was any in Joyce, and thus unfortunately deprived Mr More of his only excuse for being polite about *Ulysses*. He was afterwards to give more serious consideration to such writers as Joyce and Proust. His last volume of *Shelburne Essays* contained papers on these two novelists, which, uncongenial to More though the subjects were, show more grasp of what is really at issue in their books than most of the stuff which has been written to exalt them. The moralist in Paul Elmer More, who had always been at war with the poet and who had scored over him so crushing a victory, could usually be counted upon to formulate clearly – though of course a clear formulation may misrepresent a poet – the case of any writer, however abhorrent, who had a serious moral basis, even though the provincial prig who inseparably accompanied the moralist might prevent him from appreciating the artist's achievement. But at that time I do not think he had read *Ulysses*; and I myself was a little touchy on the subject, as my attention had just been called by Gauss to an editorial in the *New York Times* that morning in which one of their anonymous writers had ridiculed an article of mine on Joyce. Now I was further dismayed, as it seemed to me that these three men, in their fields of literature and art certainly among the ablest in the country, were themselves disposed to outlaw from literature the greatest literary artist then alive. The same confounded old academic inertia! I thought; the same old proprietary interest in the classics, which made them unwilling to believe that anything new could have great value! I remembered how thirteen years before it had been the same thing about Bernard Shaw, then already practically a classic. Dean Gauss had read *Ulysses*, but had not liked it much; and, though it turned out that Mather, the old rascal, had investigated Mrs Bloom's soliloquy, he would not commit himself on the subject. Paul Elmer More, who, as I say, had evidently not yet read Joyce, began by trying to handle the matter without heat, but when I talked about the Homeric parallel – at the suggestion of such a fellow as Joyce's having the effrontery to associate himself with one of the major Greek classics – his arrogance suddenly started up from behind his deliberate urbanity, and he sharply cut down on the discussion – (it had also been a question of whether the characters in *Ulysses* were 'purposive' or mere passive recorders of impressions): 'But Homer's Ulysses knew what he wanted. He didn't need special explanations!' It seemed to me that there were so many misconceptions lodged behind this remark of Mr More's that I had difficulty in knowing how to deal with it. The conversation became rather confused and took on a slightly acrimonious accent. Somebody changed the subject, and Mr More proposed showing us his new house.

We went upstairs. On one side of the hallway which led to Mr More's study was a bookcase entirely filled with detective stories, which I was told he systematically graded with A's, B's, C's, and D's. On the shelves of his study were Plato and Plotinus and the Fathers of the Church. Frank Mather mischievously inquired where the Acts of the Council of Chalcedon were kept, and More as usual made no reply. The study was a small unpretentious room at the very top of the house: it had one large Morris chair and a table and a desk. On the walls hung two framed photographs, yellowish-brownish: one of Perugino's *Crucifixion* and the other of two battered Greek torsos, with both arms and legs broken off, awkwardly reclining together. They faced one another across the room, the Christian world and the Greek, and seemed to neutralize one another.

Then we descended and took our leave. Still chafing at More's attitude towards Joyce, I asked him, just as we were going out the door, whether he had ever read Eliot on *Ulysses*. He replied that he had not, and I told him that Eliot considered *Ulysses* a work of the highest importance. His whole attitude towards Eliot, so friendly before, seemed, as if by reflex action, to stiffen. 'I don't see', he retorted, 'what *Ulysses* has to do with Royalism, Anglo-Catholicism, and Classicism!' – and added, 'That young man has a screw loose somewhere!' 'Would you agree with Huneker', said Mather, 'that it's impossible for the same person really to like both Raphael and Goya?' 'I don't think', Mr More replied, 'that that pair is particularly well chosen; but I should say that a capacity for enjoying certain authors made it impossible to enjoy Dante or Shakespeare or Milton – or rather, I should say that, if a man liked certain things and claimed to enjoy Shakespeare and Dante, it would be impossible that he should really appreciate them!'

On this implacable dictum we went.

The next day I took a walk on the campus. It was dreary, misty, and damp. I remembered the Mithraic bull and decided to look it up in the Museum. There it was, sure enough, right opposite the front door as I went in, shining in the dim afternoon: the white marble relief of Mithra, a naked youth in a peaked Phrygian cap, clasping the sacred bull, which had the dog and the snake that were Darkness and Evil threatening its throat and its balls. But the Sun-God was to kill the bull, and thereby to conquer the darkness and to make himself the creator of life, all the multiform life of the earth, which was to spring from the bull's ebbing blood. There they hung – once the light of those pagan caves to which the soldiers from their doomed legions had crept, once the Apollonian rivals of the Crucified – there they

hung in the Princeton Museum on a Sunday afternoon!
I went on to the glass-cases inside, but – Roman busts,
Egyptian gods, Greek marbles – almost everything was a
reproduction and gave me the impression of being de-
natured and canned. The afternoon light was grey, the
rooms were becoming chill. I turned back and stood before
the Mithra, which – round and complete and glowing –
seemed the only thing alive in the Museum. I remembered
with what amazement, a wonder that became exaltation,
I had come upon the Apollo Belvedere when I had first
visited Rome as a child – how I had turned back to stare at
its beauty.

I went over to the University Library and sat down and
wrote the *Times* a caustic letter about their sneering editorial
on Joyce.

Then I went to see if Gauss were free. He had been busy all
the afternoon and had evidently had a great many people:
Sunday visitors, college officials, protesting parents of
students whom he had disciplined. He always gave his
closest attention to anything that was submitted for his
decision and dealt with it according to his most scrupulous
judgement; and I thought his mind was tired. And now he
had to prepare his talk for the evening religious meeting.
But he revived when I told him that I had been to see the bull
and was all for going to the Museum at once. He got his
hat and coat and stick, and we set out.

'It's curious', he mused on the way, 'how closely it
paralleled Christianity. They had a sacrifice, a communion,
and an atonement. The bull was killed in a cave, and that
symbolized the resurrection.' – He spoke of his affection for
More and told me a curious story. When More had come
back recently from Italy, he had announced with gratification and assurance that he had discovered the finest picture
in Florence. Gauss had said to him: 'I'll bet I can guess what
it is! Don't tell me – I'll bet I can guess what you think is the
finest picture in Florence!' – and he guessed Perugino's
Crucifixion. He was right; More had been quite taken aback.

'But how did you know?' I asked. 'Why should he have liked that picture particularly?' 'Why, you see Christ way up there – so far above the world.'

But when we got to the Museum, it was dark, and we found that the front door had been locked. We squinted at the marble through the glass, but it was scarcely visible now: we could make out only a whitish blue at the bottom of the cavernous entrance hall. We walked around the building and found a side-door unlocked and went in. Obstinately, we climbed stairs, explored galleries, invaded classrooms and studios for classes, with their chalky plaster casts of famous statues; but all the doors into the Museum proper turned out to be locked tight for the night. A late student in one of the classrooms suggested that we might try to find the curator; but the curator was not in his office, and all the other offices were dark.

We walked back across the campus and parted. The Dean had to go to the library to look up some more about Mithra, and I remained in his office to type out my letter on Joyce.

The visit long haunted my memory, and now the news of Mr More's death has brought it back into my mind: the empty academic week-end, the new suburban house, the meetings for the discussion of religion designed to bring the students back to town, the Acts of the Council of Chalcedon, the nice old lady with her firm resolution to burn all that old stuff up, the argument over Joyce, More himself with his lifelong consecration to that great world of culture and thought which he had succeeded in making real to others but which he could never quite rejoin himself, and Gauss and I peering at Mithra though the glass.

Is Verse a Dying Technique?

THE more one reads the current criticism of poetry by poets and their reviewers, the more one becomes convinced that the discussion is proceeding on false assumptions. The writers may belong to different schools, but they all seem to share a basic confusion.

This confusion is the result of a failure to think clearly about what is meant by the words 'prose', 'verse', and 'poetry' – a question which is sometimes debated but which never gets straightened out. Yet are not the obvious facts as follows?

What we mean by the words 'prose' and 'verse' are simply two different techniques of literary expression. Verse is written in lines with a certain number of metrical feet each; prose is written in paragraphs and has what we call rhythm. But what is 'poetry', then? What I want to suggest is that 'poetry' formerly meant one kind of thing but that it now means something different, and that one ought not to generalize about 'poetry' by taking all the writers of verse, ancient, medieval, and modern, away from their various periods and throwing them together in one's mind, but to consider both verse and prose in relation to their functions at different times.

The important thing to recognize, it seems to me, is that the literary technique of verse was once made to serve many purposes for which we now, as a rule, use prose. Solon, the Athenian statesman, expounded his political ideas in verse; the *Works and Days* of Hesiod are a shepherd's calendar in verse; his *Theogony* is versified mythology; and almost everything that in contemporary writing would be put into prose plays and novels was versified by the Greeks in epics or plays.

It is true that Aristotle tried to discriminate. 'We have no common name', he wrote, 'for a mime of Sophron or Xenarchus and a Socratic conversation; and we should still be without one even if the imitation in the two instances were in trimeters or elegiacs or some other kind of verse – though it is the way with people to tack on "poet" to the name of a metre, and talk of elegiac-poets and epic-poets, thinking that they call them poets not by reason of the imitative nature of their work, but indiscriminately by reason of the metre they write in. Even if a theory of medicine or physical philosophy be put forth in a metrical form, it is usual to describe the writer in this way; Homer and Empedocles, however, have really nothing in common apart from their metre; so that, if the one is to be called a poet, the other should be termed a physicist rather than a poet.'

But he admitted that there was no accepted name for the creative – what he calls the 'imitative' – art which had for its mediums both prose and verse; and his posterity followed the custom of which he had pointed out the impropriety by calling anything in metre a 'poem'. The Romans wrote treatises in verse on philosophy and astronomy and farming. The 'poetic' of Horace's *Ars Poetica* applies to the whole range of ancient verse – though Horace did think it just as well to mingle the 'agreeable' with the 'useful' – and this essay in literary criticism is itself written in metre. 'Poetry' remained identified with verse; and since for centuries both dramas and narratives continued largely to be written in verse, the term of which Aristotle had noticed the need – a term for imaginative literature itself, irrespective of literary techniques – never came into common use.

But when we arrive at the nineteenth century, a new conception of 'poetry' appears. The change is seen very clearly in the doubts which began to be felt as to whether Pope were really a poet. Now, it is true that a critic like Johnson would hardly have assigned to Pope the position of pre-eminence he does at any other period than Johnson's own; but it is *not* true that only a critic of the latter part of the eighteenth century, a critic of an 'age of prose', would have considered Pope a poet. Would not Pope have been considered a poet in any age before the age of Coleridge?

But the romantics were to redefine 'poetry'. Coleridge, in the *Biographia Literaria*, denies that any excellent work in metre may be properly called a 'poem'. 'The final definition ...' he says, 'may be thus worded. A poem is that species of composition which is opposed to works of science by proposing for its *immediate* object pleasure, not truth; and from all other species – (having *this* object in common with it) – it is discriminated by proposing to itself such delight from the *whole* as is compatible with a distinct gratification from each component part.' This would evidently exclude the *Ars Poetica* and the *De Rerum Natura*, whose immediate objects are as much truth as pleasure. What is really happening here is that for Coleridge the function of 'poetry' is becoming more specialized. Why? Coleridge answers this question in formulating an objection which may be brought against the first part of his definition: 'But the communication of pleasure may be the immediate object of a work not metrically composed; and that object may have been in a high degree attained, as in novels and romances.' Precisely; and the novels and romances were formerly written in verse, whereas they are now usually written in prose. In Coleridge's time, tales in verse were more and more giving place to prose novels. Before long, novels in verse such as *Aurora Leigh* and *The Ring and the Book* were to seem more or less literary oddities. 'Poetry', then, for Coleridge, has become something which, unless he amends his definition, may equally well be written in prose: Isaiah and Plato and Jeremy Taylor will, as he admits, be describable as 'poetry'. Thereafter, he seems to become somewhat muddled; but he finally arrives at the conclusion that the 'peculiar property of poetry' is 'the property of exciting a more continuous and equal attention than the language of prose aims at, whether colloquial or written'.

The truth is that Coleridge is having difficulties in attempting to derive his new conception of poetry from the literature of the past, which has been based on the old conception. Poe, writing thirty years later, was able to get a good deal further. Coleridge had said – and it seems to have been really what he was principally trying to say – that 'a poem of any length neither can be, nor ought to be, all poetry'. (Yet are not the *Divine Comedy* and Shakespeare's tragedies 'all poetry'? Or rather, in the case of these masterpieces, is not the work as a whole really a 'poem', maintained, as it is, at a consistently high level of intensity and style and with the effects of the different parts dependent on one another?) Poe predicted that 'no very long poem would ever be popular again', and made 'poetry' mean something even more special by insisting that it should approach the indefiniteness of music. The reason why no very long poem was ever to be popular again was simply that verse as a technique was then passing out of fashion in every department of literature except those of lyric poetry and the short idyll. The long poems of the past – Shakespeare's plays, the *Divine Comedy*, the Greek dramatists, and Homer – were going to continue to be popular; but writers of that calibre in the immediate future were not going to write in verse.

Matthew Arnold was to keep on in Coleridge's direction, though by a route somewhat different from Poe's. He said, as we have heard so repeatedly, that poetry was at bottom a criticism of life; but, though one of the characteristics which true poetry might possess was 'moral profundity', another was 'natural magic', and 'eminent manifestations of this magical power of poetry' were 'very rare and very precious'. 'Poetry' is thus, it will be seen, steadily becoming rarer. Arnold loved quoting passages of natural magic and he suggested that the lover of literature should carry around in his mind as touchstones a handful of such topnotch passages to test any new verse he encountered. His method of presenting the poets makes poetry seem fleeting and quintessential. Arnold was not happy till he had edited Byron and Wordsworth in such a way as to make it appear that their 'poetry' was a kind of elixir which had to be distilled from

25

the mass of their work – rather difficult in Byron's case: a production like *Don Juan* does not really give up its essence in the sequences excerpted by Arnold.

There was, to be sure, some point in what Arnold was trying to do for these writers: Wordsworth and Byron both often wrote badly and flatly. But they would not have lent themselves at all to this high-handed kind of anthologizing if it had not been that, by this time, it had finally become almost impossible to handle large subjects successfully in verse. Matthew Arnold could have done nothing for Dante by reducing him to a little book of extracts – nor, with all Shakespeare's carelessness, for Shakespeare. The new specialized idea of poetry appears very plainly and oddly when Arnold writes about Homer: the *Iliad* and the *Odyssey*, which had been for the Greeks fiction and scripture, have come to appear to this critic long stretches of ancient legend from which we may pick out little crystals of moral profundity and natural magic.

And in the meantime the ideas of Poe, developed by the Symbolists in France, had given rise to the 'Art poétique' of Verlaine, so different from that of Horace: 'Music first of all ... no Colour, only the *nuance*! ... Shun Point, the murderer, cruel Wit and Laughter the impure ... Take eloquence and wring its neck! ... Let your verse be the luck of adventure flung to the crisp morning wind that brings us a fragrance of thyme and mint – and all the rest is literature.'

Eliot and Valéry followed. Paul Valéry, still in the tradition of Poe, regarded a poem as a specialized machine for producing a certain kind of 'state'. Eliot called poetry a 'superior amusement', and he anthologized, in both his poems and his essays, even more fastidiously than Arnold. He, too, has his favourite collection of magical and quintessential passages; and he possesses an uncanny gift for transmitting to them a personal accent and imbuing them with a personal significance. And as even those passages of Eliot's poems which have not been imitated or quoted often seemed to have been pieced together out of separate lines and fragments, so his imitators came to work in broken mosaics and 'pinches of glory' – to use E. M. Forster's phrase about Eliot – rather than with conventional stanzas.

The result has been an optical illusion. The critic, when he read the classic, epic, eclogue, tale, or play, may have grasped it and enjoyed it as a whole; yet when the reader reads the comment of the critic, he gets the impression, looking back on the poem, that the *Divine Comedy*, say, so extraordinarily sustained and so beautifully integrated, is remarkable mainly for Eliot-like fragments. Once we know Matthew Arnold's essay, we find that the ἀνήριθμον γέλασμα of Aeschylus and the 'daffodils that come before the swallow dares' of Shakespeare tend to stick out from their contexts in a way that they hardly deserve to. Matthew Arnold, unintentionally and unconsciously, has had the effect of making the poet's 'poetry' seem to be concentrated in the phrase or the line.

Finally, Mr A. E. Housman, in his lecture on *The Name and Nature of Poetry*, has declared that he cannot define poetry. He can only become aware of its presence by the symptoms he finds it producing: 'Experience has taught me, when I am shaving of a morning, to keep watch over my thought, because if a line of poetry strays into my memory, my skin bristles so that the razor ceases to act. This particular symptom is accompanied by a shiver down the spine; there is another which consists in a constriction of the throat and a precipitation of water to the eyes; and there is a third which I can only describe by borrowing a phrase from one of Keats's last letters, where he says, speaking of Fanny Brawne, "everything that reminds me of her goes through me like a spear". The seat of this sensation is the pit of the stomach.'

One recognizes these symptoms; but there are other things, too, which produce these peculiar sensations: scenes from prose plays, for example (the final curtain of *The Playboy of the Western World* could make one's hair stand on end when it was first done by the Abbey Theatre), passages from prose novels (Stephen Daedalus's broodings over his mother's death in the opening episode of *Ulysses* and the end of Mrs Bloom's soliloquy), even scenes from certain historians, such as Mirabeau's arrival in Aix at the end of Michelet's *Louis XVI*, even passages in a philosophical dialogue: the conclusion of Plato's *Symposium*. Though Housman does praise a few long English poems, he has the effect, like those other critics, of creating the impression that 'poetry' means primarily lyric verse, and this only at its most poignant or most musical moments.

Now all that has been said here is, of course, not intended to belittle the value of what such people as Coleridge and Poe, Arnold and Eliot have written on the subject of poetry. These men are all themselves first-class poets; and their criticism is very important because it constitutes an attempt to explain what they have aimed at in their own verse, of what they have conceived, in their age, to be possible or impossible for their medium.

Yet one feels that in the minds of all of them a certain confusion persists between the new idea of poetry and the old – between Coleridge's conception, on the one hand, and Horace's, on the other; that the technique of prose is inevitably tending more and more to take over the material which had formerly provided the subjects for compositions in verse, and that, as the two techniques of writing are beginning to appear, side by side or combined, in a single work, it is becoming more and more impossible to conduct any comparative discussion of literature on a basis of this misleading division of it into the departments of 'poetry' and of 'prose'.

One result of discussion on this basis, especially if carried on by verse-writers, is the creation of an illusion that contemporary 'poets' of relatively small stature (though of however authentic gifts) are the true inheritors of the genius and carriers-on of the tradition of Aeschylus, Sophocles and Virgil, Dante, Shakespeare and Milton. Is it not time to discard the word 'poetry' or to define it in such a way as to take account of the fact that the most intense, the most profound, the most beautifully composed, and the most comprehensive of the great works of literary art (which for these reasons are also the most thrilling and give us the most prickly sensations while shaving) have been written sometimes in verse technique, sometimes in prose technique, depending partly on the taste of the author, partly on the mere current fashion. It is only when we argue these matters that we become involved in absurdities. When we are reading, we appraise correctly. Matthew Arnold cites examples of that 'natural magic' which he regards as one of the properties of 'poetry' from Chateaubriand and Maurice de Guérin, who did not write verse but prose, as well as from Shakespeare and Keats; and he rashly includes Molière among the 'larger and more splendid luminaries in the poetical heaven', though Molière was scarcely more 'poetic' in any sense except perhaps that of 'moral profundity' when he wrote verse than when he wrote prose and would certainly not have versified at all if the conventions of his time had not demanded it. One who has first come to Flaubert at a sensitive age when he is also reading Dante may have the experience of finding that the paragraphs of the former remain in his mind and continue to sing just as the lines of the latter do. He has got the prose by heart unconsciously just as he has done with favourite passages of verse; he repeats them, admiring the form, studying the choice of words, seeing more and more significance in them. He realizes that, though Dante may be greater than Flaubert, Flaubert belongs in Dante's class. It is simply that by Flaubert's time the Dantes present their visions in terms of prose drama or fiction rather than of epics in verse. At any other period, certainly, *La Tentation de Saint Antoine* would have been written in verse instead of prose.

And if one happens to read Virgil's *Georgics* not long after having read Flaubert, the shift from verse to prose technique gets the plainest demonstration possible. If you think of Virgil with Tennyson, you have the illusion that the Virgilian poets are shrinking; but if you think of Virgil with

Flaubert, you can see how a great modern prose-writer has grown out of the great classical poets. Flaubert somewhere – I think, in the Goncourt journal – expresses his admiration for Virgil; and, in method as well as in mood, the two writers are often akin. Flaubert is no less accomplished in his use of words and rhythms than Virgil; and the poet is as successful as the novelist in conveying emotion through objective statement. The *Georgics* were seven years in the writing, as *Madame Bovary* was six. And the fact that – in *Madame Bovary* especially – Flaubert's elegiac feeling as well as his rural settings run so close to the characteristic vein of Virgil makes the comparison particularly interesting. Put the bees of the *Georgics*, for example, whose swarming Virgil thus describes:

> *aethere in alto*
> *Fit sonitus, magnum mixtae glomerantur in orbem*
> *Praecipitesque cadunt*

besides the bees seen and heard by Emma Bovary on an April afternoon: '*quelquefois les abeilles, tournoyant dans la lumière, frappaient contre les carreaux comme des balles d'or rebondissantes*'. Put

> *Et iam summa procul villarum culmina fumant,*
> *Maioresque cadunt altis de montibus umbrae*

beside: '*La tendresse des anciens jours leur revenait au cœur, abondante et silencieuse comme la rivière qui coulait, avec autant de mollesse qu'en apportait le parfum des seringas, et projetait dans leurs souvenirs des ombres plus démesurées et plus mélancoliques que celles des saules immobiles qui s'allongeaient sur l'herbe.*' And compare Virgil's sadness and wistfulness with the sadness and nostalgia of Flaubert: the melancholy of the mountainous pastures laid waste by the cattle plague:

> *desertaque regna*
> *Pastorum, et longe saltus lateque vacantes*

with the modern desolations of Paris in *L'Éducation senti-*

mentale: '*Les rues étaient désertes. Quelquefois une charrette lourde passait, en ébranlant les pavés,*' etc.; or Palinurus, fallen into the sea, swimming with effort to the coast of Italy, but only to be murdered and left there 'naked on the unknown sand', while his soul, since his corpse lies unburied, must for ever be excluded from Hades, or Orpheus still calling Eurydice when his head has been torn from his body, till his tongue has grown cold and the echo of his love has been lost among the river banks – compare these with Charles Bovary, a schoolboy, looking out on fine summer evenings at the sordid streets of Rouen and sniffing for the good country odours '*qui ne venaient pas jusqu'à lui*' – ('*tendebantque manus ripae ulterioris amore*') – or with the scene in which Emma Bovary receives her father's letter and remembers the summers of her girlhood, with the galloping colts and the bumping bees, and knows that she has spent all her illusions in maidenhood, in marriage, in adultery, as a traveller leaves something of his money at each of the inns of the road.

We find, in this connexion, in Flaubert's letters the most explicit statements. 'To desire to give verse-rhythm to prose, yet to leave it prose and very much prose,' he wrote to Louise Colet (27 March 1853), 'and to write about ordinary life as histories and epics are written, yet without falsifying the subject, is perhaps an absurd idea. Sometimes I almost think it is. But it may also be a great experiment and very original.' The truth is that Flaubert is a crucial figure. He is the first great writer in prose deliberately to try to take over for the treatment of ambitious subjects the delicacy, the precision, and the intensity that have hitherto been identified with verse. Henrik Ibsen, for the poetic drama, played a role hardly less important. Ibsen began as a writer of verse and composed many short and non-dramatic poems as well as *Peer Gynt* and *Brand* and his other plays in verse, but eventually changed over to prose for the concentrated Sophoclean tragedies that affected the whole dramatic tradition. Thereafter the dramatic 'poets' – the Chekhovs, the Synges, and the Shaws (Hauptmann had occasional relapses) – wrote almost invariably in prose. It was by such that the soul of the time was given its dramatic expression: there was nothing left for Rostand's alexandrines but fireworks and declamation.

In the later generation, James Joyce, who had studied Flaubert and Ibsen as well as the great classical verse-masters, set out to merge the two techniques. Dickens and Herman Melville had occasionally resorted to blank verse for passages which they meant to be elevated, but these flights had not matched their context, and the effect had not been happy. Joyce, however, now, in *Ulysses*, has worked out a new medium of his own which enables him to exploit verse metrics in a texture which is basically prose; and he has created in *Finnegans Wake* a work of which we cannot say whether it ought, in the old-fashioned phraseology, to be described as prose or verse. A good deal of *Finnegans Wake* is written in regular metre and might perfectly well be printed as verse, but, except for the interpolated songs, the whole thing is printed as prose. As one reads it, one wonders, in any case, how anything could be demanded of 'poetry' by Coleridge with his 'sense of novelty and freshness with old and familiar objects', by Poe with his indefiniteness of music, by Arnold with his natural magic, by Verlaine with his nuance, by Eliot with his unearthliness, or by Housman with his bristling of the beard, which the *Anna Livia Plurabelle* chapter (or canto) does not fully supply.

If, then, we take literature as a whole for our field, we put an end to many futile controversies – the controversies, for example, as to whether or not Pope is a poet, as to whether or not Whitman is a poet. If you are prepared to admit that Pope is one of the great English writers, it is less interesting to compare him with Shakespeare – which will tell you something about the development of English verse but not bring out Pope's peculiar excellence – than to compare him with Thackeray, say, with whom he has his principal theme – the vanity of the world – in common and who throws into relief the more passionate pulse and the solider art of Pope. And so the effort to apply to Whitman the ordinary standards of verse has hindered the appreciation of his careful and exquisite art.

If, in writing about 'poetry', one limits oneself to 'poets' who compose in verse, one excludes too much of modern literature, and with it too much of life. The best modern work in verse has been mostly in the shorter forms, and it may be that our lyric poets are comparable to any who have ever lived, but we have had no imaginations of the stature of Shakespeare or Dante who have done their major work in verse. The horizon and even the ambition of the contemporary writer of verse has narrowed with the specialization of the function of verse itself. (Though the novelists Proust and Joyce are both masters of what used to be called 'numbers', the verses of the first are negligible and those of the second minor.)

Would not D. H. Lawrence, for example, if he had lived a century earlier, probably have told his tales, as Byron and Crabbe did: in verse? Is it not just as correct to consider him the last of the great English romantic poets as one of the most original of modern English novelists? Must we not, to appreciate Virginia Woolf, be aware that she is trying to do the kind of thing that the writers of verse have done even more than she is trying to do what Jane Austen or George Eliot were doing?

Recently the techniques of prose and verse have been getting mixed up at a bewildering rate – with the prose technique steadily gaining. You have had the verse technique of Ezra Pound gradually changing into prose technique. You have had William Faulkner, who began by writing verse, doing his major work in prose fiction without ever quite mastering prose, so that he may at any moment upset us by interpolating a patch of verse. You have had Robinson Jeffers, in narrative 'poems' which are as much novels as some of Lawrence's, reeling out yards of what are really prose dithyrambs with a loose hexametric base; and you have had Carl Sandburg, of *The People, Yes*, producing a queer kind of literature which oscillates between something like verse and something like the paragraphs of a newspaper 'column'.

Sandburg and Pound have, of course, come out of the old *vers libre*, which, though prose-like, was either epigrammatic or had the rhythms of the Whitmanesque chant. But since the Sandburg-Pound generation, a new development in verse has taken place. The sharpness and the energy disappear; the beat gives way to a demoralized weariness. Here the 'sprung-rhythm' of Gerard Manley Hopkins has sometimes set the example. But the difference is that Hopkin's rhythms convey agitation and tension, whereas the rhythms of MacNeice and Auden let down the taut traditions of lyric verse with an effect that is often comic and probably intended to be so – these poets are not far at moments from the humorous rhymed prose of Ogden Nash. And finally – what is very strange to see – Miss Edna St Vincent Millay in *Conversation at Midnight*, slackening her old urgent pace, dimming the ring of her numbers, has given us a curious example of metrics in full dissolution, with the stress almost entirely neglected, the lines running on for paragraphs, and even the rhymes sometimes fading out. In some specimens of this recent work, the beat of verse has been so slurred and muted that it might almost as well have been abandoned. We have at last lived to see the day when the ballads of Gilbert and Hood, written without metre for comic effect in long lines that look and sound like paragraphs, have actually become the type of a certain amount of serious poetry.

You have also the paradox of Eliot attempting to revive the verse-drama with rhythms which, adapting themselves to the rhythms of colloquial speech, run sometimes closer to prose. And you have Mr Maxwell Anderson trying to renovate the modern theatre by bringing back blank verse again – with the result that, once a writer of prose dialogue distinguished by some colour and wit, he has become, as a dramatic poet, banal and insipid beyond belief. The trouble is that no verse technique is more obsolete today than blank verse. The old iambic pentameters have no longer any relation whatever to the tempo and language of our lives. Yeats was the last who could write them, and he only because he inhabited, in Ireland and in imagination, a grandiose anachronistic world. You cannot deal with contemporary events in an idiom which was already growing trite in Tennyson's and Arnold's day; and if you try to combine the rhythm of blank verse with the idiom of ordinary talk, you get something – as in Anderson's *Winterset* – which lacks the merits of either. Nor can you try to exploit the worked-out rhythm without also finding yourself let in for the antiquated point of view. The comments on the action in *Winterset* are never the expression of sentiments which we ourselves could conceivably feel in connexion with the events depicted: they are the echoes of Greek choruses and Elizabethan soliloquies reflecting upon happenings of a different kind.

Thus if the poets of the Auden-MacNeice school find verse turning to prose in their hands, like the neck of the flamingo in Lewis Carroll with which Alice tried to play croquet, Mr Anderson, returning to blank verse, finds himself in the more awkward predicament of the girl in the fairy tale who could never open her mouth without having a toad jump out.

But what has happened? What, then, is the cause of this disuse into which verse technique has been falling for at least the last two hundred years? And what are we to expect in the future? Is verse to be limited now to increasingly specialized functions and finally to go out altogether? Or will it recover the domains it has lost?

To find out, if it is possible to do so, we should be forced to approach this change from the anthropological and sociological points of view. Is verse a more primitive technique than prose? Are its fixed rules like the syntax of languages, which are found to have been stiffer and more complicated the further back one goes? Aside from the question of the requirements of taste and the self-imposed difficulties of form which have always, in any period, been involved in the production of great works of art, does the easy flexibility, say, of modern English prose bear to the versification of Horace the same relation that English syntax bears to Horace's syntax, or that Horace's bears to that of the Eskimos?

It seems obvious that one of the important factors in the history of the development of verse must have been its relations with music. Greek verse grew up in fusion with music: verse and music were learned together. It was not till after Alexander the Great that prosody was detached from harmony. The Greek name for 'prose' was 'bare words' – that is, words divorced from music. But what the Romans took over and developed was a prosody that was purely literary. This, I believe, accounts for the fact that we seem to find in Greek poetry, if we compare it with Latin poetry, so little exact visual observation. Greek poetry is mainly for the ear. Compare a landscape in one of the choruses of Sophocles or Aristophanes with a landscape of Virgil or Horace: the Greeks are *singing* about the landscape, the Romans are fixing it for the eye of the mind; and it is Virgil and Horace who lead the way to all the later picture poetry down to our own Imagists. Again, in the Elizabethan age, the English were extremely musical: the lyrics of Campion could hardly have been composed apart from their musical settings; and Shakespeare is permeated with music. When Shakespeare wants to make us see something, he is always compelling and brilliant; but the effect has been liquefied by music so that it sometimes gives a little the impression of objects seen under water. The main stream of English poetry continues to keep fairly close to music through Milton, the musician's son, and even through the less organ-voiced Dryden. What has really happened with Pope is that the musical background is no longer there and that the ocular sense has grown sharp again. After this, the real music of verse is largely confined to lyrics – songs – and it becomes more and more of a trick to write them so that they seem authentic – that is, so that they sound like some-

36

thing sung. It was the aim of the late-nineteenth-century Symbolists, who derived their theory from Poe, to bring verse closer to music again, in opposition to the school of the Parnassians, who cultivated an opaque objectivity. And the excellence of Miss Millay's lyrics is obviously connected with her musical training, as the metrical parts of Joyce – such as the Sirens episode in *Ulysses*, which attempts to render music, the response to a song of its hearer – are obviously associated with his vocal gifts. (There is of course a kind of poetry which produces plastic effects not merely by picture-making through explicit descriptions or images, but by giving the language itself – as Allen Tate is able to do – a plastic quality rather than a musical one.)

We might perhaps see a revival of verse in a period and in a society in which music played a leading role. It has long played a great role in Russia; and in the Soviet Union at the present time you find people declaiming poetry at drinking parties or while travelling on boats and trains almost as readily as they burst into song to the accordion or the balalaika, and flocking to poetry-readings just as they do to concerts. It is possible that the Russians at the present time show more of an appetite for 'poetry', if not always for the best grade of literature, than any of the Western peoples. Their language, half-chanted and strongly stressed, in many ways extremely primitive, provides by itself, as Italian does, a constant stimulus to the writing of verse.

Here in the United States, we have produced some of our truest poetry in the folk-songs that are inseparable from their tunes. One is surprised, in going through the collections of American popular songs (of Abbé Niles and W. C. Handy, of Carl Sandburg, of the various students trained by Professor Kittredge), which have appeared during the last ten or fifteen years, to discover that the peopling of the continent has had as a by-product a body of folk-verse not unworthy of comparison with the similar material that went to make Percy's *Reliques*. The air of the popular song will no doubt be carrying the words that go with it into the 'poetry' anthologies of the future when many of the set-pieces of 'poetry', which strain to catch a music gone with Shakespeare, will have come to seem words on the page, incapable of reverberation or of flight from between the covers.

Another pressure that has helped to discourage verse has undoubtedly been the increased demand for reading matter which has been stimulated by the invention of the printing press and which, because ordinary prose is easier to write than verse, has been largely supplied by prose. Modern journalism has brought forth new art-forms; and you have had not only the masterpieces of fiction of such novelists as Flaubert and Joyce, who are also consummate artists in the sense that the great classical poets were, but also the work of men like Balzac and Dickens which lacks the tight organization and the careful attention to detail of the classical epic or drama, and which has to be read rapidly in bulk. The novels of such writers are the epics of societies: they have neither the concision of the folk-song nor the elegance of the forms of the court; they sprawl and swarm over enormous areas like the city populations they deal with. Their authors, no longer schooled in the literary tradition of the Renaissance, speak the practical everyday language of the dominant middle class, which has destroyed the Renaissance world. Even a writer like Dostoyevsky rises out of this weltering literature. You cannot say that his insight is less deep, that his vision is less noble or narrower, or that his mastery of his art is less complete than that of the great poets of the past. You can say only that what he achieves he achieves by somewhat different methods.

The technique of prose today seems thus to be absorbing the technique of verse; but it is showing itself quite equal to that work of the imagination which caused men to call Homer 'divine': that recreation, in the harmony and logic of words, of the cruel confusion of life. Not, of course, that we shall have Dante and Shakespeare redone in some prose form any more than we shall have Homer in prose. In art the same things are not done again or not done again except as copies. The point is that literary techniques are tools, which the masters of the craft have to alter in adapting them to fresh uses. To be too much attached to the traditional tools may be sometimes to ignore the new masters.

*

1948. The recent work of W. H. Auden has not shown a running-to-seed of the tendencies mentioned above, but has on the contrary taken the direction of returning to the older tradition of serviceable and vigorous English verse. His *New Year Letter* must be the best specimen of purely didactic verse since the end of the eighteenth century, and the alliterative Anglo-Saxon metre exploited in *The Age of Anxiety* has nothing in common with prose. It may, however, be pointed out, for the sake of my argument above, that in the speech of the girl over the sleeping boy in the fifth section of the latter poem, the poet has found it easy to slip into the rhythms and accents of Mrs Earwicker's half-prose soliloquy at the end of *Finnegans Wake*.

In Honour of Pushkin

I. EVGENY ONEGIN*

ANYONE who has read criticism by foreigners, even well-informed criticism, of the literature of his own country knows what a large part of it is likely to be made up of either banalities or errors. In the case of a novice at Russian like the writer, this danger is particularly great; and I shall probably be guilty of many sins in the eyes of Russian readers who should happen to see this essay. But Pushkin, the hundredth anniversary of whose death is being celebrated this year by the Soviets, has in general been so little appreciated in the English-speaking countries that I may, perhaps, be pardoned for however imperfect an attempt to bring his importance home to English-speaking readers. And Evgeny Onegin, who has played such a role for the Russian imagination, really belongs among those figures of fiction who have a meaning beyond their national frontiers for a whole age of Western society. The English Hamlet was as real, and as Russian, to the Russians of the generations that preceded the Revolution as any character in Russian literature. Let us receive Evgeny Onegin as a creation equally real for us.

It has always been difficult for Westerners – except perhaps for the Germans, who seem to have translated him more successfully than anyone else – to believe in the greatness of Pushkin. We have always left him out of account. George Borrow, who visited Russia in the course of his work for the Bible Society, published some translations of Pushkin in 1835; but the conventional world of literature knew little or nothing about him. Three years after Pushkin's death (and when Lermontov's career was nearly over), Carlyle, in *Heroes and Hero Worship*, described Russia as a 'great dumb

* Written for the centenary of Pushkin's death, 29 January 1937.

monster', not yet matured to the point where it finds utterance through the 'voice of genius'. Turgenev struggled vainly with Flaubert to make him recognize Pushkin's excellence; and even Renan was so ignorant of Russian literature that it was possible for him to declare on Turgenev's death that Russia had at last found her voice. Matthew Arnold, in writing about Tolstoy, remarked complacently that 'the crown of literature is poetry' and that the Russians had not yet had a great poet; and T. S. Eliot, not long ago, in a discussion of the importance of Greek and Latin, was insisting on the inferior educational value of what he regarded as a merely modern literature like Russian, because 'half a dozen great novelists' – I quote from memory – 'do not make a culture'. Even today we tend to say to ourselves, 'If Pushkin is really as good as the Russians think he is, why has he never taken his place in world literature as Dante and Goethe have, and as Tolstoy and Dostoyevsky have?'

The truth is that Pushkin *has* come through into world literature – he has come through by way of the Russian novel. Unlike most of the poets of his period, he had the real dramatic imagination, and his influence permeates Russian fiction – and theatre and opera as well. Reading Pushkin for the first time, for a foreigner who has already read later Russian writers, is like coming for the first time to Voltaire after an acquaintance with later French literature: he feels that he is tasting the pure essence of something which he has found before only in combination with other elements. It is a spirit whose presence he has felt and with whom in a sense he is already familiar, but whom he now first confronts in person.

For the rest, it is true that the poetry of Pushkin is particularly difficult to translate. It is difficult for the same reason that Dante is difficult: because it says so much in so few words, so clearly and yet so concisely, and the words themselves and their place in the line have become so much more important than in the case of more facile or rhetorical writers.

It would require a translator himself a poet of the first order to reproduce Pushkin's peculiar combination of intensity, compression, and perfect ease. A writer like Pushkin may easily sound 'flat', as he did to Flaubert in French, just as Cary's translation of Dante sounds flat. Furthermore, the Russian language, which is highly inflected and able to dispense with pronouns and prepositions in many cases where we have to use them and which does without the article altogether, makes it possible for Pushkin to pack his lines (separating modifiers from substantives, if need be) in a way which renders the problem of translating him closer to that of translating a tightly articulated Latin poet like Horace than any modern poet that we know. Such a poet in translation may sound trivial just as many of the translations of Horace sound trivial – because the weight of the words and the force of their relation have been lost with the inflections and the syntax.

So that, failing any adequate translation, we have tended, if we have thought about Pushkin at all, to associate him vaguely with Byronism: we have heard that *Evgeny Onegin* is an imitation of *Don Juan*. But this comparison is very misleading. Pushkin was a great artist: he derived as much from André Chénier as from Byron. *Don Juan* is diffuse and incoherent, sometimes brilliant, sometimes silly; it has its unique excellence, but it is the excellence of an improvisation. Byron said of some of the cantos that he wrote them on gin, and essentially it is a drunken monologue by a desperately restless, uncomfortable man, who does not know what is the matter with him or what he ought to do with himself, who wants to tell stories about other things or to talk about himself in such a way as to be able to laugh and curse and grieve without looking into anything too closely. Byron's achievement, certainly quite remarkable, is to have raised the drunken monologue to the dignity of a literary form. But the achievement of Pushkin is quite different. He had, to be sure, learned certain things from Byron – for example, the tone of easy negligence with which

Evgeny Onegin begins and the habit of personal digression; but both of these devices in Pushkin are made to contribute to a general design. *Evgeny Onegin* is the opposite of *Don Juan* in being a work of unwavering concentration. Pushkin's 'novel in verse' came out of Pushkin's deepest self-knowledge and was given form by a long and exacting discipline. The poet had adopted a compact speech and a complicatee stanza-form as different as possible from Byron's doggerel; and he worked over the three hundred and eighty-nine stanzas which fill about two hundred pages through a period of eight years (1823–31) and was still, with every successive edition, revising them and cutting them down up to the time of his death.

One can convey a much more accurate impression of what Pushkin's actual writing is like by comparing him to Keats than to Byron. There are passages in *Evgeny Onegin*, such as those that introduce the seasons, which have a felicity and a fullness of detail not unlike Keats's *Ode to Autumn* – or, better perhaps, the opening of *The Eve of St Agnes*, which resembles them more closely in form:

> St Agnes' Eve – ah, bitter chill it was!
> The owl, for all his feathers, was a-cold;
> The hare limp'd trembling through the frozen grass,
> And silent was the flock in woolly fold:
> Numb were the Beadsman's fingers while he told
> His rosary, and while his frosted breath,
> Like pious incense from a censer old,
> Seem'd taking flight for heaven without a death,
> Past the sweet Virgin's picture, while his prayer he saith.

Here is Pushkin's description of the coming of winter:

'Already now the sky was breathing autumn, already the dear sun more seldom gleamed, shorter grew the day, the forest's secret shadow was stripped away with sighing sound, mist lay upon the fields, the caravan of loud-tongued geese stretched toward the south: drew near the duller season; November stood already at the door.

'Rises the dawn in cold murk; in the fields the sound of work is still; the wolf with his hungry mate comes out upon the road; sniffing, the road-horse snorts – and the traveller who is wise makes full speed up the hill; the herdsman now at last by morning light no longer drives his cattle from the byre; at midday to their huddle his horn no longer calls them; inside her hut, the farm girl, singing, spins, while – friend of winter nights – her little flare of kindling snaps beside her.

'And now the heavy frosts are snapping and spread their silver through the fields . . . smoother than a smart parquet glistens the ice-bound stream. The merry mob of little boys with skates cut ringingly the ice; on small red feet the lumbering goose, hoping to float on the water's breast, steps carefully but slips and topples; gaily the first snow flashes and whirls about, falling in stars on the bank.'

If you can imagine this sort of thing, which I have translated more or less literally, done in something like Keats's marrowy line, you will get some idea of what Pushkin is like. He can make us see and hear things as Keats can, but his range is very much greater: he can give us the effect in a few lines of anything from the opening of a bottle of champagne or the loading and cocking of pistols for a duel to the spinning and skipping of a ballet girl – who 'flies like fluff from Aeolus' breath' – or the falling of the first flakes of snow. And as soon as we put the *Eve of St Agnes* (published in 1820) beside *Evgeny Onegin*, it seems to us that Keats is weakened by an element of the conventionally romantic, of the mere storybook picturesque. But Pushkin can dispense with all that: here everything is sharp and real. No detail of country life is too homely, no phase of city life too worldly, for him to master it by the beauty of his verse. Artistically, he has outstripped his time; and neither Tennyson in *In Memoriam* nor Baudelaire in *Les Fleurs du Mal* was ever to surpass Pushkin in making poetry of classical precision and firmness out of a world realistically observed.

I should note also – what I have never seen mentioned – that the passages of social description often sound a good deal more like Praed than like Byron. It is not likely that Pushkin was influenced by Praed, since Praed's poems began to appear in *Knight's Quarterly* only in 1823, the year that *Onegin* was begun, and his characteristic vein of *vers de société* seems to date only from 1826, in which year Pushkin completed his sixth chapter. But the stanza in Chapter Two, with its epitaph, on the death of Tatyana's father might have been imitated from Praed's poem *The Vicar*, and if you can imagine Praed's talent raised to a higher power and telling a long story in his characteristically terse and witty stanzas (Pushkin's measure is shorter than Byron's, a rapid tetrameter like Praed's), you will be closer to Pushkin than *Don Juan* will take you:

> Good night to the Season! – the dances,
>   The fillings of hot little rooms,
> The glancings of rapturous glances,
>   The fancyings of fancy costumes;
> The pleasures which Fashion makes duties,
>   The praisings of fiddles and flutes,
> The luxury of looking at Beauties,
>   The tedium of talking to Mutes;
> The female diplomatists, planners
>   Of matches for Laura and Jane;
> The ice of her Ladyship's manners,
>   The ice of his Lordship's champagne.

To have written a novel in verse, and a novel of contemporary manners, which was also a great poem was Pushkin's unprecedented feat – a feat which, though anticipated on a smaller scale by the tales in verse of Crabbe and several times later attempted by nineteenth-century poets, was never to be repeated. And when we think of *Evgeny Onegin* in connexion with *Don Juan* or *The Ring and the Book* or *Aurora Leigh* or *Evangeline* we find that it refuses to be classed with them. Pushkin's genius, as Maurice Baring has said, has more in common with the genius of Jane Austen than

with the general tradition of the nineteenth-century novel.
It is classical in its even tone of comedy which is at the same
time so much more serious than the tragedies of Byron ever
are, in its polishing of the clear and rounded lens which
focuses the complex of human relations.

But Pushkin is much more vigorous than Jane Austen:
the compression and rigour of the verse cause the characters
to seem to start out of the stanzas. And he deals with more
violent emotions. *Evgeny Onegin* is occupied with Byronism
in a different way than that of deriving from Byron: it is
among other things an objective study of Byronism. Both
in the poem itself and in a letter that Pushkin wrote while
he was working on it, he makes significant criticisms of
Byron. 'What a man this Shakespeare is!' he exclaims.
'I can't get over it. How small the tragic Byron seems beside him! – that Byron who has been able to imagine but a
single character: his own . . . Byron simply allots to each of
his characters some characteristic of his own: his pride to
one, his hatred to another, his melancholy to a third, etc.,
and thus out of a character which is in itself rich, sombre,
and energetic, he makes several insignificant characters;
but that is not tragedy.' And in *Evgeny Onegin*, he speaks of
Byron's 'hopeless egoism'. Pushkin has been working away
from his early romantic lyricism towards a Shakespearean
dramatization of life, and now he is to embody in objective creations, to show involved in a balanced conflict,
the currents of the age which have passed through him.
Evgeny Onegin is presented quite differently from any of
the romantic heroes of Byron or Chateaubriand or Musset:
when Byron dropped the attitudes of Childe Harold, the
best he could do with Don Juan was to give him the innocence
of Candide. Evgeny differs even from his immediate successor and kinsman, Lermontov's Hero of Our Time –
because Lermontov, though he tells his story with the dis-
tinctive Russian realism absent in the other romantic
writers, is really involved to a considerable degree with the
attitudes of his hero; whereas Pushkin, in showing us Evgeny,

neither exalts him in the perverse romantic way nor yet, in exposing his weakness, hands him over to conventional morality. There is, I think, but one creation of the early nineteenth century who is comparable to Evgeny Onegin: Stendhal's Julien Sorel; and the poem is less akin to anything produced by the romantic poets than it is to *Le Rouge et le Noir* and *Madame Bovary*.

Our first glimpse of Pushkin's hero is not an ingratiating one: he has just been summoned to the bedside of a dying uncle, whose estate he is going to inherit, and he is cursing at the tiresome prospect of sitting around till the old man dies. But the scene is shifted at once to his previous life in St Petersburg. He has been a young man about town, who has had everything society can give him. We see him at the restaurant, the opera, the ball; in one masterly passage we are shown him falling asleep after a round of the pleasures of the capital while the Petersburg of the merchants and cabmen and peddlers is just waking up for the day. But Evgeny is intelligent: he gets tired of his friends, tired of his love affairs. He is infected with the 'English spleen' and grows languid and morose like Childe Harold. He shuts himself up to write, but he finds it terribly hard and gives it up. Then his uncle dies, and he inherits the estate and goes to live in the country.

The country bores him, too. Being a man of liberal ideas, he tries to lighten the lot of his serfs, and the neighbours decide he is a dangerous fellow. Then there appears in the neighbourhood a young man named Lensky with whom Evgeny finds he has something in common. Lensky has just come back from Göttingen and is saturated with German idealism; and he is a poet in the German-romantic vein. Evgeny thinks him callow and naïve, but tries not to throw cold water on his illusions. He likes Lensky, and they go riding and have long arguments together.

Lensky is in love in the most idealistic fashion with a girl whom he has known since childhood and to whom he has always been faithful. She is pretty but entirely uninteresting: Pushkin tells us that she is just like the heroines of all the popular love stories of the day. Lensky goes to see her every evening – she lives with her sister and her widowed mother on a nearby estate – and one day takes Evgeny with him. Evgeny has sarcastically told Lensky in advance what the refreshments and the conversation will be like – the Larins will be just a 'simple Russian family'; and on the drive back home he remarks that the face of Lensky's worshipped sweetheart is lifeless, red, and round 'like this silly moon over this silly horizon', and remarks that if *he* were a poet like Lensky, he would have preferred the older sister, who had sat sadly by the window and said nothing.

This older sister, Tatyana, is 'wild, melancholy, silent, and shy' and not so pretty as Olga. As a child, she hadn't liked games and hadn't been fond of dolls; she had thought it was funny to mimic her mother by lecturing her doll on how young ladies ought to comport themselves. Now her head is full of Richardson and Rousseau, and she likes to get up before dawn and watch the stars fade and the distance grow bright and feel the morning wind. And now, from the first moment she sees him, she falls furiously in love with Evgeny. She waits for a time in silence; then, as Evgeny does not come to call again, she sits down and writes him a letter, in which, painfully, uncontrollably, innocently, she confesses to him her love. This chapter, which deals with Tatyana's letter, is one of the great descriptions of first love in literature. Pushkin renews for us as we read all the poignancy and violence of those moments when for the first time the emotional forces of youth are released by another human being and try to find their realization through him. All the banal and deluded things that young people say and feel – that Evgeny is the one man in the world for her, the man for whom she has been waiting all her life, that he has been appointed by God to be her protector, that she is all alone and that no one understands her – poor Tatyana believes them all and puts them all into her letter; and Pushkin has succeeded in giving them to us in all their banality and deludedness, with no romantic sentimentalization, and yet making them move us profoundly. We enter into the emotions of Tatyana as we do into those of Juliet, yet at the same time Pushkin has set the whole picture in a perspective of pathetic irony which is not in that early play of Shakespeare's: there is nothing to indicate that Shakespeare's lovers might not have been ideally happy if it had not been for the family feud; but, in the case of Tatyana, we know from the first moment that her love is hopelessly misplaced in Evgeny. And the whole thing is set off and rooted in life by a series of marvellous touches – Tatyana's conversation with the nurse, the song she hears the serf-girls singing – and saturated with the atmosphere of the country estate where Tatyana has spent her whole life and where – so amazing is Pushkin's skill at evoking a complete picture through suggestion, needing only a few hundred lines where a novelist would take as many pages – we feel by the time she leaves it that we have lived as long as she.

Evgeny does not answer the letter, but two days afterwards he comes to see her. The role of the seducer is *passé*: it went out with periwigs and red heels; and for Evgeny the time for great passions is past: it is too much trouble to do anything about Tatyana. He conducts himself honourably, he talks to her kindly. He tells her that, if he had any desire for family life, she would certainly be the woman he would choose for a wife. But he was not created for happiness, such satisfactions are foreign to his soul. As a husband, he would be gloomy and disagreeable, and he would eventually cease to love her. He makes quite a long speech about it. And he tells her that she ought to learn to control herself: another man might not understand as he does. Tatyana listens silently, in tears. He gives her his arm and leads her back to the house.

But now Evgeny takes an unexpected turn. The Larins give a big evening party to celebrate Tatyana's Saint's Day.

Evgeny goes and sits opposite Tatyana and realizes that she is still in love with him and frightened to death in his presence. He thinks that he is angry with Lensky because the party has turned out a bore and Lensky has brought him there on false pretences. He has for months been watching Lensky moon over Olga with his eternal romantic devotion which treats the beloved object with a reverence almost religious and never makes any practical advances; and he sets out now to annoy the young poet by getting Olga away from him for the evening. Evgeny makes Olga dance with him repeatedly, pays her animated attentions – to which, as she is incapable of saying no, she almost automatically responds. Lensky is deeply hurt and furious; he leaves the party and goes straight home and writes Evgeny a note calling him out.

Evgeny's first impulse, when he receives the challenge, is to set things right with Lensky, not to let the young man make a fool of himself. But then he is moved, as he tells himself, by the fear of public opinion: the second by whom Lensky has sent the challenge, though a thoroughly disreputable individual, is an old-fashioned fancier and promoter of duels. The night before they are to meet, Lensky sits up till morning writing poetry. Evgeny sleeps sound and late; he arrives on the field with his French valet, whom he insolently presents as his second. The adversaries are stationed by their seconds and take their paces toward one another. Evgeny, as he is still approaching, quietly raises his pistol, and he shoots while Lensky is aiming. Lensky falls: in a remarkable simile, characteristically realistic and exact, Pushkin tells us how the young man's heart, in which a moment before all the human passions were dwelling, becomes suddenly like an abandoned house blinded and dark and silent, with the windows covered with chalk and the owner gone away. Evgeny has killed in the most cynical fashion a man whose friend he had believed himself to be and whom he had thought he did not want to kill. Now at last we are sure of what Pushkin, who has always given us Evgeny's version of his own motives, has only so far in various ways suggested: that, for all Lensky's obtuseness and immaturity, Evgeny has been jealous of him, because Lensky has been able to feel for Olga an all-absorbing emotion whereas Evgeny, loved so passionately by Tatyana, has been unable to feel anything at all. Lensky, the author now tells us, might or might not have become a good poet; but the point is, as he lets us know without telling us, that it is the poet in Lensky whom Evgeny has hated. Evgeny had wanted to write; but when he had sat down with the paper before him, he had found it was too much trouble.

After the duel, Evgeny leaves the countryside. Lensky is soon forgotten by Olga. She says yes to an uhlan, who takes her off when he goes to join his regiment. Tatyana is left alone. She walks over to Evgeny's house and gets the caretaker to let her in: and there she returns day after day and reads the books – so much more up to date than Richardson and Rousseau – which she has found in Evgeny's library. There are a picture of Byron on the wall and a little iron statue of Napoleon; and, for the first time, Tatyana reads Byron, as well as several fashionable novels which reflect the fashionable attitudes of the day. Evgeny has marked them and made notes in the margin: and now his lecture to her after her letter begins to have the sound of an echo of all the things he has read.

But Tatyana continues to languish, doesn't get married. Her mother decides to take her to Moscow. There follows a wonderful description of the Larin family travelling to Moscow. Pushkin, with his infinite sympathy and his equally universal detachment, puts on record characteristics and customs of the Russians which are still striking to a foreigner today. The Larins set several dates to get off, but they never get off on those dates. Then at last they do get off and get there. Now the leafy and mazy and timeless estate is far behind Tatyana, and she sees the gold crosses of the churches and then the people and shops and palaces of Moscow. The shift from country to town is beautifully handled by Pushkin; and there is nothing in fiction more remarkable in its way than the account of Tatyana's first days in Moscow. It is the

forerunner of the social scenes in *War and Peace*, and Natasha
Rostova and her family seem related to Tatyana and hers,
just as Tolstoy's Moscow originals must have been to Pushkin's. The Moscow cousin, to whose house Tatyana and her
mother first go and where an old Kalmuck in a ragged caftan
and spectacles lets them in, had been in love, before she was
married, with a dandy whom she had thought another Sir
Charles Grandison; and now the first thing she says to
Tatyana's mother, in whom she had used to confide, is,
'Cousin, do you remember Grandison?' ' What Grandison?
Oh, Grandison! – of course, I remember: where is he?' 'He's
living in Moscow now; he came to see me at Christmas; he
married off his son not long ago.' – But the fashion of the
younger generation – we are not told whether or not Tatyana
makes this reflection – is for Byron instead of Grandison.

Tatyana cannot at first take her place in this world. Her
cousins, though urban, are nice; they look her over and decide
she is nice. They confide in her, but she cannot return their
confidences: she moves among them detached, distracted.
She goes to dinner to be shown to her grandparents: '"How
Tanya has grown! " they say. "Wasn't it just the other day I
christened you? and *I* used to carry you in my arms! And *I*
boxed your ears! And *I* used to feed you gingerbread!" And
the old ladies in chorus would keep repeating: "How our
years fly by!" – But they – in them she could see no change;
it was all on the same old pattern: her aunt, the Princess
Helena, still had the same tulle bonnet, Lukerya Lvovna
still powdered herself just as much, Lyubov Petrovna still
told the same lies, Ivan Petrovich was still just as silly, Semen
Petrovich was still just as stingy, Pelagya Nikolavna still had
the same friend, M. Finemouche, and the same Pomeranian
and the same husband; and her husband was just as punctual
at his club and just as meek and just as deaf as ever, and still
ate and drank enough for two.' One night at a ball, her
solicitous aunt whispers to her to look to the left. An im-
portant-looking general is staring at her. 'Who?' she asks.
'That fat general?'

When Evgeny returns from his travels and goes into society again, he sees at a ball an extraordinarily smart lady who combines perfect naturalness with great dignity, whom everybody wants to speak to and to whom everybody defers; and he gasps at her resemblance to Tatyana. He inquires who she is of a man he knows. 'My wife,' the friend replies. It is Tatyana, now a princess; the man is the pompous general. Tatyana meets Evgeny without batting an eyelash: she asks him whether he has been long in St Petersburg and whether he doesn't come from her part of the world.

Evgeny pays her court, follows her everywhere; but she refuses to recognize him. He writes her a letter, which is the counterpart of hers: now the roles are reversed – it is he who is putting himself at her mercy. She doesn't answer: he writes again and again. Then he shuts himself up in his house, cuts himself off from society, and gives himself up to serious reading: history and moral philosophy. But Lensky gets between him and the page, and he hears a voice that says, 'What, killed?' and he sees all the malicious gossips and the mean cowards and the young jilts and bitches whom he has known in Petersburg society and whom he has wanted to get away from and forget, and he sees Tatyana in the country house, sitting silent beside the window, as on the day when he first called.

Suddenly, one day when the winter snow is melting, he gets into his sleigh and drives off to her house. There is no one in the hall: he walks in. He finds her reading his letters. He throws himself at her feet. She looks at him without anger or surprise; she sees how sick and pitiful he is; the girl who loved him so in the country wakens again in her heart; she does not take her hand from his lips. Then, after a moment, she makes him get up. 'I must be frank with you,' she tells him. 'Do you remember in the orchard how submissively I listened to your rebuke? Now it's my turn. I was younger then, and better. I loved you, and you were severe with me. The love of a humble country girl was not exciting for you. Good heavens! my blood still chills when I remember the

53

cold look and the sermon you gave me. You didn't like me then in the country, and why do you run after me now? Because I'm rich and well known? because my husband has been wounded on the battlefield? because we're in favour at court? Isn't it because my shame would now be known to everybody, and would give you a reputation as a rake? Don't you think I would a thousand times rather be back with the orchard and my books and the places where I first saw you and the graveyard with my nurse's grave, than play this role in this noisy masquerade? But it's too late to do anything now. From the moment when you wouldn't have me, what did it matter to me what became of me? And now you're a man of honour; and although I love you still – why should I pretend? – I've given myself to another and I shall always be faithful to him.'

She goes; and Evgeny stands thunderstruck, and then he hears the clank of the general's spurs. And there Pushkin leaves him.

The truth about Evgeny's fatal weakness has for the first time been fully driven home in Tatyana's speech: he has never been able to judge for himself of the intrinsic value of anything; all his values are social values; he has had enough independence, he has been enough superior to his associates, to be dissatisfied with the life of society, but, even in his disaffection, he has only been able to react into the disaffected attitude that is fashionable; his misanthropy itself has been developed in terms of what people will think of him, and, even trying to escape to the country, he has brought with him the standards of society. He had had enough sense of real values to know that there was something in Tatyana, something noble about her passion for him, to recognize in his heart that it was she who was the true unquiet brooding spirit, the true rebel against the conventions, where his quarrel with the world had been half a pose; but he had not had quite enough to love her just as she was: he had only been able to shoot Lensky.

Pushkin has put into the relations between his three central characters a number of implications. In one sense, they may be said to represent three intellectual currents of the time: Evgeny is Byronism turning worldly and dry; Lensky, with his Schiller and Kant, German romantic idealism; Tatyana, that Rousseauist Nature which was making itself heard in romantic poetry, speaking a new language and asserting a new kind of rights. And from another point of view they represent different tendencies in Russia itself: both Evgeny and Lensky are half foreigners, they think in terms of the cultures of the West, whereas Tatyana, who has spent her whole life on the wild old feudal estate, is for Pushkin the real Russia. Tatyana, like Pushkin, who said he owed so much to the stories of his Russian nurse, has always loved old wives' tales and is full of country superstitions. Before the fatal Saint's-Day party and after her conversation with Onegin, she has an ominous dream, which is recounted at length. Tatyana's subconscious insight, going to the bottom of the situation and clothing it with the imagery of folk-tales, reveals to her a number of things which the others do not yet know about themselves: that there is something bad about Evgeny and that there is an antagonism between him and Lensky; in her dream, she sees Onegin stab Lensky. It is the sensitive though naïve Russian spirit, always aware of the hidden realities, with which Tolstoy and Dostoyevsky were later on still attempting to make contact in their reaction against Western civilization. Yet with Pushkin, as Gide says of Dostoyevsky, the symbols are perfectly embodied in the characters; they never deform the human being or convert him into an uninteresting abstraction. *Evgeny Onegin* has been popular because it has for generations been read by young Russians as a story, a story in which the eternal reasoning male is brought up against the eternal instinctive woman – like Elizabeth Bennet and Mr Darcy; and in which the modest heroine – who, besides, is Cinderella and will end up expensively dressed and with the highest social position – gets morally all the best of it.

But there is still another aspect which the characters in *Evgeny Onegin* present. Pushkin speaks, at the end, of the years which have elapsed since he first saw Evgeny dimly, before the 'free novel' which was to shape itself could be discerned 'through the magic crystal'. This magic crystal was Pushkin's own mind, which figures in the poem in a peculiar way. The poet, when he talks about himself, is not wilful and egoistic like Byron; his digressions, unlike Byron's or Sterne's, always contribute to the story: they will begin by sounding like asides, in which the author is merely growing garrulous on the subject of some personal experience, but they will eventually turn out to merge into the experience of one of his characters, which he has been filling-in in this indirect way. Yet the crystal sphere is always there: it is inside it that we see the drama. Pushkin, throughout this period, had been tending to get away from his early subjective lyricism and to produce a more objective kind of art. After *Evgeny Onegin*, he was to write principally stories in prose. And in *Evgeny Onegin* it is almost as if we had watched the process – as we can see in the life-cell the nucleus splitting up into its separate nuclei and each concentrating its filaments and particles about it – by which the several elements of his character, the several strands of his experience, have taken symmetry about the foci of distinct characters. Pushkin had finally transfused himself into a dramatic work of art as none other of his romantic generation had done – for his serenity, his perfect balance of tenderness for human beings with unrelenting respect for reality, show a rarer quality of mind than Stendhal's.

Yet *Evgeny Onegin*, for all its lucidity, all its objectification, has behind it a conflict no less desperate than those which the other romantics were presenting so much more hysterically. Though Pushkin had triumphed as an artist as Byron was never able to do, he is otherwise a figure more tragic than the man who died at Missolonghi. For, after all, the chief disaster of *Evgeny Onegin* is not Evgeny's chagrin or Lensky's death: it is that Tatyana should have been caught up irrevocably by that empty and tyrannical social world from which Evgeny had tried to escape and which she had felt and still feels so alien. Pushkin married, the same year that *Onegin* was finished, a young and pleasure-loving wife who submerged him in the expenses of social life; and before he was out of his thirties, he got himself killed in a duel by a man whom he suspected of paying her attentions. It was as if in those generations where Byron, Shelley, Keats, Leopardi, and Poe were dead in their twenties or thirties or barely reached forty, where Coleridge and Wordsworth and Beddoes and Musset burned out while still alive, where Lermontov, like Pushkin, was killed in a duel, before he was twenty-seven – it was as if in that great age of the bourgeois ascendancy – and even in still feudal Russia – it were impossible for a poet to survive. There was for the man of imagination and moral passion a basic maladjustment to society in which only the student of society – the social philosopher, the historian, the novelist – could find himself and learn to function. And to deal with the affairs of society, he had to learn to speak its language: that is, giving up the old noble language, he had – as Goethe and Hugo did, and as Pushkin did just before he died – to train himself to write in prose.

Yet Pushkin, who had done for the Russian language what Dante had done for the Italian and who had laid the foundations of Russian fiction, had, in opposing the natural humanity of Tatyana to the social values of Evgeny, set a theme which was to be developed through the whole of Russian art and thought, and to give it its peculiar power. Lenin, like Tolstoy, could only have been possible in a world where this contrast was acutely felt. Tatyana, left by Pushkin with the last word, was actually to remain triumphant.

II. THE BRONZE HORSEMAN

In attempting a new translation of A. S. Pushkin's great poem, *The Bronze Horseman*, it may be useful to make a few explanations.

The poem deals with the tragic contradiction between the right to peace and happiness of the ordinary man and the right to constructive domination of the state. (The Bronze Horseman, which symbolizes the latter, is Falconet's well-known statue of Peter the Great, which has figured in several Soviet films.) What is present to the minds of Russian readers but what may not be equally familiar to foreign ones is the background of the history of St Petersburg. This new capital was built by Peter the Great – the 'He' of the first part of the poem – at the beginning of the eighteenth century, on the swampy shores and islands of the Neva. The difficulties involved in the feat were prodigious, and neither then nor with a view to the future did Peter stint himself in the expenditure of human life. Of the artisans whom he compelled to come north to lay the foundations of the city, thousands died of hardship and disease; and the city, in its unnatural location, was at the mercy of terrible floods caused by the breaking-up of the ice of Lake Ladoga just east of it or – as on the occasion described in the poem – by the west wind blowing back the Neva. There had been one such flood in 1777, there was another in 1824, and they continued after Pushkin's time.

Pushkin contributed anonymously to the victims of 1824, and it is with this disaster that *The Bronze Horseman* deals. But the poem was not written until 1833. The poet, who had spent seven of the best years of his youth in exile and under surveillance as a result of his revolutionary verses and who, finally allowed to return to St Petersburg, was still obliged to submit all his writings and movements to the obstructive control of the Tsar, knew well what it was to have one's life in the hands of a ruthless authority. And he had recently married a young wife who was bringing him into the circle of the Court, where the obligations imposed by the Tsar were weighing on him more heavily than ever and where, it has been supposed, the attentions of the Tsar to his wife were among factors in the sequence of events which drove Pushkin, hardly more than three years later, to issue the challenge to his fatal duel.

In *The Bronze Horseman*, as in *Evgeny Onegin*, we can see very clearly the process by which the creations which Pushkin in the beginning has identified more or less with himself become detached from the author, turn into sharply outlined characters and dramatize the impulse which engendered them in a purely objective way. The original intention of Pushkin had been to continue *Evgeny Onegin*. In this sequel Evgeny was to have played some role in connexion with the Decembrist revolt of 1825, in consequence of which so many of Pushkin's friends had been executed or sent to Siberia. He wrote his tenth canto in cipher and then, still fearing that it might get him into trouble, burned most of the manuscript. Then he embarked on an entirely new poem in the same stanza-form as *Evgeny Onegin* and with a hero whose first name was still Evgeny, but whose family name was different and who was in fact a quite different person. The new Evgeny is the descendant of an illustrious old boyar family – Pushkin begins with a long genealogy – whose possessions and credit have terribly dwindled. Evgeny himself is a clerk; and Pushkin in his original draft conducted a long argument with imaginary opponents over his right to choose so humble a personage, in defiance of the romantic fashion, as the hero of a narrative poem. The situation of the new Evgeny was a caricature of Pushkin's own. He himself was the descendant of boyars – the early Pushkins had been among the electors of the first Romanov – and now he found himself a socially insignificant person in a *haut monde* where neither his ancient blood nor his genius as a poet was much respected. He had been put under a terrible strain since his marriage to keep up his establishment from his literary earnings.

And, as Pushkin begins to develop his real theme, the new Evgeny evolves entirely out of the *Evgeny Onegin* frame. Pushkin drops the genealogy, the *vers de société* stanza-form, the amusing man-of-the-world digressions. He drops the imaginary argument, of which he has apparently gotten the better. The former family-glories of the hero, which we are told he spends no time regretting, are alluded to in half a dozen lines; and the poet in two words says curtly that Evgeny avoids the nobility. The life of upper-class St Petersburg figures only in an introduction, in which Pushkin describes its attractions in his own conventional character; and his deeper feelings have obviously been canalized in the character of the unfortunate desk-worker who hopes to own two chairs and a table. Indeed, Pushkin has used already in regard to himself, in one of the rejected parts of *Evgeny Onegin*, exactly the same phrases about wanting only to be master in his own house with a pot of cabbage soup, which he now assigns to the second Evgeny. At the beginning of *Evgeny Onegin*, we see Evgeny, the Petersburg dandy, returning home after a night of gaiety just as the common people of the capital are getting up and going about their tasks. The new Evgeny is now one of these common people: Pushkin has dropped even the literary avocations which he gave him in his original version. And he has made out of Evgeny's collision with the power and pride of St Petersburg a poem which has been put by Russian critics beside the longer masterpiece that preceded it – which has indeed been described by D. S. Mirsky as probably the greatest Russian poem ever written.

It would be impossible to reproduce in English the peculiar poetic merits of *The Bronze Horseman*. The terseness and compactness of Pushkin's style, which constitute one of the chief difficulties of translating him, reach a point in this poem where, as Mirsky says, 'the words and their combinations' are 'charged to breaking-point with all the weight of meaning they can bear'. The two terrific themes of violence: the oppressive power of the city, made solid in stone and metal, the liquid force and fury of the flood, are embodied in language of a density and energy which are hardly to be found in English outside the first books of *Paradise Lost*:

> He scarce had finisht, when such murmur fill'd
> Th' assembly, as when hollow rocks retain
> The sound of blust'ring winds, which all night long

Had rous'd the sea, now with hoarse cadence lull
Sea-faring men o'er watcht. . . .

Or,

Rocks, caves, lakes, fens, bogs, dens, and shades of death. . . .

Yet I believe it is worth while to make an attempt to present *The Bronze Horseman* in English. There has, so far as I know, been only one English translation – that of Professor Oliver Elton, included by Mr Avrahm Yarmolinsky in his *Poems, Prose, and Plays of Pushkin*. This translation is a very respectable performance: it has certain merits which mine cannot pretend to. Professor Elton, following Pushkin's rhymed verse, has been able to succeed far better than I in catching the tumult and movement of the poem, and he has occasionally struck off a fine Pushkinian line; but he has blurred the effect of the whole by diluting it with a kind of stock romantic verbiage.

I have tried the experiment of translating the poem into prose with an iambic base. This at least makes it possible to avoid the woolliness which is the bane of translations of Pushkin – who is the least woolly of poets – since one is not obliged to pad out the spare and rapid phrases of the original with half-a-dozen words or more for every two of the text and with adjectives and images which are not Pushkin's. (I have used a different text from Professor Elton's: that of P. E. Shchegolev.)

But the main point is that this tale in verse is certainly one of the most enlightening things ever written about Russia by a Russian. It is not only in the portrayal of chaos, the resounding accents of power, that Pushkin is comparable to Milton. Pushkin's poor clerk Evgeny, too, is defying Eternal Order. But his defiance no longer appears under the aspect of a theological struggle; it is the great theme of the nineteenth century: the struggle of the individual with society – the theme of which, in terms of the bourgeois world, the great artistic presentation is in Ibsen. But Pushkin had dramatized it in terms of a society partly modernized and yet basically and belatedly feudal. Evgeny has lost his position as a gentleman through the incompetence of his father as a landlord (this appears from the genealogical fragment which Pushkin broke off and published separately), but he has not become a middle-class man. He is the pettiest of *petits bourgeois*; with his two chairs and his pot of cabbage soup, he has been reduced practically to a working-class level. The distance between him and the Statue, and what the Statue represents, is immense. He will be crushed, and his protest will never be heard – or rather, it would never have been heard if it had not been transmitted by Pushkin, whose poet's vocation it was to hear and to give a voice to the voiceless.

The Tsar was to do his best to prevent it from being heard: *The Bronze Horseman* was suppressed by the censorship and not published till after Pushkin's death. And one wonders, in reading it today, what repercussions it may have in Soviet Russia. After all, the construction of the White Sea canal has been accomplished by forced labour not much different from the forced labour with which Peter the Great built St Petersburg; and, after all, Peter the Great is the figure to whom the laureates of Stalin most willingly compare him and to whom he is said to be most willing to be compared. The dissident and the irreverent, like Evgeny, hear behind them a horseman, not of bronze but of steel, and no matter where they go, they cannot escape him; he drives them into the prisons of the GPU just as surely as he drove Evgeny into the Gulf of Finland; and just as Evgeny took off his hat and slunk aside where he had formerly hissed a threat, so the guilt of simple opposition puts them ultimately at the mercy of the 'Idol' and compels them to confess to crimes which they have unquestionably never committed. Between the power that builds the State and the Idol that represents it, on the one hand, and the ordinary man, on the other, the distance is still very great.

Not of course that Soviet Russia is not an advance beyond Tsarist Russia. The gains of the Revolution and the potentialities of its programme should be no more destructible by the policies of however narrow and harsh an administration than the gains of the American Revolution and the potentialities of our republic were destroyed by Harding and Hoover. And not, on the other hand, that government of any sort, whether tsarist or capitalist or socialist, may not give rise to the same kind of conflict between the individual and the corporate interest which Pushkin presents in this poem. But it is well to remember nowadays that the attempt to establish socialism in Russia has had to be carried out in a society conditioned by despotism.

It is also well to remember that Pushkin makes Evgeny's defiance take place in Senate Square, the scene of the Decembrist revolt, which occurred the year after the flood; and that, however discouraged the poet may have been by the suppression of the revolt and by his own eclipse, that defiance was ultimately made good – in November 1917.

The Bronze Horseman

A PETERSBURG TALE

The incident described in this tale is based on fact. The details are taken from contemporary magazines. The curious may verify them from the material compiled by V. I. Berkh. – Foreword by Pushkin.

Beside the desolate waves stood *He*, and, thronged with mighty thoughts, stared out. Before him, broad, the river rushed along; a poor skiff plied upon it, solitary. Along the mossy marshy bank, the cabins, here and there, showed black: roofs for the wretched Finn; and forests, never brightened by the mist-enshrouded sun, were roaring all around.

Thought *He*: 'We shall from hence strike terror to the Swede. Here shall a town be reared to that arrogant neighbour's woe. Here, for our greatness, Nature has ordained that we shall break a window through to Europe; shall stand with foot set firm beside the sea. Hither, by waters they have never known, all flags shall come to be our guests, and we shall glory in our scope.'

A hundred years went by, and that young city, of northern lands the beauty and the marvel, from dark of forests, damp of bogs, rose up in all its grandeur and its pride; where once the Finnish fisher, Nature's sullen stepchild, had all alone beside low-lying shores let down his ragged nets, today by bustling docks, crowd, strong and shapely, bulks of tower and palace; ships swarm from all earth's ends to that rich port; Neva has clothed herself in stone; bridges have spanned her waters; her isles with groves dark-green are covered over; and now before the younger capital, old Moscow dims – as, before the new Tsarina, the widow of the purple.

I love thee, masterpiece of Peter – I love thine aspect, graceful and severe, Neva's mighty stream, her granite banks, stiff lace of iron fences, the limpid dusk and moonless radiance of nights so full of thought, when lampless in my room I write and read, and sleeping masses of deserted streets show clear, and the Admiralty's needle gleams, and, never suffering the shade of night to dim the golden sky, one glow makes haste to take the other's place, leaves night but half an hour. I love thy cruel winters, the frost and moveless air, the racing of the sleighs beside broad Neva, the girls with faces brighter bit than roses, the balls with all their glitter, stir, and chatter, and bachelor feasts, with fizz of foaming goblets and azure flame of punch. I love the warlike liveliness of playing-fields of Mars, monotonous beauty of the Horse and Foot in ranks that sway in rhythm, streaming triumphant banners, the glinting of their bronze war-riddled helmets. I love, O martial capital, thy fort's loud smoke and thunder, when the Empress of the North gives the Imperial house a son, or Russia greets, exulting, her foeman's fresh defeat, or Neva, breaking through the dark blue ice, forth sweeps it to the sea and, smelling spring days, rejoices.

Be splendid, Peter's City, and stand, like Russia, strong – for lo, the very conquered element has made her peace with thee at last; their ancient hate and bondage may the Finnish waves forget, nor vex with impotent anger Peter's eternal sleep!

A dreadful time there *was* – of that I tell. And may my story, friends, be but, for you, a grisly fireside tale, no legend of bad omen. . . .

I

On Petrograd, all clouded over, November breathed the autumn cold. Splashing with loud waves against her handsome banks, Neva threshed about, a sick man on his restless bed. The hour was late and dark; angry, the rain against the window beat, the dolorous wind drove howling. That evening from the house of friends returned the young Evgeny. We shall call our hero so: the name rings nicely; my pen is friendly to it from of old. No need to give his surname – though in former times it may have shone, and sounded from the pen of Karamzin among our country's annals; today the world of gossip has forgot it. Our hero lodges in a little room. He works somewhere or other, shuns the gentry, pines after neither his departed relatives nor old days now forgotten.

And so, come home, he shook his overcoat, undressed, and went to bed, but long he could not sleep, disturbed by divers thoughts. What thoughts? That he was poor; that he had to work for decent independence; that God might make him cleverer and richer; that there were certain lucky idle fellows, who loafed and took no thought and found life light enough; that he must wait two years perhaps to get promotion; that the river was all bloated, that the weather got no better; that the bridges might perhaps be taken up, and that in that case his Parasha would surely miss him. . . . Here he was filled with ardent tenderness, his fancy like a poet's, soared away.

Get married? Well, why not? Why not, indeed? 'I shall make myself a modest little corner and there I shall give Parasha peace. A bed, two chairs, a pot of cabbage soup, and I the master of the house . . . What more should I want? We shall coddle no caprices; I shall take Parasha out for country walks on summer Sundays; humble I'll be and sly: they'll give me a snug berth; Parasha will keep house, bring up the children . . . And so we'll live and so go down to death, still hand in hand, and be buried by our grandsons. . . .'

So he mused. And yet that night he was melancholy, and he wished that the wind would not sound so dreary, that the rain would not sound so angry, as it beat against the pane.

Sleepy, he closed his eyes at last. And lo! the dark of that foul night is thinning, and pale day is at hand . . . Ah, dreadful day!

All night had Neva plunged against the storm to reach the sea, but, worsted by that fury, she now could fight no more. . . . At morning to her shores the people flocked in crowds, in wonder at the spray, the mountainous swell, the foam of raging waters. But Neva, by the Gulf winds' driving taxed now beyond her force, fell back in rage and tumult; flooded the islands; fiercer and fiercer grew; reared up and roared; like a caldron, boiled, breathed steam; and, frenzied, fell at last upon the town. All fled before her – all was left abandoned – and now the waves were breaking through the streets, and now invading basements; Neva's canals were all one sea with her, and like a Triton, Petropol emerged, waist-deep in water.

A siege! A storming! Waves, like savage beasts, climb to the windows. Boats, pell-mell borne along, strike the glass with their sterns. Bridges swept loose by the deluge, fragments of cabins, timbers, roofs, the thrifty merchant's wares, the wretched chattels of the poor, the wheels of city droshkies, the coffins from the graveyard, washed afloat – all these drift through the town!

The people see the wrath of God and wait their execution. Alas! all ruined: roof and food! Where will it end?

The late Tsar in that terrible year still gloriously ruled Russia. Distressed and baffled now, he sought the balcony and spoke: 'To tsars it is not given to curb the elements, for they belong to God.' With mournful brooding eyes, he watched the dreadful work. The public squares were lakes, and into them the streets were pouring rivers. The palace seemed a dismal isle. The Tsar's command went forth: his generals, far and wide, through stormy waters on a perilous course, plunged through the streets and sought to save the people, gone mad with panic, drowning in their houses.

Now at this time in Peter's Square, where a new corner-house had risen, where on the perron high, lifelike with lifted paw, two ornamental lions stand – astride one marble beast, hatless, with arms tight folded, rigid and deathly pale, Evgeny perched. Not for himself, poor fellow, did he fear. He did not notice how the greedy billows rose till they lapped his soles nor how his face was dashed with rain nor how the wildly howling wind had suddenly snatched his hat. His eyes were fixed far out in one strained desperate stare. *There* reared and raged the waves, like mountains, from the outraged deep; *there* raved the storm, *there* broken things were tossed. . . . And *there* – God! God! – alas! within the billows' reach, by the Gulf's very brink – the paintless fence, the willow, the little flimsy house – and they, the widow and her daughter, *there* – his dear Parasha, all his hope. . . . Or is it all a dream that he beholds? Or is our life, then, nothingness – as empty as a dream, Fate's mockery of man? As if bewitched, fast rooted to the marble, he can't dismount! About him stretches water – water now and nothing else. And, back turned towards him, steady on its height above defiant Neva, rears on its steed of bronze, with outstretched arm, the idol.

II

But now, with ruin sated, with insolent uproar spent, Neva crept back, well pleased to have wreaked her fury and heedlessly abandoning her booty. So, with his villainous band invading town, the ruffian breaks in, wrecks, ransacks, cuts throats: cries, grindings, violence, oaths, alarms, and howls! . . . And, burdened with their plunder, fearing pursuit and tired, the robbers hurry home and drop their loot along the road.

The water sank, the pavements cleared again, and my Evgeny hastes with fainting spirit, hoping, fearing, yearning, to the river scarce grown tame. But, still exulting fiercely in the fullness of their triumph, still wickedly the waters boil; still does the foam o'erspread them, and like a warhorse running from a battle, heavily Neva breathes. Evgeny looks: he sees a boat, a godsend; he runs, calls out to the boatman – he, careless of danger, is ready enough to take him across the terrible waters for ten kopecks.

And long the practised oarsman contends with the tossing waves and momently the skiff with its rash sailors seems like to plumb the abyss between their ranks – and now at last it makes the land.

The poor wretch runs along the familiar street to find the familiar place. He looks – oh, dreadful sight! – he knows it not. All lies a heap before him; part tumbled down, part swept away; some of the little houses knocked awry, some quite destroyed, some shifted by the waves – and all about, as on a field of battle, bodies are strewn. Evgeny rushes headlong – uncomprehending, faint with horror – where Fate awaits him with the unseen tidings as if with a sealed letter. And now he is in that last outlying suburb, and here's the Gulf, and here's the house hard by it . . . What's this? . . . He stops – goes back, returns. He stares . . . advances . . . stares again. Here is the place their house stood; here is the willow. Here were the gates – so they've been carried off. But where's the house? And, full of black foreboding, he prowls and prowls about, talks loudly to himself – then suddenly, striking his brow, he bursts out laughing.

Night's darkness fell upon the frightened town; and long the people did not sleep, but talked of the day just past.

The morning's ray, from pale and haggard clouds, shone on a quiet capital and found no trace of yesterday's disaster; with royal purple now the hurt was overspread. And all took up the old routine. Already through the streets, now clear again, with cold indifference flowed the crowd. The clerks, quitting their lodgings, went to their desks. Hardy trade, not downed, explored his cellars, plundered by the river, preparing to revenge his heavy losses out of his neighbour's pocket. And people took the boats out of the courtyards.

And Khostov, poet, favourite of the heavens, already sang in verses never to die the griefs of Neva's shores.

But ah, my poor Evgeny ... alas! his baffled wits gave way before these blows. The mutinous roar of Neva and the winds were now resounding in his ears. Possessed by dreadful thoughts he could not utter, he strayed from place to place. Some dream was preying on him. A week, and then a month had passed – he never from that day went home. His empty lodging, when the lease expired, the landlord rented out to a poor poet. Evgeny never came to claim his things. The world forgot him soon. All day he tramped, at night slept on the docks; his food was morsels handed out from windows. His shabby clothes were torn and wearing out. The cruel children stoned him as he passed. Often he felt the coachmen's whips, for all was thoroughfare to him alike – courtyard or street, he never paid attention, always submerged in some strange inner terror. And so he dragged his miserable life, not beast nor man, not this nor that, no dweller on the earth nor yet departed spirit. . . .

One night he slept on a landing of the Neva. The summer days inclined towards fall. A foul wind blew. The dark surf dashed on the wharf, muttering grief and beating the smooth steps, like a suppliant at the door of a deaf court. The poor wretch fell asleep. The dark had come; the rain was dripping down; the wind was dreary; from far away the sentry through the thickness of the night returned its cry ... Evgeny leapt from sleep; his horror had come on him; quickly he rose and started on his wandering. Then suddenly he stopped and, standing very still, his face aghast with terror, began to gaze about. The great house with its columns rose before him. And on the perron high, lifelike with lifted paw, the ornamental lions stood; and right before him, from its fenced-in rock, with outstretched arm, uprearing in the darkness, the idol sat its copper steed.

A shudder shook Evgeny. His thoughts grew terribly clear. He knew this place where the flood had had its sport, where the waves had flocked like beasts of prey about him, ruthless, in full rebellion – and he knew these lions and this square, and him he knew who, fixed and still forever, held high in the murk of night his copper head – himself whose fateful will had based the city on the sea. . . . How dreadful now in all-enveloping mist! What power of thought upon his brow! What force within! And in that steed what fire! Where dost thou gallop, haughty steed? And where wilt thou plant thy hoof? O thou who, in thy might, didst master Destiny! Didst not just so, aloft, above the very precipice, with iron curb make Russia rear?

The poor crazed fellow prowled about the pedestal, cast wild looks on the image of the lord of half the world. His chest grew tight. He pressed his brow against the cold grate; his eyes blurred with mist; a flame flashed through his heart; his blood boiled up. Sombre he stood before the arrogant statue, and, clinching teeth and fists, possessed by some black force: 'Good! wonderworking builder!' with quivering hate, he hissed. 'You'll reckon with me yet!' – And headlong took to flight. The terrible Tsar, on the instant hot with wrath, had seemed all soundlessly to turn his head.

And through the empty square he plunges wildly, and hears behind – like rattling thunderclap – against the pounded pave a heavy-ringing gallop. And, dark in the pale moon, one arm flung up, the Copper Horseman comes behind, his charger's gallop ringing brass; and all night long, turn where Evgeny will, the Copper Horseman's clattering hoofbeats hammer – pursuing, still impend.

Thereafter, if he chanced upon the Square, his face, dismayed, would darken. Quick he would press his hand against his heart as if to calm its fluttering, remove his shabby cap, cast down his gaze, and slink away.

A little isle there is that lies offshore. Sometimes the fisher moors there with his net, belated at the haul, and cooks his humble supper, or some dreaming Sunday boatman puts in at the desert place. No blade of grass has ever sprouted there. But there the sportive flood had brought a flimsy cottage. Like a blackened bush it showed above the water. Last spring they took it up aboard a barque. It was empty, all a wreck; but on its threshold they dragged up my madman, and there for Charity's sake they buried his cold corpse.

A. E. Housman

The Voice, Sent Forth, Can Never Be Recalled

WHEN A. E. Housman's *Introductory Lecture* delivered in 1892 'Before the Faculties of Arts and Laws and of Science in University College, London' was reprinted in 1933, Housman characteristically wrote of it as follows: 'The Council of University College, not I, had the lecture printed.' He described it as 'rhetorical and not wholly sincere' and put upon the title page, *Nescit vox missa reverti*.

The little essay is curious in largely evading the questions it raises and taking the direction of a piece of special pleading for the author's own pursuits. Both the sciences and the arts, says Housman, are ordinarily defended by arguments which make their interests appear mutually antagonistic. But the arguments on both sides are mistaken. Science is said to be useful; but what is the use, for example, of a great deal of astronomical research? And the businessmen who make practical use of the results of scientific study are usually not scientists at all. (They do make use of them, nevertheless; and the results of the most gratuitous researches are always likely to turn out to be useful.) The Humanities, on the other hand, are supposed to 'transform and beautify our inner nature by culture'. Yet the proportion of the human race capable of being benefited by classical studies is certainly very small, and these 'can attain the desired end without that minute and accurate study of the classical tongues which affords Latin professors their only excuse for existing'. Not even the great critics of the classics are genuine classical scholars: 'When it comes to literary criticism, heap up in one scale all the literary criticism that the whole nation of professed scholars ever wrote, and drop into the other the thin green volume of Matthew Arnold's *Lectures on Translating Homer*, which has

72

long been out of print because the British public does not care to read it, and the first scale, as Milton says, will straight fly up and kick the beam.' (We shall look into the assumptions here in a moment.)

The arts and the sciences alike are only to be defended, says Housman, on the ground that the desire for knowledge is one of the normal human appetites, and that men suffer if they do not have it gratified. And 'once we have recognized that knowledge in itself is good for man, we shall need to invent no pretexts for studying this subject or that; we shall import no extraneous considerations of use or ornament to justify us in learning one thing rather than another. If a certain department of knowledge specially attracts a man, let him study that, and study it because it attracts him; and let him not fabricate excuses for that which requires no excuse, but rest assured that the reason why it most attracts him is that it is best for him.'

This is certainly true in so far as it means that we should follow the direction of our aptitudes; but it seems to imply that there is no difference in value between one department of learning and another or between the different points of view from which the various kinds of research can be conducted. There is no conception in Housman's mind, as there would have been in Whitehead's, for example, of relating the part to the whole, understanding the organism through the cell. Knowledge seems to be regarded by Housman as a superior sort of pastime – 'good for man' because it gives him pleasure and at most because 'it must in the long run be better for a man to see things as they are than to be ignorant of them; just as there is less fear of stumbling or of striking against corners in the daylight than in the dark'. ('*The thoughts of others Were light and fleeting, Of lovers' meeting Or luck or fame; Mine were of trouble And mine were steady, So I was ready When Trouble came.*') The disillusionment of western man in regard to his place in the universe, finding 'that he has been deceived alike as to his origin and his expectations, that he neither springs of the high lineage he fancied, nor will inherit the vast estate he looked for', is described in an eloquent passage; and the activities of the 'Arts and Laws and Science' are finally characterized as 'the rivalry of fellow soldiers in striving which can most victoriously achieve the common end of all, to set back the frontier of darkness'.

In other words, there is no role for creation in Housman's scheme of things. Indeed, if one had read only his poetry, one might be surprised to find that he even believed that it was possible or of any importance to set back the frontier of darkness. In this poetry, we find only the realization of man's smallness on his turning globe among the other revolving planets and of his own basic wrongness to himself, his own inescapable anguish. No one, it seems, can do anything about this universe which 'ails from its prime foundation': we can only, like Mithridates, render ourselves immune to its poisons by compelling ourselves to absorb them in small quantities in order that we may not succumb to the larger doses reserved for us by our fellows, or face the world with the hard mask of stoicism, 'manful like the man of stone'. For the rest, 'let us endure an hour and see injustice done'. And now we learn that for Housman knowledge itself meant at most the discovery of things that were already there – of those sharp corners which it was just as well not to bump into, of facts that were as invariable and as inert as the astronomical phenomena which are always turning up in his poems and which form the subject of the poem of Manilius to which he devoted so much of his life. He does not look to the sciences and arts for the births of new worlds of thought, of new possibilities for men themselves. It is characteristic of him that he should speak, in this essay, of Milton as a greater artist than Shakespeare, of Shakespeare, in fact, as not 'a great artist' – as if the completeness and richness of Shakespeare's dramatic imagination, a kind of genius which Milton, by comparison, seems hardly to possess at all, were not important enough to be taken into account in estimating his greatness as an artist – as if those stretches of *Paradise Lost* where everything is dead but the language were not the result of artistic deficiency.

Again, the creation of life has no place in the universe of Housman.

Housman's practice in his own field of scholarship is an astonishing proof of this. The modern English classical scholar of the type of A. W. Verrall or Gilbert Murray is a critic not merely of texts but of the classics in their quality as literature and of literature in its bearing on history. This school on one of its sides sometimes merges with the anthropology of J. G. Frazer; and it deals with ancient Greece and Rome in relation to the life of its own time, restates them in terms of its own time. The danger, of course, with a Verrall or a Murray is that, with something of the poet's imagination himself, he may give way, in the case of Greek drama, for example, to inventing new plays of his own and trying to foist them on Euripides or Aeschylus. With Housman we do not run this danger. Housman is the opposite kind of scholar; he is preoccupied with the emendation of texts. He could never have been guilty of the extravagances of a Gilbert Murray or a Verrall, but he was not capable of their kind of illumination. Note his assumption, in the passage quoted above, that 'the minute and accurate study of the classical tongues', with which he himself is exclusively preoccupied, 'affords Latin professors their only excuse for existing'. Have those classical scholars who write history, who write criticism, who make translations – Gibbon and Renan and Verrall and Murray and Jowett and Mackail (to take in the whole field of the classics) – no excuse for existing, then? Is it so certain that, if their literary criticism were put into the scales with Matthew Arnold on Homer, the scholars would kick the beam? Or are such persons not scholars at all? In either case, it is plain that, for Housman, their activities lie outside the periphery of the sphere which he has chosen for himself.

Not, however, that Housman in this limited sphere has left the poet of *The Shropshire Lad* behind him. On the contrary, the peculiar genius which won him a place beside Porson and Bentley, which established him in his own time as almost supreme, with, apparently, only Wilamowitz as a rival, was derived from his ability to combine with the most 'minute and accurate' mastery of language a first-hand knowledge of how poets express themselves. 'The task of editing the classics', he wrote in his preface to Juvenal, 'is continually attempted by scholars who have neither enough intellect nor enough literature. Unless a false reading chances to be unmetrical or ungrammatical they have no means of knowing that it is false.' And he himself seemed able with a miraculous sureness to give the authors back their lines as they had written them. So, for example, despite a unanimity of manuscripts which read '*Omnis ab hac cura mens relavata mea est*', Housman restored to Ovid from an inscription one of the latter's characteristic turns of style: '*Omnis ab hac cura cura levata mea est*'. ('*And set you at your threshold down, Townsman of a stiller town*'; '*Runners whom renown outran And the name died before the man*'; '*By Sestos tower, in Hero's town, On Hero's heart Leander lies.*') So, slightly emending the text, he turned a meaningless accepted reading of Juvenal, '*Perditus ac vilis sacci mercator olentis*', into a characteristically vivid satiric stroke: '*Perditus ac similis sacci mercator olentis*' – the money-chasing merchant, on a stormy voyage, turns as yellow as his bag of saffron. ('*They shook, they stared as white's their shirt: Them it was their poison hurt.*') So, without even an emendation and simply by indicating a new relation between three words of Virgil's, he was able to save Virgil's style in a phrase – *fallax herba veneni* – which had always up to then been read as if it had been written with neither style nor grammar: substituting for 'the deceitful plant of poison' 'the plant that dissembles its venom'. ('*And bear from hill and valley The daffodil away That dies on Easter day*'; '*Lie long, high snowdrifts in the hedge That will not shower on me*'; '*Snap not from the bitter yew His leaves that live November through.*') Several of his readings, I understand, have been confirmed by the subsequent discovery of manuscripts which Housman had never seen.

To this rescue of the Greek and Roman poets from the

negligence of the Middle Ages, from the incompetence and insensitivity of the scholars, A. E. Housman brought an unremitting zeal which may almost be described as a passion. It has been said of the theorems of Newton that they cause the pulse to beat faster as one follows them. But the excitement and satisfaction afforded by the classical commentary of Housman must be unique in the history of scholarship. Even the scraping of the rust from an old coin is too tame an image to convey the experience of pursuing one of his arguments to its climax. It is as if, from the ancient author, so long dumb with his language itself, his very identity blurred or obliterated, the modern classicist were striking a new spark of life – as if the poet could only find his tongue at the touch across Time of the poet. So far is Housman the scholar a giver of life – yet it is only as re-creator. He is only, after all, again, discovering things that were already there. His findings do not imply a new vision.

It was a queer destiny, and one that cramped him – if one should not say rather that he had cramped himself. (Not to dispute, however, with Housman, who thought that human beings were all but helpless, the problem of natural fate and free will.)

The great work of A. E. Housman's life in the field of classical scholarship was his edition of the five books of Manilius, the publication of which alone extended from 1903 to 1930. We are told in a memoir of Housman by his colleague, Professor A. S. F. Gow of Cambridge, that Housman regarded Manilius as 'a facile and frivolous poet, the brightest facet of whose genius was an eminent aptitude for doing sums in verse'. And the layman may be disposed to assume that by Housman's time the principal Latin poets had already been covered so completely that there was nobody left except third-rate ones like Manilius. But it turns out from Professor Gow that Housman's real favourite was Propertius, and that he had done a great deal of valuable work on him and had at one time contemplated a complete edition.

Professor Gow says that presumably Housman saw in Manilius and Lucan (Lucan he seems also to have despised) 'more opportunity than in Propertius of displaying his special gifts, and more hope of approaching finality in the solution of the problems presented', but adds that he 'cannot help regretting that he [Housman] abandoned a great and congenial poet on whom so much time had already been lavished'.

The elegist of *The Shropshire Lad*, then, deliberately and grimly chose Manilius when his real interest was in Propertius. There is an element of perversity, of self-mortification, in Housman's career all along. (Gow tells how up to the time of his death 'he would be found reading every word of books whose insignificance must have been apparent in ten pages, and making remorseless catalogues of their shortcomings'.) And his scholarship, great as it is in its way, is poisoned in revenge by the instincts which it seems to be attempting to destroy, so that it radiates more hatred for his opponents than love for the great literature of antiquity. Housman's papers on classical subjects, which shocked the sense of decorum of his colleagues, are painful to the admirers of his poetry. The bitterness here *is* indecent as in his poetry it never is. In a prose, old-fashioned and elaborate, which somewhat resembles Pope's, he will attack the German professors who have committed the unpardonable sin of editing the Latin authors inadequately with sentences that coil and strike like rattlesnakes, or that wrap themselves around their victims and squeeze them to death like boa constrictors. When English fails, he takes to scurrilous Latin. And the whole thing is likely at any moment to give way to some morose observation on the plight of the human race: 'To believe that wherever a best MS. gives possible readings it gives true readings, and that only when it gives impossible readings does it give false readings, is to believe that an incompetent editor is the darling of Providence, which has given its angels charge over him lest at any time his sloth and folly should produce their natural results and incur their appropriate penalty. ... How the world is managed, and why it was created, I cannot tell; but it is no feather-bed for the repose of sluggards.' And not only, he continues, has the notion been imposed that 'inert adhesion to one authority is methodical criticism', but 'rational criticism has been branded with a term of formal reprobation.' 'But still there is a hitch. Competent editors exist; and side by side with those who have embraced "the principles of criticism", there are those who follow the practice of critics: who possess intellects, and employ them on their work. Consequently their work is better done, and the contrast is mortifying. This is not as it should be. As the wise man dieth, so dieth the fool: why then should we allow them to edit the classics differently? If nature, with flagitious partiality, has given judgement and industry to some men and left other men without them, it is our evident duty to amend her blind caprice; and those who are able and willing to think must be deprived of their unfair advantage by stringent prohibitions. In Association football you must not use your hands, and similarly in textual criticism you must not use your brains. Since we cannot make fools behave like wise men, we will insist that wise men should behave like fools: by these means only can we redress the injustice of nature and anticipate the equality of the grave.'

And here is the sombre and threatening, the almost Isaian, utterance to which he is moved by the failure of one of the compilers of a German-Latin dictionary to include in the article on *aelurus*, the Latinized Greek word for *cat*, any mention of an instance of its occurrence arrived at by an emendation in Juvenal and believed by Housman to be the first extant: 'Everyone can figure to himself the mild inward glow of pleasure and pride which the author of this unlucky article felt while he was writing it and the peace of mind with which he said to himself, when he went to bed that night, "Well done, thou good and faithful servant." This is the felicity of the house of bondage, and of the soul which is so fast in prison that it cannot go forth; which commands no outlook on the past or the future, but believes that the fashion of the present, unlike all fashions heretofore, will endure perpetually and that its own flimsy tabernacle of second-hand opinions is a habitation for everlasting.'

Even when Housman is saying something positive the emotion is out of proportion to its object: he speaks feverishly, seems unnaturally exalted. Here is a passage on Bentley from the preface to the first volume of his Manilius: '*Lucida tela diei*: these are the words that come into one's mind when one has halted at some stubborn perplexity of reading or inter-pretation, has witnessed Scaliger and Gronovius and Huetius fumble at it one after another, and then turns to Bentley and sees Bentley strike his finger on the place and say *thou ailest here, and here* . . . The firm strength and piercing edge and arrowy swiftness of his intellect, his matchless facility and adroitness and resource, were never so triumphant as where defeat seemed sure; and yet it is other virtues that one most admires and welcomes as one turns from the smoky fire of Scaliger's genius to the sky and air of Bentley's: his lucidity, his sanity, his great and simple and straightforward fashion of thought.' Transferring Arnold's words for Goethe to Bentley is not perhaps comparing great things with small, but in the substitution for the 'physician of the Iron Age' of the physician of mangled texts, there is a narrowing of scope almost comic. The preface to the first book of Manilius, from which the above passage has been quoted, magnificent as it is in its way, has also something monstrous about it.

Yet some acquaintance with the classical work of Housman greatly increases one's estimate of his stature. One encounters an intellectual pride almost Dantesque or Swiftian. 'You would be welcome to praise me', he writes, 'if you did not praise one another'; and 'the reader whose good opinion I desire and have done my utmost to secure is the next Bentley or Scaliger who may chance to occupy himself with Manilius'. His arrogance is perhaps never more ferocious than when he is judging himself severely: when a friend who had ventured to suggest the publication of a paper on Swinburne which Housman had read before a college literary society had been told by Housman that he was leaving directions to have it destroyed after his death and had retorted that if the writer really thought it so bad, he would already himself have destroyed it, Housman replied: 'I do not think it bad: I think it not good enough for me.' And he put on the title page of his edition of Juvenal, *editorum in usum edidit*, to indicate that this feat of erudition – according to his own announcement, unprecedented – was merely intended as a hint to future scholars who might tackle the subject as to how they might accomplish their task in a thoroughgoing fashion.

Is this the spectacle of a great mind crippled? Certainly it is the spectacle of a mind of remarkable penetration and vigour, of uncommon sensibility and intensity, condemning itself to duties which prevent it from rising to its full height. Perhaps it is the case of a man of genius who has never been allowed to come to growth. Housman's anger is tragic like Swift's. He is perhaps more pitiable than Swift, because he has been compelled to suppress himself more completely. Even when Swift had been exiled to Ireland, he was able to take out his fury in crusading against the English. But A. E. Housman, giving up Greek in order to specialize in Latin because he 'could not attain to excellence in both', giving up Propertius, who wrote about love, for Manilius, who did not even deal with human beings, turning away from the lives of the Romans to rivet his attention to the difficulties of their texts, can only flatten out small German professors with weapons which would have found fit employment in the hands of a great reformer or a great satirist. He is the hero of *The Grammarian's Funeral* – the man of learning who makes himself impressive through the magnitude, not the importance, of his achievement. After all, there was no need for another Bentley.

It is only in the Latin verses – said to have been called by Murray the best since the ancient world – which Housman prefixed to his Manilius, in his few translations from Latin and Greek, and in his occasional literary essays, that the voice of the Shropshire Lad comes through – that voice which, once sped on its way, so quickly pierced to the hearts and the minds of the whole English-speaking world and which went on vibrating for decades, disburdening hearts with its music that made loss and death and disgrace seem so beautiful, while poor Housman, burdened sorely for ever, sat grinding and snarling at his texts. Would he have called back that voice if he could, as he recalled, or tried to recall, so much else? There are moments when his ill humour and his pedantry, his humility which is a perverse kind of pride, almost make us think that he would.

At this point Professor Gow is able to throw some further light on his friend. It seems that Housman had marked the following passage from Colonel Lawrence's *Seven Pillars of Wisdom*, which he had come across in a review:

'There was my craving to be liked – so strong and nervous that never could I open myself friendly to another. The terror of failure in an effort so important made me shrink from trying; besides, there was the standard; for intimacy seemed shameful unless the other could make the perfect reply, in the same language, after the same method, for the same reasons.

'There was a craving to be famous; and a horror of being known to like being known. Contempt for my passion for distinction made me refuse every offered honour. I cherished my independence almost as did a Bedouin, but my impotence of vision showed me my shape best in painted pictures, and the oblique overheard remarks of others best taught me my created impression. The eagerness to overhear and oversee myself was my assault upon my own inviolate citadel.'

Housman had written in the margin, 'This is me.' Both had been compelled by their extreme sensibility to assume in the presence of their fellows eccentric or repellent masks. Both had been led by extreme ambition to perform exploits which did not do them justice, exploits which their hearts were but half in: Professor Gow says that Housman's prime motive in undertaking his edition of Manilius was the ambition to 'build' himself 'a monument'. And just as

Lawrence was always losing the manuscripts of his books, limiting their circulation, making the pretence of suppressing them altogether, so Housman kept his poems out of anthologies, made the gestures of a negative attitude in regard to the reprinting of his other writings, and left instructions that his classical papers, of which Gow says there are something like a hundred, should never be collected in a volume (instructions which it is to be hoped will be disobeyed).

Both were products of the English universities; and it would take an Englishman properly to account for them. But their almost insane attempts to conceal their blazing lights under bushels are recognizable as exaggerations of the Englishman's code of understatement in connexion with his achievements and conquests. And both obviously belong to the monastic order of English university ascetics. The company to which Housman refers himself is that of Walter Pater, Lewis Carroll, Edward Fitzgerald, and Gerard Manley Hopkins – and, earlier, Thomas Gray. Hopkins, converted at Oxford, entered the Jesuit order; Pater and Dodgson stayed on there as dons; Fitzgerald and Gray, when they had finished at Cambridge, continued to haunt the place: they remained men of the monastery all their lives. Are their humility, which seems imposed by moral principles, their shyness in relation to the extra-collegiate world, derived from the ages when learning was the possession of pious brotherhoods and shut away between the walls of foundations?

Certainly their failure to develop emotionally is due to that semi-monastic training. All seem checked at some early stage of growth, beyond which the sensibility and the intellect – even, in Lawrence's case, the ability to manage men – may crystallize in marvellous forms, but after which there is no natural progress in the experience of human relationships. Their works are among the jewels of English literature rather than among its great springs of life; and Alice and the Shropshire Lad and Marius the Epicurean are all the beings of a looking-glass world, either sexless or with an unreal sex which turns only towards itself in the mirror of art. Isn't the state of mind indicated by Lawrence in the first of the paragraphs quoted above essentially an adolescent one? We are told, in a recent memoir, that Housman used to rail against marriage and child-bearing. 'My father and my mother,' he makes one of his hanged heroes say, 'They had a likely son, And I have none.'

It would not be true to say of Housman, as it would be of Fitzgerald or Gray, that his achievement has been merely to state memorably certain melancholy commonplaces of human existence without any real presentation of that existence as we live it through. There *is* immediate emotional experience in Housman of the same kind that there is in Heine, whom he imitated and to whom he has been compared. But Heine, for all his misfortunes, moves at ease in a larger world. There is in his work an exhilaration of adventure – in travel, in love, in philosophy, in literature, in politics. Doleful though his accents may sometimes be, he always lets in air and light to the mind. But Housman is closed from the beginning. His world has no opening horizons; it is a prison that one can only endure. One can only come the same painful cropper over and over again and draw from it the same bitter moral.

And Housman has managed to grow old without in a sense ever knowing maturity. He has somehow never arrived at the age when the young man decides at last to summon all his resources and try to make something out of this world he has never made.

The Politics of Flaubert

GUSTAVE FLAUBERT has figured for decades as the great glorifier and practitioner of literary art at the expense of human affairs both public and personal. We have heard about his asceticism, his nihilism, his consecration to the search for *le mot juste*. His admirers have tended to praise him on the same assumption on which his critics have found him empty and sterile: the assumption that he had no moral or social interests. At most, *Madame Bovary* has been taken as a parable of the romantic temperament.

Really Flaubert owed his superiority to those of his contemporaries – Gautier, for example, who professed the same literary creed – to the seriousness of his concern with the large questions of human destiny. It was a period when the interest in history was intense; and Flaubert, in his intellectual tastes as well as in his personal relations, was almost as close to the historians Michelet, Renan, and Taine, and to the biographical critic Sainte-Beuve, as to Gautier and Baudelaire. In the case of Taine and Sainte-Beuve, he came to deplore their preoccupation in their criticism with the social aspects of literature at the expense of all its other values; but he himself seems always to see humanity in social terms and historical perspective. His point of view may be gauged pretty accurately from his comments in one of his letters on Taine's *History of English Literature*: 'There is something else in art beside the milieu in which it is practised and the physiological antecedents of the worker. On this system you can explain the series, the group, but never the individuality, the special fact which makes him this person and not another. This method results inevitably in leaving *talent* out of consideration. The masterpiece has no longer any significance except as a historical document. It is the old critical method of La Harpe exactly turned around. People used to believe that literature was an altogether personal thing and that books fell out of the sky like meteors. Today they deny that the will and the absolute have any reality at all. The truth, I believe, lies between the two extremes.'

But it was also a period in France – Flaubert's lifetime, 1820–81 – of alternating republics and monarchies, of bogus emperors and defeated revolutions, when political ideas were in much confusion. The French historians of the Enlightenment tradition, which was the tradition of the Revolution, were steadily becoming less hopeful; and a considerable group of the novelists and poets held political and social issues in contempt and staked their careers on art as an end in itself: their conception of their relation to society was expressed in their damnation of the bourgeois, who gave his tone to all the world, and their art was a defiance of him. The Goncourts in their journal have put the attitude on record: 'Lying phrases, resounding words, hot air – that's just about all we get from the political men of our time. Revolutions are a simple *déménagement* followed by the moving-back of the same ambitions, corruptions, and villainies into the apartment which they have just been moved out of – and all involving great breakage and expense. No political morals whatever. When I look about me for a disinterested opinion, I can't find a single one. People take risks and compromise themselves on the chance of getting future jobs. ... You are reduced, in the long run, to disillusion, to a disgust with all beliefs, a tolerance of any power at all, an indifference to political passion, which I find in all my literary friends, and in Flaubert as in myself. You come to see that you must not die for any cause, that you must live with any government that exists, no matter how antipathetic it may be to you – you must believe in nothing but art and profess only literature. All the rest is a lie and booby-trap.' In the field of art, at least, it was possible, by heroic effort, to prevent the depreciation of values.

This attitude, as the Goncourts say, Flaubert fully shared. 'Today', he wrote Louise Colet in 1853, 'I even believe that a thinker (and what is an artist if he is not a triple thinker?) should have neither religion nor fatherland nor even any social conviction. It seems to me that absolute doubt is now indicated so unmistakably that it would almost amount to an absurdity to take the trouble to formulate it.' And: 'The citizens who work themselves up for or against the Empire or the Republic', he wrote George Sand in 1869, 'seem to be just about as useful as the ones who used to argue about efficacious grace and efficient grace.' Nothing exasperated him more – and we may sympathize with him today – than the idea that the soul is to be saved by the profession of correct political opinions.

Yet Flaubert is an idealist on a grandiose scale. 'The idea' which turns up in his letters of the fifties – 'genius like a powerful horse drags humanity at her tail along the roads of the idea', in spite of all that human stupidity can do to rein her in – is evidently, under its guise of art, none other than the Hegelian 'Idea' which served Marx and so many others under a variety of different guises. There are great forces in humanity, Flaubert feels, which the present is somehow suppressing but which may some day be gloriously set free. 'The soul is asleep today, drunk with the words she has listened to, but she will experience a wild awakening, in which she will give herself up to the ecstasies of liberation, for there will be nothing more to constrain her, neither government nor religion, not a formula; the republicans of all shades of opinion seem to me the most ferocious pedagogues, with their dreams of organizations, of legislations, of a society constructed like a convent.'

When he reasons about society – which he never does except in his letters – his conceptions seem incoherent. But Flaubert, who believed that the artist should be triply ('to the *n*th degree') a thinker and who had certainly one of the great minds of his time, was the kind of imaginative writer who works directly in concrete images and does not deal at all in ideas. His informal expressions of his general opinions are as unsystematized and impromptu as his books are well-built and precise. But it is worth while to quote a few from his letters, because, though he never came anywhere near to expounding a social philosophy – when George Sand accused him of not having one, he admitted it – they do indicate the instincts and emotions which are the prime movers in the world of his art.

Flaubert is opposed to the socialists because he regards them as materialistic and because he dislikes their authoritarianism, which he says derives straight from the tradition of the Church. Yet they have 'denied *pain*, have blasphemed three-quarters of modern poetry, the blood of Christ, which quickens in us'. And: 'O socialists, there is your ulcer: the ideal is lacking to you; and that very matter which you pursue slips through your fingers like a wave; the adoration of humanity for itself and by itself (which brings us to the doctrine of the useful in Art, to the theories of public safety and reason of state, to all the injustices and all the intolerances, to the immolation of the right, to the levelling of the Beautiful), that cult of the belly, I say, breeds wind.' One thing he makes clear by reiteration through the various periods in his life: his disapproval of the ideal of equality. What is wanted, he keeps insisting, is 'justice'; and behind this demand for justice is evidently Flaubert's resentment, arising from his own experience, against the false reputations, the undeserved rewards, and the stupid repressions of the Second Empire. And he was sceptical of popular education and opposed to universal suffrage.

Yet among the men of his time whom Flaubert admired most were democrats, humanitarians, and reformers. 'You are certainly the French author', he wrote Michelet, 'whom I have read and reread most'; and he said of Victor Hugo that Hugo was the living man 'in whose skin' he would be happiest to be. George Sand was one of his closest friends: *Un Coeur simple* was written for her – apparently in answer to her admonition that art was 'not merely criticism and satire' and to show her that he, too, had a heart.

When we come to Flaubert's books themselves, we find a much plainer picture of things.

It is not true, as is sometimes supposed, that he disclaimed any moral intention. He deliberately refrained in his novels from commenting on the action in his own character: 'the artist ought not to appear in his work any more than God in nature'. But, like God, he rules his universe through law; and the reader, from what he hears and sees, must infer the moral system.

What *are* we supposed to infer from Flaubert's work? His general historical point of view is, I believe, pretty well known. He held that 'the three great evolutions of humanity' had been '*paganisme, christianisme, muflisme* [muckerism]', and that Europe was in the third of these phases. Paganism he depicted in *Salammbô* and in the short story *Hérodias*. The Carthaginians of *Salammbô* had been savage and benighted barbarians: they had worshipped serpents, crucified lions, sacrificed their children to Moloch, and trampled armies to death with herds of elephants; but they had slaughtered, lusted, and agonized superbly. Christianity is represented by the two legends of saints, *La Tentation de Saint Antoine* and *La Légende de Saint Julien l'Hospitalier*. The Christian combats his lusts, he expiates human cruelty; but this attitude, too, is heroic: Saint Anthony, who inhabits the desert, Saint Julien, who lies down with the leper, have pushed to their furthest limits the virtues of abnegation and humility. But when we come to the *muflisme* of the nineteenth century – in *Madame Bovary* and *L'Éducation sentimentale* – all is meanness, mediocrity, and timidity.

The villain here is, of course, the bourgeois; and it is true that these two novels of Flaubert ridicule and damn the contemporary world, taking down its pretensions by comparing it with Carthage and the Thebaid. But in these pictures of modern life there is a complexity of human values and an analysis of social processes which does not appear in the books that deal with older civilizations; and this social analysis of Flaubert's has, it seems to me, been too much disregarded – with the result that *L'Éducation sentimentale*, one of his most remarkable books, has been rather underestimated.

In *Madame Bovary*, Flaubert is engaged in criticizing that very longing for the exotic and the faraway which played such a large part in his own life and which led him to write *Salammbô* and *Saint Antoine*. What cuts Flaubert off from the other romantics and makes him primarily a social critic is his grim realization of the futility of dreaming about the splendours of the Orient and the brave old days of the past as an antidote to bourgeois society. Emma Bovary, the wife of a small country doctor, is always seeing herself in some other setting, imagining herself someone else. She will not face her situation as it is, and the result is that she is eventually undone by the realities she has been trying to ignore. The upshot of all Emma's yearnings for a larger and more glamorous life is that her poor little daughter, left an orphan by Emma's suicide and the death of her father, is sent to work in a cotton mill.

The socialist of Flaubert's time might perfectly have approved of this: while the romantic individualist deludes himself with unrealizable fantasies, in the attempt to evade bourgeois society, and only succeeds in destroying himself, he lets humanity fall a victim to the industrial-commercial processes, which, unimpeded by his dreaming, go on with their deadly work.

Flaubert had more in common with, and had perhaps been influenced more by, the socialist thought of his time than he would ever have allowed himself to confess. In his novels, it is never the nobility – indistinguishable for mediocrity from the bourgeois – but the peasants and working people whom he habitually uses as touchstones to show up the pretensions of the bourgeois. One of the most memorable scenes in *Madame Bovary* is the agricultural exhibition at which the pompous local dignitaries award a medal to an old farm servant for forty-five years of service on the same farm. Flaubert has told us about the bourgeois at length, made us listen to a long speech by a town councillor on the flourishing state of France; and now he describes the peasant – scared by the flags and drums and by the gentlemen in black coats, and not understanding what is wanted of her. Her long and bony hands, with which she has worked all her life in stable dust, lye, and greasy wool, still seem dirty, although she has just washed them, and they hang at her sides half open, as if to present a testimony of toil. There is no tenderness or sadness in her face: it has a rigidity almost monastic. And her long association with animals has given her something of their placidity and dumbness. 'So she stood up before those florid bourgeois, that half-century of servitude.' And the heroine of *Un Coeur simple*, a servant who devotes her whole life to the service of a provincial family and gets not one ray of love in return, has the same sort of dignity and pathos.

It is, however, in *L'Éducation sentimentale* that Flaubert's account of society comes closest to socialist theory. Indeed, his presentation here of the Revolution of 1848 parallels in so striking a manner Marx's analysis of the same events in *The Eighteenth Brumaire of Louis Napoleon* that it is worth while to focus together the diverse figures of Flaubert and Marx in order to recognize how two of the most searching minds of the century, pursuing courses so apparently divergent, arrived at almost identical interpretations of the happenings of their own time.

When we do this, we become aware that Marx and Flaubert started from very similar assumptions and that they were actuated by moral aims almost equally uncompromising. Both implacably hated the bourgeois, and both were resolved at any cost of worldly success to keep outside the bourgeois system. And Karl Marx, like Flaubert, shared to some degree the romantic bias in favour of the past. The author of *Das Kapital* can hardly, of course, be said to have had a very high opinion of any period of human history; but in comparison with the capitalist nineteenth century, he did betray a certain tenderness for Greece and Rome and the

Middle Ages. He pointed out that the slavery of the ancient world had at least purchased the 'full development' of the masters, and that a certain Antipater of Thessalonika had joyfully acclaimed the invention of the water wheel for grinding corn because it would set free the female slaves who had formerly had to do this work, whereas the bourgeois economists had seen in machinery only a means for making the workers work faster and longer in order 'to transform a few vulgar and half-educated upstarts into "eminent cotton spinners", "extensive sausage makers", and "influential blacking dealers".' And he had also a soft spot for the feudal system before the nobility had revolted against the Crown and while the rights of all classes, high and low, were still guaranteed by the king. Furthermore, the feudal lords, he insisted, had spent their money lavishly when they had it, whereas it was of the essence of capitalism that the capitalist saved his money and invested it, only to save and reinvest the profits.

Karl Marx's judgement on his age was the *Communist Manifesto*. Let us examine the implications of Flaubert's political novel. The hero of *L'Éducation sentimentale*, Frédéric Moreau, is a sensitive and intelligent young man equipped with a moderate income; but he has no stability of purpose and is capable of no emotional integrity. He becomes aimlessly, will-lessly, involved in love affairs with different types of women and he is unable to make anything out of any of them: they simply get in each other's way till in the end he is left with nothing. Frédéric is most in love from the very beginning of the story with the virtuous oval-faced wife of a sort of glorified drummer, who is engaged in more or less shady business enterprises; but, what with his timidity and her virtue, he never gets anywhere with her – even though she loves him in return – and leaves her in the hands of the drummer. Flaubert makes it plain to us, however, that Frédéric and the vulgar husband at bottom represent the same thing: Frédéric is only the more refined as well as the more incompetent side of the middle-class mediocrity of which the dubious promoter represents the more flashy and active aspect. And so in the case of the other characters, the journalists and the artists, the members of the various political factions, the remnants of the old nobility, Frédéric finds the same shoddiness and lack of principle which are gradually revealed in himself – the same qualities which render so odious to him the banker M. Dambreuse, the type of the rich and powerful class. M. Dambreuse is always ready to trim his sails to any political party, monarchist or republican, which seems to have a chance of success. 'Most of the men who were there', Flaubert writes of the guests at the Dambreuse house, 'had served at least four governments; and they would have sold France or the human race in order to guarantee their fortune, to spare themselves an anxiety or a difficulty, or even from simple baseness, instinctive adoration of force.' '*Je me moque des affaires!*' cries Frédéric when the guests at M. Dambreuse's are complaining that criticism of the government hurts business; but he cannot give up going to the house, because he always hopes to profit by Dambreuse's investments and influence.

The only really sympathetic characters in *L'Éducation sentimentale* are, again, the representatives of the people. Rosanette, Frédéric's mistress, is the daughter of poor workers in the silk mills, who sold her at fifteen as mistress to an old bourgeois. Her liaison with Frédéric is a symbol of the disastrously unenduring union between the proletariat and the bourgeois, of which Karl Marx had written in *The Eighteenth Brumaire*. After the suppression of the workers' insurrection during the June days of '48, Rosanette gives birth to a weakly child, which dies at the same time that Frédéric is already arranging a love affair with the dull wife of the banker. Frédéric believes that Mme Dambreuse will be able to advance his interests. And bourgeois socialism gets a very Marxist treatment – save in one respect, which we shall note in a moment – in the character of Sénécal, who is eternally making himself unpleasant about communism and the welfare of the masses, for which he is ready to fight to the last barricade. When, later, Sénécal gets a job as foreman in a pottery factory, he at once becomes a harsh little tyrant; and as soon as it begins to appear, after the putting-down of the June riots, that the reaction is sure to triumph, he decides, like certain radicals turned fascists, that the strong centralization of the government is already a kind of communism and that authority is in itself a great thing.

You have, on the other hand, the clerk Dussardier, a strapping and obtuse fellow, who is one of the few honest characters in the book. When we first see him, he has just knocked down a policeman in a political brawl on the street. Later, when the National Guard, of which Dussardier is a member, turns against the proletariat in the interests of law and order, Dussardier fells one of the insurgents from the top of a barricade and gets at the same time a bullet in the leg, thereby becoming a great hero of the bourgeois. But the poor fellow himself is unhappy. The boy that he had knocked down had wrapped the tricolor around him and shouted to the National Guard: 'Are you going to fire on your brothers?' Dussardier is not at all sure that he ought not to have been on the other side. His last appearance is at the climax of the story, constitutes, indeed, the climax: he turns up in a proletarian street riot, which the cavalry and the police are putting down. Dussardier refuses to move, crying ' *Vive la République!* '; and Frédéric comes along just in time to see one of the policemen kill him. Then he recognizes this policeman: it is the socialist, Sénécal.

L'Éducation sentimentale, unpopular when it first appeared, is likely, if we read it in youth, to prove baffling and even repellent. The title may have given the impression that we are going to get a love story, but the love affairs turn out invariably to be tepid or incomplete, and one finds oneself depressed or annoyed. Is it a satire? The characters are too close to life, and a little too well rounded, for satire. Yet they are not quite vitalized enough, not quite responsive enough, to seem the people of a straight novel. But we find that it sticks in our crop. If it is true, as Bernard Shaw has said, that

Das Kapital makes us see the nineteenth century 'as if it were a cloud passing down the wind, changing its shape and fading as it goes', so that we are afterwards never able to forget that 'capitalism, with its wage slavery, is only a passing phase of social development, following primitive communism, chattel slavery, and feudal serfdom into the past' – so Flaubert's novel plants deep in our mind an idea which we never quite get rid of: the suspicion that our middle-class society of manufacturers, businessmen, and bankers, of people who live on or deal in investments, so far from being redeemed by its culture, has ended by cheapening and invalidating all the departments of culture, political, scientific, artistic, and religious, as well as corrupting and weakening the ordinary human relations: love, friendship, and loyalty to cause – till the whole civilization seems to dwindle.

But fully to appreciate the book, one must have had time to see something of life and to have acquired a certain interest in social and political dramas as distinct from personal ones. If one rereads it in middle age, one finds that the author's tone no longer seems quite so acrid, that one is listening to a muted symphony of which the varied instrumentation and the pattern, the marked rhythms and the melancholy sonorities, had been hardly perceptible before. There are no hero, no villain, to arouse us, no clowns to entertain us, no scenes to wring our hearts. Yet the effect is deeply moving. It is the tragedy of nobody in particular, but of the poor human race itself reduced to such ineptitude, such cowardice, such commonness, such weak irresolution – arriving, with so many fine notions in its head, so many noble words on its lips, at a failure which is all the more miserable because those who have failed in their roles have even forgotten what roles they were cast for. We come to understand the statement of Mr Ford Madox Ford that he has found it is not too much to read the book fourteen times. Though *L'Éducation sentimentale* is less attractive on the surface and less exciting as a story than *Madame Bovary*, it is certainly the book of Flaubert's which is most ambitiously planned and into which he has tried to put most. And once we have got the clue to the immense and complex drama which unrolls itself behind the half-screen of the detached and monotonous style, we find it as absorbing and satisfying as a great play or a great piece of music.

The one conspicuous respect in which Flaubert's point of view on the events of 1848 *diverges* from that of Marx has been thrown into special relief by the events of our own time. For Marx, the evolution of the socialist into a proletarian-persecuting policeman would have been blamed on the bourgeois in Sénécal; for Flaubert, it is a development of socialism implicit in socialist beginnings. He distrusted, as I have shown above, the authoritarian aims of the socialists. It is Flaubert's conception that Sénécal, given his bourgeois hypocrisy, is still carrying out a socialist principle – or rather, that his behaviour as a policeman and his yearnings towards socialist control are both derived from his impulse towards despotism.

We may not be prepared to conclude that the evolution of Sénécal represents the whole destiny of socialism, but we must recognize that Flaubert had here brought to our attention a danger of which Marx was not aware. We have had the opportunity to see how even a socialism which has come to power as the result of a proletarian revolution can breed a political police of almost unprecedented ruthlessness – how the example of Marx himself, with his emphasis on dictatorial control rather than on democratic processes, has contributed to produce this disaster. Flaubert, who believed that the artist should rid himself of social convictions, has gauged the tendencies of a political doctrine as the greatest of doctrinaires could not; and here the attitude he proposed has been justified.

The war of 1870 was a terrible shock to Flaubert: the nervous disorders of his later years have been attributed to it. He had the Prussians in his house at Croisset and had to bury his manuscripts. When he made a trip to Paris after the

Commune, he came back to the country deeply shaken. 'This would never have happened', he said when he saw the wreck of the Tuileries, 'if they had only understood *L'Éducation sentimentale.*' What Flaubert meant, no doubt, was that if the French had seen the falsity of their politics, they would never have fought about them so fiercely. 'Oh, how tired I am', he writes George Sand, 'of the ignoble worker, the inept bourgeois, the stupid peasant, and the odious ecclesiastic.'

But in his letters of this period, which are more violent than ever, we see him taking a new direction. The effect of the Commune on Flaubert, as on so many of the other French intellectuals, was to bring out in him the class-conscious bourgeois. Basically bourgeois his life had always been, with his mother and his little income. He had, like Frédéric Moreau himself, been 'cowardly in his youth', he wrote George Sand. 'I was *afraid* of life.' And, even moving amongst what he regarded as the grandeurs of the ancient world, he remains a moderate Frenchman of the middle nineteenth century, who seems to cultivate excess, systematically and with a certain self-consciousness, in the hope of horrifying other Frenchmen. Marcel Proust has pointed out that Flaubert's imagery, even in books which do not deal with the bourgeois, tends to be rather banal. It was the enduring tradition of French classicism which had saved him from the prevailing shoddiness: by discipline and objectivity, by heroic application to the mastery of form, he had kept the enemy at a distance. But now when a working-class government had held Paris for two months and a half and had wrecked monuments and shot bourgeois hostages, Flaubert found himself as fierce against the Communards as any respectable 'grocer'. 'My opinion is', he wrote George Sand, 'that the whole Commune ought to have been sent to the galleys, that those sanguinary idiots ought to have been made to clean up the ruins of Paris, with chains around their necks like convicts. That would have wounded *humanity*, though. They treat the mad dogs with tenderness, but not the people whom they have bitten.' He raises his old cry for 'justice'. Universal suffrage, that 'disgrace to the human spirit', must first of all be done away with; but among the elements of civilization which must be given their due importance he now includes 'race and even money' along with 'intelligence' and 'education'.

For the rest, certain political ideas emerge – though, as usual, in a state of confusion. 'The mass, the majority, are always idiotic. I haven't got many convictions, but that one I hold very strongly. Yet the mass must be respected, no matter how inept it is, because it contains the germs of an incalculable fecundity. Give it liberty, but not power. I don't believe in class distinctions any more than you do. The castes belong to the domain of archaeology. But I do believe that the poor hate the rich and that the rich are afraid of the poor. That will go on for ever. It is quite useless to preach the gospel of love to either. The most urgent need is to educate the rich, who are, after all, the strongest.' 'The only reasonable thing to do – I always come back to that – is a government of mandarins, provided that the mandarins know something and even that they know a great deal. The people is an eternal minor, and it will always (in the hierarchy of social elements) occupy the bottom place, because it is unlimited number, mass. It gets us nowhere to have large numbers of peasants learn to read and no longer listen to their priest; but it is infinitely important that there should be a great many men like Renan and Littré who can live and be listened to. Our salvation now is in a *legitimate aristocracy*, by which I mean a majority which will be made up of something other than numerals.' Renan himself and Taine were having recourse to similar ideas of the salvation of society through an 'élite'. In Flaubert's case, it never seems to have occurred to him that his hierarchy of mandarins and his project for educating the rich were identical with the notions of Saint-Simon, which he had rejected with scorn years before on the ground that they were too authoritarian. The Commune has stimulated in Flaubert a demand for his own kind of despotism.

He had already written in 1869: 'It's no longer a question of imagining the best form of government possible, because they are all alike, but of making sure that science prevails. That is the most urgent problem. Everything else will inevitably follow. The purely intellectual type of man has done more for the human race than all the Saint Vincent de Pauls in the world! And politics will remain idiotic for ever so long as it does not derive from science. The government of a country ought to be a department of the Institute, and the least important of all.' 'Politics', he reiterated in 1871, 'must become a positive science, as war has already become'; and, 'The French Revolution must cease to be a dogma and become part of the domain of science, like all the rest of human affairs.' Marx and Engels were not reasoning otherwise; but they believed, as Flaubert could not do, in a coming-of-age of the proletariat which would make possible the application of social science. To Flaubert the proletariat made a certain pathetic appeal, but it seemed to him much too stupid to act effectively in its own behalf; the Commune threw him into such a panic that he reviled the Communards as criminals and brutes. At one moment he writes to George Sand: 'The International may end by winning out, but not in the way that it hopes, not in the way that people are afraid of'; and then, two days later, 'the International will collapse, because it is on the wrong path. No ideas, nothing but envy!'

Finally, he wrote her in 1875: 'The words "religion" or "Catholicism", on the one hand, "progress", "fraternity", "democracy", on the other, no longer answer the spiritual needs of the day. The dogma of equality – a new thing – which the radicals have been crying up, has been proved false by the experiments of physiology and by history. I do not at the present time see any way of setting up a new principle, any more than of still respecting the old ones. So I search unsuccessfully for the central idea from which all the rest ought to depend.'

In the meantime, his work becomes more misanthropic. 'Never, my dear old chap,' he had written Ernest Feydeau, 'have I felt so colossal a disgust for mankind. I'd like to drown the human race under my vomit.' His political comedy, *Le Candidat*, produced in 1874, is the only one of his works which does not include a single character for whom one can feel any sympathy. The rich parvenu who is running for deputy not only degrades himself by every form of truckling and trimming in order to win the election, but sacrifices his daughter's happiness and allows himself to be cuckolded by his wife. The audiences would not have it; the actor who played the candidate came off the stage in tears. And, reading the play today, one cannot but agree with the public. It has some amusing and mordant passages, but one's gorge rises against it.

Flaubert then embarked on *Bouvard et Pécuchet*, which occupied him – with only one period of relief, when he indulged his suppressed kindliness and idealism in the relatively human *Trois Contes* – for most of the rest of his life. Here two copyists retire from their profession and set out to cultivate the arts and sciences. They make a mess of them all. The book contains an even more withering version of the events of 1848, in which the actors and their political attitudes are reduced to the scale of performing fleas. (There is one bitter scene, however, which has a terrible human force: that in which, the revolution having failed and the reaction having entrusted to the clergy the supervision of public education, the village priest visits the village schoolmaster, a freethinker who has been on the revolutionary side, and compels him, by threatening to dismiss him from the job which he needs to support his children, to consent to betray his principles by teaching catechism and sacred history.) When Bouvard and Pécuchet find at last that everything has 'cracked in their hands', they go back to copying again. Flaubert did not live to finish the book; but he had already compiled some of the materials which he had intended to use in the second part: a collection of ridiculous statements and idiotic sentiments that Bouvard and Pécuchet were to find in the works they should copy.

This last uncompleted novel has somewhat mystified those critics who have taken it for an attack on the bourgeois like *L'Éducation sentimentale* – though there would not have been much point in Flaubert's simply doing the same thing again in a smaller and drier way. But. M. René Dumesnil, one of the principal authorities on Flaubert, believes that *Bouvard et Pécuchet* was to have had a larger application. The anthology of *idées reçues* was to have not merely a credo of the bourgeois: it was to have included, also, many lapses by distinguished men of the past as well as the present, of writers, in certain cases, whom Flaubert immensely admired, and some passages, even, from Flaubert himself (in the first part of the book, it is obvious that the author is caricaturing his own ideas along with those of everybody else). Bouvard and Pécuchet, having realized the stupidity of their neighbours and discovered their own limitations, were to be left with a profound impression of the general imbecility and ignorance. They were themselves to assemble this monument of the inanity of the human mind.

If this be true – and the papers left by Flaubert seem to make his intention clear – he had lifted the blame from a social class and for the first time written a work of the type of *Gulliver's Travels*: a satire on the human race. The bourgeois has ceased to preach to the bourgeois: as the first big cracks begin to show in the structure of the nineteenth century, he shifts his complaint to the incompetence of humanity, for he is unable to believe in, or even to conceive, any non-bourgeois way out.

The Ambiguity of Henry James

A DISCUSSION of Henry James's ambiguity may appropriately begin with *The Turn of the Screw*. This story, which seems to have proved more fascinating to the general reading public than anything else of James's except *Daisy Miller*, perhaps conceals another horror behind the ostensible one. I do not know who first suggested this idea; but I believe that Miss Edna Kenton, whose insight into James is profound, was the first to write about it,* and the water-colourist Charles Demuth did a set of illustrations for the tale that were evidently based on this interpretation.

The theory is, then, that the governess who is made to tell the story is a neurotic case of sex repression, and that the ghosts are not real ghosts but hallucinations of the governess.

Let us see how the narrative runs. This narrative is supposed to have been written by the governess herself, but it begins with an introduction in which we are told something about her by a man whose sister's governess she had been after the time of the story. The youngest daughter of a poor country parson, she struck him, he explains, as 'awfully clever and nice ... the most agreeable woman I've ever known in her position' and 'worthy of any whatever'. (Now, it is a not infrequent trick of James's to introduce sinister characters with descriptions that at first sound flattering, so this need not throw us off.) Needing work, she had come up to London to answer an advertisement and had found someone who wanted a governess for an orphaned nephew and niece. 'This prospective patron proved a gentleman, a bachelor in the prime of life, such a figure as had never risen,

* In *The Arts*, November 1924. This issue contains also photographs of the Demuth illustrations.

save in a dream or an old novel, before a fluttered, anxious girl out of a Hampshire vicarage.' It is made clear that the young woman has become thoroughly infatuated with her employer. He is charming to her and lets her have the job on condition that she will take all the responsibility and never bother him about the children; and she goes down to the house in the country where they have been left with a house-keeper and some other servants.

The boy, she finds, has been sent home from school for reasons into which she does not inquire but which she colours, on no evidence at all, with a significance somehow ominous. She learns that her predecessor left, and that the woman has since died, under circumstances which are not explained but which are made in the same way to seem queer. The new governess finds herself alone with the good but illiterate housekeeper and the children, who seem innocent and charming. As she wanders about the estate, she thinks often how delightful it would be if one should come suddenly round the corner and see the master just arrived from London: there he would stand, handsome, smiling, approving.

She is never to meet her employer again, but what she does meet are the apparitions. One day when his face has been vividly in her mind, she comes out in sight of the house and, looking up, sees the figure of a man on a tower, a figure which is not the master's. Not long afterwards, the figure appears again, towards the end of a rainy Sunday. She sees him at closer range and more clearly: he is wearing smart clothes but is obviously not a gentleman. The housekeeper, meeting the governess immediately afterwards, behaves as if the governess herself were a ghost: 'I wondered why she should be scared.' The governess tells her about the apparition and learns that it answers the description of one of the master's valets, who had stayed down there and who had sometimes stolen his clothes. The valet had been a bad character, had used 'to play with the boy ... to spoil him'; he had finally been found dead, having apparently slipped on the ice coming out of a public house – though one couldn't say he hadn't been murdered. The governess cannot help believing that he has come back to haunt the children.

Not long afterwards, she and the little girl are out on the shore of a lake, the child playing, the governess sewing. The latter becomes aware of a third person on the opposite side of the lake. But she looks first at little Flora, who is turning her back in that direction and who, she notes, has 'picked up a small flat piece of wood, which happened to have in it a little hole that had evidently suggested to her the idea of sticking in another fragment that might figure as a mast and make the thing a boat. This second morsel, as I watched her, she was very markedly and intently attempting to tighten in its place.' This somehow 'sustains' the governess so that she is able to raise her eyes: she sees a woman 'in black, pale and dreadful'. She concludes that it is the former governess. The housekeeper, questioned, tells her that this woman, although a lady, had had an affair with the valet. The boy had used to go off with the valet and then lie about it afterwards. The governess concludes that the boy must have known about the valet and the woman – the boy and girl have been corrupted by them.

Observe that there is never any reason for supposing that anybody but the governess sees the ghosts. She believes that the children see them, but there is never any proof that they do. The housekeeper insists that she does not see them; it is apparently the governess who frightens her. The children, too, become hysterical; but this is evidently the governess's doing. Observe, also, from the Freudian point of view, the significance of the governess's interest in the little girl's pieces of wood and of the fact that the male apparition first takes shape on a tower and the female apparition on a lake. There seems here to be only a single circumstance which does not fit into the hypothesis that the ghosts are mere fancies of the governess: the fact that her description of the masculine ghost at a time when she knows nothing of the valet should be identifiable as the valet by the housekeeper. And when we look back, we see that even this has perhaps been left open to a double interpretation. The governess has never heard of the valet, but it has been suggested to her in a conversation with the housekeeper that there has been some other male about who 'liked everyone young and pretty', and the idea of this other person has been ambiguously confused with the master and with the master's possible interest in her, the present governess. And may she not, in her subconscious imagination, taking her cue from this, have associated herself with her predecessor and conjured up an image who wears the master's clothes but who (the Freudian 'censor' intervening) looks debased, 'like an actor', she says (would he not have to stoop to love her)? The apparition had 'straight, good features' and his appearance is described in detail. When we look back, we find that the master's appearance has never been described at all: we have merely been told that he was 'handsome', and it comes out in the talk with the housekeeper that the valet was 'remarkably handsome'. It is impossible for us to know how much the phantom resembles the master – the governess, certainly, would never tell.

The new apparitions now begin to be seen at night, and the governess becomes convinced that the children get up to meet them, though they are able to give plausible explanations of the behaviour that has seemed suspicious. The housekeeper now says to the governess that, if she is seriously worried about all this, she ought to report it to the master. The governess, who has promised not to bother him, is afraid he would think her insane; and she imagines 'his derision, his amusement, his contempt for the breakdown of my resignation at being left alone and for the fine machinery I had set in motion to attract his attention to my slighted charms'. The housekeeper, hearing this, threatens to send for the master herself; the governess threatens to leave if she does. After this, for a considerable period, the visions no longer appear.

But the children become uneasy: they wonder when their uncle is coming, and they try to communicate with him – but the governess suppresses their letters. The boy finally asks her frankly when she is going to send him to school, intimates that if he had not been so fond of her, he would have complained to his uncle long ago, declares that he will do so at once.

This upsets her: she thinks for a moment of leaving, but decides that this would be deserting them. She is now, it seems, in love with the boy. Entering the schoolroom, after her conversation with him, she finds the ghost of the other governess sitting with her head in her hands, looking 'dishonoured and tragic', full of 'unutterable woe'. At this point the new governess feels – the morbid half of her split personality is now getting the upper hand of the other – that it is she who is intruding upon the ghost: 'You terrible miserable woman!' she cries. The apparition disappears. She tells the housekeeper, who looks at her oddly, that the soul of the woman is damned and wants the little girl to share her damnation. She finally agrees to write to the master, but no sooner has she sat down to the paper than she gets up and goes to the boy's bedroom, where she finds him lying awake. When he demands to go back to school, she embraces him and begs him to tell her why he was sent away; appealing to him with what seems to her desperate tenderness but in a way that disquiets the child, she insists that all she wants is to save him. There is a sudden gust of wind – it is a stormy night outside – the casement rattles, the boy shrieks. She has been kneeling beside the bed: when she gets up, she finds the candle extinguished. 'It was I who blew it, dear!' says the boy. For her, it is the evil spirit disputing her domination. She cannot imagine that the boy may really have blown out the candle in order not to have to tell her with the light on about his disgrace at school. (Here, however, occurs a detail which is less easily susceptible of double explanation: the governess has *felt* a 'gust of frozen air' and yet sees that the window is 'tight'. Are we to suppose she merely fancied that she felt it?)

The next day, the little girl disappears. They find her beside the lake. The young woman for the first time now speaks openly to one of the children about the ghosts. 'Where, my pet, is Miss Jessel?' she demands – and immediately answers herself: 'She's there, she's there!' she cries, pointing across the lake. The housekeeper looks with a 'dazed blink' and asks where she sees anything; the little girl turns upon the governess 'an expression of hard, still gravity, an expression absolutely new and unprecedented and that appeared to read and accuse and judge me'. The governess feels her 'situation horribly crumble' now. The little girl breaks down, becomes feverish, begs to be taken away from the governess; the housekeeper sides with the girl and hints that the governess had better go. But the young woman forces her, instead, to take the little girl away; and she tries to make it impossible, before their departure, for the children to see one another.

She is now left alone with the boy. A strange and dreadful scene ensues. 'We continued silent while the maid was with us – as silent, it whimsically occurred to me, as some young couple who, on their wedding-journey, at the inn, feel shy in the presence of the waiter.' When the maid has gone, and she presses him to tell her the reason for his expulsion from school, the boy seems suddenly afraid of her. He finally confesses that he 'said things' – to 'a few', to 'those he liked'. It all sounds sufficiently harmless: there comes to her out of her 'very pity the appalling alarm of his being perhaps innocent. It was for the instant confounding and bottomless, for if he *were* innocent, what then on earth was I?' The valet appears at the window – it is 'the white face of damnation'. (But is it really the spirits who are damned or the governess who is slipping to damnation herself?) She is aware that the boy does not see it. 'No more, no more, no more!' she shrieks to the apparition. 'Is she *here*?' demands the boy in panic. (He has, in spite of the governess' efforts, succeeded in seeing his sister and has heard from her of the incident at the lake.) No, she says, it is not the woman: 'But it's at the window – straight before us. It's *there*!' ... 'It's *he*?' then whom does he mean by 'he'?

' "Peter Quint – you devil!" His face gave again, round the

room, its convulsed supplication. "Where?" " 'What does he matter now, my own?' she cries. 'What will he *ever* matter? *I* have you, but he has lost you for ever!' Then she shows him that the figure has vanished: 'There, *there*!' she says, pointing towards the window. He looks and gives a cry; she feels that he is dead in her arms. From the governess' point of view, the final disappearance of the spirit has proved too terrible a shock for the child and 'his little heart, dispossessed, has stopped'; but if we study the dialogue from the other point of view, we see that he must have taken her 'There, *there*!' as an answer to his own 'Where?' Instead of persuading him that there is nothing to be frightened of, she has, on the contrary, finally convinced him either that he has actually seen or that he is just about to see some horror. He gives 'the cry of a creature hurled over an abyss'. She has literally frightened him to death.

When one has once got hold of the clue to this meaning of *The Turn of the Screw*, one wonders how one could ever have missed it. There is a very good reason, however, in the fact that nowhere does James unequivocally give the thing away: almost everything from beginning to end can be read equally in either of two senses. In the preface to the collected edition, however, as Miss Kenton has pointed out, James does seem to want to give a hint. He asserts that *The Turn of the Screw* is 'a fairy-tale pure and simple' – but adds that the apparitions are of the order of those involved in witchcraft cases rather than those in cases of psychic research. And he goes on to tell of his reply to one of his readers who objected that he had not characterized the governess sufficiently. At this criticism, he says, 'One's artistic, one's ironic heart shook for the instant almost to breaking'; and he answered: 'It was "*déjà très-joli*" . . . please believe, the general proposition of our young woman's keeping crystalline her record of so many intense anomalies and obscurities – *by which I don't of course mean her explanation of them, a different matter* . . . She has "authority", which is a good deal to have given her . . .' The italics above are mine: these words seem impossible to explain except on the hypothesis of hallucination (though this is hardly consistent with the intention of writing 'a fairy-tale pure and simple') And note too, that in the collected edition James has not included *The Turn of the Screw* in the volume with his other ghost stories but with stories of another kind: between *The Aspern Papers* and *The Liar* – the first a study of a curiosity which becomes a mania and menace (to which we shall revert in a moment), the second a study of a pathological liar, whose wife protects his lies against the world, acting with very much the same sort of 'authority' as the governess in *The Turn of the Screw*.

When we look back in the light of these hints, we are inclined to conclude from analogy that the story is primarily intended as a characterization of the governess: her sombre and guilty visions and the way she behaves about them seem to present, from the moment we examine them from the obverse side of her narrative, an accurate and distressing picture of the poor country parson's daughter, with her English middle-class class-consciousness, her inability to admit to herself her natural sexual impulses, and the relentless English 'authority' which enables her to put over on inferiors even purposes which are totally deluded and not at all in the other people's best interests. Remember, also, in this connexion, the peculiar psychology of governesses, who, by reason of their isolated position between the family and the servants, are likely to become ingrown and morbid. One has heard of actual cases of women who have frightened a household by opening doors or smashing mirrors and who have succeeded in torturing parents by mythical stories of kidnappers. The traditional 'poltergeist' who breaks crockery and upsets furniture has been for centuries a recurring phenomenon. First a figure of demonology, he later became an object of psychic research, and is now a recognized neurotic type.

Once we arrive at this conception of *The Turn of the Screw*, we can see in it a new significance in its relation to Henry James's other work. We find that it is a variation on one of his familiar themes: the thwarted Anglo-Saxon spinster; and we remember unmistakable cases of women in James's fiction who deceive themselves and others about the origins of their aims and emotions. One of the most obvious examples is that remarkable and too little read novel, *The Bostonians*. The subject of *The Bostonians* is the struggle for the daughter of a poor evangelist between a young man from the South who wants to marry her and a well-to-do Boston lady with a Lesbian interest in her. The strong-minded and strong-willed spinster is herself apparently quite in the dark as to the real character of her feeling for the girl: she is convinced that her desire to dominate her, to have her always living with her, to teach her to make speeches on women's rights and to prevent the young Southerner from marrying her, is a disinterested ardour for the Feminist cause. But the reader is not left in doubt; and Olive Chancellor is shown us in a setting of other self-deluded New England idealists.

There is a theme of very much the same kind in the short story called *The Marriages*, which amused R. L. Stevenson so hugely. But here the treatment is frankly comic. A young and rather stupid girl, described as of the unmarriageable type, but much attached to her widower father and obsessed by the memory of her mother, undertakes to set up an obstacle to her father's proposed second marriage. Her project, which she carries out, is to go to his fiancée and tell this lady that her father is an impossible character who had made her late mother miserable. She thus breaks up the projected match; and when her brother calls her a raving maniac, she is not in the least disquieted in her conviction that, by frustrating her father, she has proved faithful in her duty to her mother.

James's world is full of these women. They are not always emotionally perverted. Sometimes they are apathetic – like the charming Francie Dosson of *The Reverberator*, who, though men are always falling in love with her, seems not really ever to have grasped what courtship and marriage mean and is apparently quite content to go on all the rest of her life eating *marrons glacés* with her family in a suite in a Paris hotel. Or they are longing, these women, for affection but too inhibited or passive to obtain it for themselves, like the pathetic Milly Theale of *The Wings of the Dove*, who wastes away in Venice and whose doctor recommends a lover.

II

James's men are not precisely neurotic; but they are the masculine counterparts of his women. They have a way of missing out on emotional experience, either through timidity or prudence or through heroic renunciation.

The extreme and fantastic example is the hero of *The Beast in the Jungle*, who is finally crushed by the realization that his fate is to be the man in the whole world to whom nothing at all is to happen. Some of these characters are presented ironically: Mr Acton of *The Europeans*, so smug and secure in his clean-swept house, deciding not to marry the baroness who has proved such an upsetting element in his little New England community, is an amusing and accurate portrait of a certain kind of careful Bostonian. Others are made sympathetic, such as the starved Lambert Strether of *The Ambassadors*, who comes to Paris too late in life.

Sometimes, however, the effect is ambiguous. Though the element of irony in Henry James is often underestimated by his readers, there are stories which leave us in doubt as to whether or not the author could foresee how his heroes would strike the reader. Is the fishy Bernard Longueville, for example, of the early novel called *Confidence* really intended for a sensitive and interesting young man or is he a prig in the manner of Jane Austen? This is not due to a beginner's uncertainty, for some of James's later heroes make us uneasy in a similar way. The very late short story *Flickerbridge*, in which a young American painter decides not to marry a young newspaper woman (the men are always deciding *not* to marry the women in Henry James) because he fears that she will spoil by publicizing it a delightful old English house, the property of a cousin of hers, which she herself has not yet seen but at which he has enjoyed visiting – this story is even harder to swallow, since it is all too evident here that the author approved of his hero.

But what are we to think of *The Sacred Fount*? This short novel, surely James's most curious production, inspired when it first appeared a parody by Owen Seaman which had a certain historical significance because the book seemed to mark the point at which James, for the general public, had definitely become unassimilable, and therefore absurd or annoying. *The Sacred Fount* was written not long after *The Turn of the Screw* and is a sort of companion piece to it. Here we have the same setting of an English country house, the same passages of a strange and sad beauty, the same furtive subversive happenings in an atmosphere of clarity and brightness, the same dubious central figure, the same almost inscrutable ambiguity. As in the case of *The Turn of the Screw*, the fundamental question presents itself and never seems to get properly answered: What is the reader to think of the protagonist? – who is here a man instead of a woman.

It would be tedious to analyse *The Sacred Fount* as I have done *The Turn of the Screw* – and it would prove, I think, somewhat more difficult. The book is not merely mystifying but maddening. Yet I believe that if one got to the bottom of it, a good deal of light would be thrown on the author. Rebecca West, in her little book on James, has given a burlesque account of this novel as the story of how 'a week-end visitor spends more intellectual force than Kant can have used on the *The Critique of Pure Reason* in an unsuccessful attempt to discover whether there exists between certain of his fellow-guests a relationship not more interesting among these vacuous people than it is among sparrows'. This visitor, who himself tells the story, observes that, among the other guests, a man and a woman he knows, both of them middle-aged, appear to have taken a new lease of life, whereas a younger man and woman appear to have been depleted.

He evolves a theory about them: he imagines that the married couples have been forming new combinations and that the younger man and woman have been feeding the older pair from the sacred fount of their youth at the price of getting used up themselves.

This theory seems rather academic – and does James really mean us to accept it? Do not the narrator's imaginings serve to characterize the narrator just as the governess' ghosts serve to characterize the governess? As this detached and rather eerie individual proceeds to spy on and question his friends in order to find out whether the facts fit his hypothesis, we decide, as we do with *The Turn of the Screw*, that there are two separate stories to be kept distinct: a romance which the narrator is spinning and a reality which we are supposed to divine from what he tells us about what actually happens. We remember the narrator of *The Aspern Papers*, another prying and importunate fellow, who is finally foiled and put to rout by the old lady whose private papers he is trying by fraud to get hold of. In the case of *The Aspern Papers*, there is no uncertainty whatever as to what we are to think of the narrator: the author is quite clear that the papers were none of the journalist's business, and that the rebuff he received served him right. Now, the amateur detective of *The Sacred Fount* is also foiled and rebuffed, and in very much the same manner, by one of his recalcitrant victims. 'My poor dear, you *are* crazy, and I bid you good night!' she says to him at the end of the story. 'Such a last word,' the narrator remarks, 'the word that put me altogether nowhere – was too inacceptable not to prescribe afresh that prompt test of escape to other air for which I had earlier in the evening seen so much reason. I *should* certainly never again, on the spot, quite hang together, even though it wasn't really that I hadn't three times her method. What I too fatally lacked was her tone.' But *why* did he lack her tone? – *why* would he not hang together? What view are we supposed to take of the whole exploit of this singular being?

Mr Wilson Follett, the only writer, so far as I know, who

has given special attention to *The Sacred Fount*,* believes that the book is a parable – even a conscious parody – of James's own role as an artist. The narrator may or may not have been right as to the actual facts of the case. The point is that, in elaborating his theory, he has constructed a work of art, and that you cannot test the validity of works of art by checking them against actuality. The kind of reality that art achieves, made up of elements abstracted from experience and combined in a new way by the artist, would be destroyed by a collision with the actual, and the artist would find himself blocked.

Now it may very well be true that James has put himself into *The Sacred Fount* – that he has intended some sort of fable about the brooding imaginative mind and the material with which it works. But it seems to me that Mr Follett's theory assumes on James's part a conception of artistic truth which would hardly be worthy of him. After all, the novelist must pretend to know what people are actually up to, however much he may rearrange actuality; and it is not clear in *The Sacred Fount* whether the narrator really knows what he is talking about. If the book is, then, merely a parody, what is the point of the parody? Why should James have represented the artist as defeated by the breaking-in of life?

The truth is, I believe, that Henry James was not clear about the book in his own mind. Already, with *The Turn of the Screw*, he has carried his ambiguous procedure to a point where we almost feel that the author does not want the reader to get through to the hidden meaning. See his curious replies in his letters to correspondents who write him about the story: when they challenge him with leading questions, he seems to give evasive answers, dismissing the

---

* *Henry James's* 'Portrait of Henry James' in the *New York Times Book Review*, 23 August 1936. (Since my own essay was first written, Mr Edward Sackville West, in the *New Statesman and Nation* of 4 October 1947, has taken issue with the views here expressed in the best defence of this book I have seen.)

tale as a mere 'pot-boiler', a mere *jeu d'esprit*. There was no doubt in *The Bostonians*, for example, as to what view the reader was intended to take of such a character as Olive Chancellor: Olive, though tragic perhaps, is definitely unhealthy and horrid, and she is vanquished by Basil Ransom. But James does leave his readers uncomfortable as to what they are to think of the governess. And now, in *The Sacred Fount*, we do not know whether the week-end guest, though he was unquestionably obnoxious to the other guests, is intended to be taken as one of the élite, a fastidious, highly civilized sensibility, or merely as a little bit cracked and a bore. The man who tried to get the Aspern papers was a fanatic, a cad, and a nuisance; but many of James's inquisitive observers who never take part in the action are presented as superior people, and Henry James had confessed to being an inquisitive observer himself. Ambiguity was certainly growing on him. It was eventually to pass all bounds in those scenes in his later novels (of which the talks in *The Turn of the Screw* between the housekeeper and the governess are only comparatively mild examples) in which he compels his characters to carry on long conversations with each of the interlocutors always mistaking the other's meaning and neither ever yielding to the impulse to say one of the obvious things that would clear the situation up.

What if the hidden theme of *The Sacred Fount* is simply sex again? What if the real sacred fount, from which the narrator's acquaintances have been drawing their new vitality, is love, sexual love, instead of youth? They have something which he has not had, know something which he does not know; and, lacking the clue of experience, he can only misunderstand them and elaborate pedantic hypotheses; while they, having the forces of life on their side, are in a position to frighten him away. This theory may be dubious, also; but there is certainly involved in *The Sacred Fount*, whether or not Henry James quite meant to put it there, the conception of a man shut out from love, condemned to peep at other people's activities and to speculate about them rather barrenly, who will be shocked and put to rout when he touches the live current of human relations.

Hitherto, as I have said, it has usually been plain what James wanted us to think of his characters; but now there appears in his work a relatively morbid element which is not always handled objectively and which seems to have invaded the storyteller himself. It is as if at this point he had taken to dramatizing the frustrations of his own life without being willing to confess it, without fully admitting it even to himself.

But before we go further with this line of inquiry, let us look at Henry James in another connexion.

III

Who *are* these characters of James's about whom we come to be less certain as to precisely what we ought to think?

The type of Henry James's observers and sometimes of his heroes is the cultivated American bourgeois, like Henry James himself, who lives on an income derived from some form of business activity, usually left rather vague, but who has rarely played any part in the efforts which have created the business. These men turn their backs on the commercial world; they disdain its vulgarity and dullness, and they attempt to enrich their experience through the society and art of Europe. But they bring to these the bourgeois qualities of timidity, prudence, primness, the habits of mind of a puritan morality, which, even when they wish to be men of the world, make it too easy for them to be disconcerted. They wince alike at the brutalities of the aristocracy and at the coarseness of the working class; they shrink most of all from the 'commonness' of the less polished bourgeoisie, who having acquired their incomes more recently, are not so far advanced in self-improvement. The women have the corresponding qualities: they are innocent, conventional, and rather cold – sometimes they suffer from Freudian complexes or a kind of arrested development, sometimes they are neglected or cruelly cheated by the men to whom they have given their hearts. And even when James's central characters are English, they assimilate themselves to these types.

It is enlightening in this connexion to compare James's point of view with Flaubert's. The hero of *L'Éducation sentimentale* is a perfect Henry James character: he is sensitive, cautious, afraid of life; he lives on a little income and considers himself superior to the common run. But Flaubert's attitude towards Frédéric Moreau is devastatingly ironic. Frédéric has his aspects of pathos, his occasional flashes of spirit: but Flaubert is quite emphatic in his final judgement of Frédéric. He considers Frédéric a worm.

Now, James has his own kind of irony, but it is not Flaubert's kind. Frédéric Moreau, in a sense, is the hero of many of James's novels, and you can see how the American's relation to him usually differs from the Frenchman's if you compare certain kinds of scenes which tend to recur in Henry James with certain scenes in *L'Éducation sentimentale* of which they sometimes seem like an echo: those ominous situations in which we find the sensitive young man either immersed in some sort of gathering or otherwise meeting successively a number of supposed friends, more worldly and unscrupulous persons, who are obviously talking over his head, acting behind his back, without his being able, in his innocence, quite to make out what they are up to. You have this same situation, as I say, in James and in Flaubert; but the difference is that, whereas with James the young man is made wondering and wistful and is likely to turn out a pitiful victim, with Flaubert he is quietly and cruelly made to look like a fool and is as ready to double-cross these other people who seem to him so inferior to himself as they are to double-cross him.

In this contrast between Flaubert's treatment of Frédéric Moreau and James's treatment of, say, Hyacinth Robinson in *The Princess Casamassima* is to be found perhaps one of the reasons for James's resentment of Flaubert. James had known Flaubert, had read him when young, had obviously been impressed by his work; he had it in common with the older man that he wanted to give dignity and integrity to the novel of modern life by imposing on it rigorous aesthetic form. Yet there is something about Flaubert that sticks in his crop, and he keeps up a sort of running quarrel with him, returning to the subject again and again in the course of his critical writing. But though it is plain that James cannot help admiring the author of *Madame Bovary*, he usually manages before he has done to give the impression of belittling him – and he is especially invidious on the subject of *L'Éducation sentimentale*. His great complaint is that Flaubert's characters are intrinsically so ignoble that they do not deserve to be treated at length or to have so much art expended on them and that there must have been something wrong with Flaubert for him ever to have supposed that they did. James does not seem to understand that Flaubert *intends* all his characters to be 'middling' and that the greatness of his work arises from the fact that it constitutes a criticism of something bigger than they are. James praises the portrait of Mme Arnoux: let us thank God, at least, he exclaims, that Flaubert was able here to command the good taste to deal delicately with a fine-grained woman! He does not seem to be aware that Mme Arnoux is treated as ironically as any of the other characters – that the virtuous bourgeois wife with her inhibitions and superstitions is pathetic only as a part of the failure of a civilization. Henry James mistakes Mme Arnoux for a refined American woman and he is worried because Frédéric isn't one of his own American heroes, quietly vibrating and scrupulously honourable. Yet it probably makes him uncomfortable to feel that Flaubert is flaying remorselessly the squeamish young man of this type; and it may be that Henry James's antagonism to Flaubert has something to do with the fact that the latter's all-permeating criticism of the pusillanimity of the bourgeois soul has touched Henry James himself. The protagonists of the later James are always regretting having lived too meagrely; and James distils from these non-participants all the sad self-effacing nobility, all the fine wan beauty, they are good for. Flaubert extracts something quite different from Frédéric Moreau – a kind of acrid insecticide: when Frédéric and his friend, both middle-aged by now, recall at the end of the book their first clumsy and frightened visit to a brothel as the best that life has had to offer them, it is a damnation of their whole society.

But there was another kind of modern society which Gustave Flaubert did not know and which Henry James did. Henry James was himself that new anomalous thing, an American. He had, to be sure, lived a good deal in Europe both in childhood and early manhood, and he had to a considerable extent become imbued with the European point of view – so that the monuments of antiquity and feudalism, the duchesses and princesses and princes who seem to carry on the feudal tradition, are still capable of having the effect for him of making modern life look un-distinguished. But the past, in the case of James, does not completely dwarf the present, as the vigil of Flaubert's Saint Anthony and the impacts of his pagan armies diminish Frédéric Moreau. The American in Henry James asserts himself insistently against Europe. After all, Frédéric Moreau and the respectable Mme Arnoux are the best people of Albany and Boston! – but in America they are not characters in Flaubert. Their scruples and renunciations have a real moral value here – for Frédéric Moreau at home possesses a real integrity; and when these best people come over to Europe, they judge the whole thing in a quite new way. James speaks somewhere of his indignation at an Englishwoman's saying to him in England, in connexion with something they were discussing: 'That is true of aristocracy, but in one's own class it is quite different.' As an American and the grandson of a millionaire, it had never occurred to James that anyone could consider him a middle-class person. When Edith Wharton accused him in his later years of no longer appreciating Flaubert and demanded of him why Emma Bovary, the choice of whom as a heroine he had always deplored, was not just as good a subject for fiction as Tolstoy's Anna Karenina, he replied: 'Ah, but one paints the fierce passions of a luxurious aristocracy; the other deals with the petty miseries of a little bourgeoise in a provincial town!' But if Emma Bovary is small potatoes, what about Daisy Miller? Why, Daisy Miller is an American girl! Emma Bovary has her longings and her debts and her adulteries, but she is otherwise a conventional person, she remains in her place in the social scheme even when she dreams of rising out of it. So great is the prestige for her of the local nobility that when she goes to the château for the ball, the very sugar in the sugar bowl seems to her whiter and finer than the sugar she has at home; whereas a girl like Daisy Miller as well as one like Isabel Archer represents a human species that had been bred outside of Europe and that cannot be accommodated or judged inside the European frame. When this species comes back to Europe, it tends to disregard the social system. Europe is too much for Daisy Miller: she catches cold in the Coliseum, where according to European conventions she oughtn't to have been at that hour. But the great popularity of her story was certainly due to the fact that her creator had somehow conveyed the impression that her spirit went marching on.

There evidently went on in the mind of James a debate that was never settled between the European and the American points of view; and this conflict may have had something to do with his inability sometimes to be clear as to what he wants us to think of a certain sort of person. It is quite mistaken to talk as if James had uprooted himself from America in order to live in England. He had travelled so much from his earliest years that he had never had real roots anywhere. His father had himself been a wandering intellectual, who had oscillated back and forth between Europe and the United States; and even in America the

Jameses were always oscillating between New York and Boston. They were not New Englanders even by ancestry, but New Yorkers of Irish and Scotch-Irish stock, and they had none of the tight New England local ties – they always came to Boston from a larger outside world and their point of view about it was objective and often rather ironical. To this critical attitude on Henry's part was probably partly due the failure of *The Bostonians*; and this failure seems to mark the moment of his abandonment of his original ambition of becoming the American Balzac, as it does that of his taking up his residence in England and turning, for the subjects of his fiction, from the Americans to the English. He had been staying for some time in London, and he found he liked living in London better than in New York or New England, better than in Paris or Rome. His parents in the States had just died, and his sister came over to join him.

IV

And this brings us to what seems to have been the principal crisis in Henry James's life and work. We know so little about his personal life from any other source than himself, and even in his memoirs and letters he tells us so little about his emotions, that it is impossible to give any account of it save as it reflects itself in his writings.

Up to the period of his playwriting, his fiction has been pretty plain sailing. He has aimed to be a social historian, and, in a limited field, he has succeeded. His three long novels of the later eighties – *The Bostonians*, *The Princess Casamassima*, and *The Tragic Muse* – are, indeed, as social history, his most ambitious undertakings, and from the conventional point of view – that of the reporting of the surface of life – by far his most successful. The first hundred pages of *The Bostonians*, with the arrival of the young Southerner in Boston and his first contacts with the Boston reformers, is, in its way, one of the most masterly things that Henry James ever did. *The Princess Casamassima*, with its opening in the prison and its revolutionary exiles in London, deals with issues and social contrasts of a kind that James had never before attempted. The familiar criticism of Henry James – the criticism made by H. G. Wells: that he had no grasp of politics or economics – does not, in fact, hold true of these books. Here his people do have larger interests and functions aside from their personal relations: they have professions, missions, practical aims; and they also engage in more drastic action than in his novels of any other period. Basil Ransom pursues Verena Tarrant and rescues her from the terrible Olive Chancellor; Hyacinth Robinson pledges himself to carry out a political assassination, then commits suicide instead; Miriam Rooth makes her career as a great actress. One finds in all three of these novels a will to participate in life, to play a responsible role, quite different from the passive ones of the traveller who merely observes or the victim who merely suffers, that had seemed characteristic of James's fiction. Up to a point these books are brilliant.

But there is a point – usually about half-way through – at which every one of these novels begins strangely to run into the sands; the excitement of the story lapses at the same time as the treatment becomes more abstract and the colour fades from the picture. The ends are never up to the beginnings. This is most obvious – even startling – in *The Tragic Muse*, the first volume of which, as we read it, makes us think that it must be James's best novel, so solid and alive does it seem. Here are areas of experience and types of a kind that James has never before given us: a delicately comic portrait of a retired parliamentarian, which constitutes, by implication, a criticism of British Liberal politics; a really charged and convincing scene between a man and a woman (Nick Dormer and Julia Dallow) in place of the mild battledore-and-shuttlecock that we are accustomed to getting from James; and, in Miriam Rooth, the Muse, a character who comes nearer to carrying the author out of the bounds of puritan scruples and prim prejudices on to the larger and more dangerous stage of human creative effort than any other he has hitherto drawn. Here at last we are among complete people, who have the appetites and ambitions that we recognize – and in comparison, the characters of his earlier works only seem real in a certain convention. Then suddenly the story stops short: after the arrival of Miriam in London, *The Tragic Muse* is almost a blank. Of the two young men who have been preoccupied with Miriam, one renounces her because she will not leave the stage and the other doesn't, apparently, fall in love with her. Miriam, herself, to be sure, makes a great success as an actress, but we are never taken into her life, we know nothing at first hand of her emotions. The only decisions that are looming are negative ones, and the author himself seems to lose interest.

These earlier chapters of *The Tragic Muse* are the high point of the first part of James's career, after which something snaps. He announces that he will write no more long novels, but only fiction of shorter length; and it may be that he has become aware of his failure in his longer novels to contrive the mounting-up to a climax of intensity and revelation which, in order to be effective, this kind of full-length fiction demands. At any rate, he applied himself to writing plays, and for five years he produced little else; but one wonders when one reads these plays – in the two volumes he called *Theatricals* – why James should have sacrificed not only his time but also all the strength of his genius for work that was worse than mediocre. He had had reason to complain at this period that he had difficulty in selling his fiction, and he confessed that his plays were written in the hope of a popular success, and that they were intended merely as entertainment and were not to be taken too seriously – seeking to excuse that which 'would otherwise be inexplicable' by invoking 'the uttermost regions of dramatic amiability, the bland air of the little domestic fairy-tale'. Yet the need for money and even for fame is surely an insufficient explanation for the phenomenon of a novelist of

James's gifts almost entirely abandoning the art in which he has perfected himself to write plays that are admittedly trivial.

That there was something insufficient and unexplained about James's emotional life seems to appear unmistakably from his novels. I believe that it may be said that there have not been up to this point any consummated love affairs in his fiction – that is, none among the principal characters and while the action of the story is going on; and this deficiency must certainly have contributed to his increasing loss of hold on his readers. It is not merely that he gave in *The Bostonians* an unpleasant picture of Boston, and in *The Tragic Muse*, on the whole, a discouraging picture of the English; it is not merely that *The Princess Casamassima* treated a social-revolutionary subject from a point of view that was non-political and left neither side a moral advantage. It was not merely that he was thus at this period rather lost between America and England. It was also that you cannot enchant an audience with stories about men wooing women in which the parties either never get together or are never seen functioning as lovers. And you will particularly dampen your readers with a story – *The Tragic Muse* – which deals with two men and a girl but in which neither man ever gets her. There is, as I have said, in *The Tragic Muse*, one of his more convincing man-and-woman relationships. Julia Dallow is really female and she behaves like a woman with Nick Dormer; but here the woman's political ambitions get between Nick and her, so that this, too, never comes to anything: here the man, again, must renounce. (In Henry James's later novels, these healthily female women – Kate Croy and Charlotte Stant – are to take on a character frankly sinister.) Years later, Henry James explained in his preface to *The Tragic Muse* that the prudery, in the eighties, of the American magazines had made it impossible for Miriam Rooth to follow the natural course of becoming Nick Dormer's mistress; and certainly the skittishness of a public that was scandalized by *Jude the Obscure* is not to be underestimated. But, after all, Hardy did write about Jude, and Meredith about Lord Ormont and his Aminta, and let the public howl; and it might well have enhanced Henry James's reputation – to which he was by no means indifferent – if he had done the same thing himself. Problems of sexual passion in conflict with convention and law were beginning to be subjects of burning interest. But it is probable that James had by this time – not consciously, perhaps, but instinctively – come to recognize his unfittedness for dealing with them and was far too honest to fake.

One feels about the episode of his playwriting that it was an effort to put himself over, an effort to make himself felt, as he had never succeeded in doing. His brother William James wrote home in the summer of 1889, at the beginning of this playwriting period, that Henry, beneath the 'rich sea-weeds and rigid barnacles and things' of 'strange heavy alien manners and customs' with which he had covered himself like a 'marine crustacean', remained the 'same dear old, good, innocent, and at bottom very powerless-feeling Harry'. He had seriously injured his back in an accident in his boyhood, and it was necessary for him still, in his forties, to lie down for regular rests. And now it is as if he were trying to put this 'broken back', as he once called it, into making an impression through the drama as he had never been able to put it into a passion. His heroine Miriam Rooth has just turned away from the Philistine English world which rejects her and taken into the theatre the artist's will with which she is to conquer that world; and her creator is now to imitate her.

But his plays were either not produced or not well received. At the first night of *Guy Domville* (5 January 1895), he ran foul of a gallery of hooligans, who booed and hissed him when he came before the curtain. Their displeasure had evidently been partly due to a feeling of having been let down by one of James's inevitable scenes of abdication of the lover's role: the hero, at the end of the play, had rejected a woman who adored him and an estate he had just inherited in order to enter the Church. These five years of unsuccessful playwriting had put Henry James under a strain, and this was the final blow. When he recovers from his disappointment, he is seen to have passed through a crisis.

Now he enters upon a new phase, of which the most obvious feature is a subsidence back into himself. And now sex *does* appear in his work – even becoming a kind of obsession – in a queer and left-handed way. We have *The Turn of the Screw* and *The Sacred Fount*; *What Maisie Knew* and *In the Cage*. There are plenty of love affairs now and plenty of irregular relationships, but there are always thick screens between them and us; illicit appetites, maleficent passions, now provide the chief interest, but they are invariably seen from a distance.

For the Jamesian central observer who has become a special feature of his fiction – the reflector by whose consciousness is registered all that we know of events – has undergone a diminution. This observer is less actively involved and is rarely a complete and a full-grown person: we have a small child who watches her elders, a female telegraph operator who watches the senders of telegrams and lives vicariously through them, a week-end guest who seems not to exist in any other capacity whatever except that of week-end guest and who lives vicariously through his fellow guests. The people who surround this observer tend to take on the diabolic values of the spectres of *The Turn of the Screw*, and these diabolic values are almost invariably connected with sexual relations that are always concealed and at which we are compelled to guess. The innocent Nanda Brookenham of *The Awkward Age*, a work of the same period and group, is hemmed in by a whole host of goblins who beckon and hint and whisper and exhale a creepy atmosphere of scandal. It has for the time become difficult for James to sustain his old objectivity: he has relapsed into a dreamy interior world, where values are often uncertain and where it is not even possible any longer for him to judge his effect on his audience – on the audience which by this time has shrunk to a relatively small band of initiated readers. One is dismayed, in reading his comments on *The Awkward Age*, which he regarded as a technical triumph, to see that he was quite unaware of the inhuman aspect of the book which makes it a little repellent. The central figure of *The Sacred Fount* may perhaps have been presented ironically; but James evidently never suspected how the ordinary reader would feel about this disembowelled gibbering crew who hover around Nanda Brookenham with their shadowy sordid designs.

This phase of Henry James's development is also distinguished by a kind of expansion of the gas of the psychological atmosphere – an atmosphere which has now a special flavour. With *What Maisie Knew*, James's style, as Ford Madox Ford says, first becomes a little gamey. He gets rid of some of his old formality and softens his mechanical hardness; and, in spite of the element of abstraction which somewhat dilutes and dims his writing at all periods, his language becomes progressively poetic.

With all this, his experience of playwriting has affected his fiction in a way which does not always seem quite to the good. He had taken as models for his dramatic work the conventional 'well made' French plays of the kind that Bernard Shaw was ridiculing as 'clock-work mice'; and when he took to turning his plays into novels (*Covering End* and *The Outcry*), their frivolity and artificiality became even more apparent (it was only in *The Other House*, which he also made into a novel, that he had dared to be at all himself, and had produced a psychological thriller that had something in common with *The Turn of the Screw*; *Guy Domville*, too, was evidently more serious, but the text has never been published). Even after he had given up the theatre, he went on casting his novels in dramatic form – with the result that *The Awkward Age*, his supreme effort in this direction, combines a lifeless trickery of logic with the equivocal subjectivity of a nightmare.

In this period also originates a tendency on James's part to exploit his sleight-of-hand technique for the purpose of diverting attention from the inadequacies of his imagination. This has imposed on some of James's critics and must of course have imposed on James himself. One can see from his comments at various periods how a method like that of Tolstoy became more and more distasteful to him. Tolstoy, he insisted, was all over the shop, never keeping to a single point of view but entering the minds of all his characters and failing to exercise sufficiently the principle of selection, and James was even reckless enough, in his preface to *The Tragic Muse*, to class *War and Peace* with *Les Trois Mousquetaires* and *The Newcomes*, as 'large loose baggy monsters, with ... queer elements of the accidental and the arbitrary' — though the truth was, of course, that Tolstoy had spent six years on his novel, had reduced it by a third of its original length and made of every little scene a masterpiece of economy and relevance. He speaks in the same preface of the difficulty he has found himself in handling a complex subject – though it is only a problem here of going into the minds of two of the characters. The truth is, of course, that the question of whether or not the novelist enters into a variety of points of view has nothing necessarily to do with his technical mastery of his materials or even with his effect of concentration. Precisely one trouble with *The Tragic Muse* is that James does not get inside Miriam Rooth; and if he fails even to try to do so, it is because, in his experience of the world and his insight into human beings, he is inferior to a man like Tolstoy. So, in *The Wings of the Dove*, the 'messengering', as the drama courses say, of Kate Croy's final scene with Merton Densher is probably due to James's increasing incapacity for dealing directly with scenes of emotion rather than to the motives he alleges. And so his recurring complaint that he is unable to do certain things because he can no longer find space within his prescribed limits has the look of another excuse. Henry James never seems aware of the amount of space he is wasting through the long abstract formulations that do duty for concrete details, the unnecessary circumlocutions and the gratuitous meaningless verbiage – the *as it were's* and *as we may say's* and all the rest – all the words with which he pads out his sentences and which themselves are probably symptomatic of a tendency to stave off his main problems, since they are a part of the swathing process with which he makes his embarrassing subjects always seem to present smooth contours.

v

But after this a new process sets in. In *The Ambassadors*, *The Wings of the Dove*, and *The Golden Bowl*, the psychological atmosphere thickens and fills up the structure of the novel, so carefully designed and contrived, with the fumes of the Jamesian gas; and the characters, though apprehended as recognizable human entities, loom obscurely through a phantasmagoria of dreamlike similes and metaphors that seem sometimes, as Miss West has said, more vivid and solid than the settings.

But a positive element reappears. The novels of *The Awkward Age* period were written not merely from an international limbo between Europe and the United States but in the shadow of defeat and self-doubt. Yet in these queer and neurotic stories (some of them, of course – *The Turn of the Screw* and *What Maisie Knew* – among James's masterpieces) moral values begin to reassert themselves. These present themselves first in an infantile form, in Maisie Farrange and in Nanda Brookenham, whose innocence is a touchstone for the other characters. Then, in the longer novels that follow, embodied in figures of a more mature innocence, they come completely to dominate the field. These figures are now always Americans. We have returned to the pattern of his earlier work, in which the typical dramatic conflict took place between glamorous people who were worldly and likely to be wicked, and people of superior scruples who were likely to be more or less homely, and in which the glamorous characters usually represented Europe and the more honourable ones the United States. In those earlier novels of James, it had not been always – as in *The Portrait of a Lady* – the Americans who were left with the moral advantage; the Europeans – as in the story with that title – had been sometimes made the more sympathetic. But in these later ones it is always the Americans who command admiration and respect – where they are pitted against a fascinating Italian prince, a charming and appealing French lady, and a formidable group of rapacious English. Yes: there *was* a beauty and there was also a power in the goodness of these naïve but sensitive people – there *were* qualities which did not figure in Flaubert's or Thackeray's picture. This *was* something new in the world which did not fit into the formulas of Europe. What if poor Lambert Strether *had* missed in Woollett, Mass., many things he would have enjoyed in Paris: he had brought to Paris something it lacked. And the burden of James's biography of William Wetmore Story, which came out at the same time as these novels, the early years of the century – rather different from that of his study of Hawthorne, published in 1880 – is that artists like Story who left Boston for Europe eventually found themselves in a void and might better have stayed at home.

And now Henry James revisits America, writes *The American Scene*, and, for the first time since the rejected *Bostonians*, lays the scene of a novel – *The Ivory Tower*, which he dropped and did not live to finish – entirely in the United States.

In another unfinished novel, the fantasia called *The Sense of the Past*, he makes a young contemporary American go back into eighteenth-century England. Here the Jamesian ambiguity serves an admirable artistic purpose. Is it the English of the past who are ghosts or the American himself who is only a dream? – will the moment come when *they* will vanish or will he himself cease to exist? And, as before, there is a question of James's own asking at the bottom of the ambiguity: Which is real – America or Europe? – a question which was apparently to be answered by the obstinate survival of the American in the teeth of the spectres who would drag him back. (It is curious, by the way, to compare *The Sense of the Past* with Mark Twain's *Connecticut Yankee*: the two books have a good deal in common.)

Yes: in spite of the popular assumption, founded on his expatriation and on his finally becoming a British citizen, it is the ideals of the United States which triumph in James's work. His warmest tributes to American genius come out of these later years. Though he could not, in *Notes of a Son and Brother*, resist the impulse to remove references to Lincoln as 'old Abe' from William James's early letters of the wartime, this autobiographical reverie contains pages on Lincoln's death of a touching appreciation and pride. 'It was vain to say', he writes of Andrew Johnson, of whom he declares that the American people felt him unworthy to represent them, 'that we had deliberately invoked the "common" in authority and must drink the wine we had drawn. No countenance, no salience of aspect nor composed symbol, could superficially have referred itself less than Lincoln's mould-smashing mask to any mere matter-of-course type of propriety; but his admirable unrelated head had itself revealed a type – as if by the very fact that what made in it for roughness of kind looked out only less than what made in it for splendid final stamp; in other words for commanding Style.' And of the day when the news reached Boston: 'I was fairly to go in shame of its being my birthday. These would have been the hours of the streets if none others had been – when the huge general gasp filled them like a great earth-shudder and people's eyes met people's eyes without the vulgarity of speech. Even this was, all so strangely, part of the lift and the swell, as tragedy has but to be of a pure enough strain and a high enough connexion to sow with its dark hand the seed of greater life. The collective sense of what had occurred was of a sadness too noble not somehow to inspire, and it was truly in the air that, whatever we had as a nation produced or failed to produce, we could at least gather round this perfection of classic woe.' In *The American Scene*, he writes of Concord: 'We may smile a little as we "drag in" Weimar, but I confess myself, for my part, much more satisfied than not by our happy equivalent, "in American money", for Goethe and Schiller. The money is a potful in the second case as in the first, and if Goethe, in one, represents the gold and Schiller the silver, I find (and quite putting aside any bimetallic prejudice) the same good relation in the other between Emerson and Thoreau. I open Emerson for the same benefit for which I open Goethe, the sense of moving in large intellectual space, and that of the gush, here and there, out of the rock, of the crystalline cupful, in wisdom and poetry, in *Wahrheit* and *Dichtung*; and whatever I open Thoreau for (I needn't take space here for the good reasons) I open him oftener than I open Schiller.' Edith Wharton says that he used to read Walt Whitman aloud 'in a mood of subdued ecstasy' and with tremendous effect on his hearers.

James's visit to the United States in 1904-5, after nearly a quarter of a century's absence, had been immensely exciting to him. He had plunged into his sensations with a gusto, explored everything accessible with a voracity, and delivered himself of positive ideas (the presence and the opinions of William must partly have stimulated this, as a passage in Henry's note-books suggests) at a rate that seems almost to transform the personality of the modest recluse of Lamb House, with his addiction to the crepuscular and the dubious. One realizes now for the first time, as he was realizing for the first time himself, how little of America he had seen before. He had never been West or South. He had known only New York, Boston, and Newport. But he now travelled all the way south to Florida and all the way west to California, apparently almost drunk with new discoveries and revelations. His account of his trip in *The American Scene*, published in 1907, has a magnificent solidity and brilliance quite different from the vagueness of impressionism which had been making the backgrounds of his novels a little unsatisfactory; and the criticism of the national life shows an incisiveness, a comprehensiveness, a sureness in knowing his way about, a grasp of political and economic factors, that one might not have expected of Henry James returning to Big Business America. It is probably true that James – as W. H. Auden has suggested – had never approached Europe with anything like the same boldness. In Italy, France, or England, he had been always a 'passionate pilgrim' looking for the picturesque. But with long residence abroad, as he tells us, the romance and the mystery had evaporated, and America, of which he had been hearing such sensational if sometimes dismaying news, had in its turn been coming to seem romantic. What is exhilarating and most surprising is the old-fashioned American patriotism which – whether he is admiring or indignant – throbs in every pulse of *The American Scene*. It would be difficult to understand why James should have been credited in the United States with being an immoderate Anglophile – even if the implications of *The Wings of the Dove* had been missed – after *The American Scene* had appeared, if one did not have to allow for the shallowness of professional criticism and the stupid indifference of the public that marked that whole period in the United States. The truth is that he returns to America with something like an overmastering homesickness that makes him desire to give it the benefit of every doubt, to hope for the best from what shocks or repels him. He is not at the mercy of his wincings from the elements that are alien and vulgar. The flooding-in of the new foreign population, though he has to make an effort to accept it, does not horrify him or provoke him to sneers, as it did that professional explorer but professional Anglo-Saxon, Kipling – after all, the James family themselves had not been long in the United States and were so nearly pure Irish that Henry speaks of their feeling a special interest in the only set of their relatives that represented the dominant English blood. He thinks it a pity that the immigrants should be standardized by barren New York, but he is gratified at the evidence that America has been able to give them better food and clothing. The popular consumption of candy, in contrast to the luxury and privilege that sweets have always been in Europe, seems to please him when he attends the Yiddish theatre. He is angry over the ravages of commercialism – the exploitation of real-estate values and the destruction of old buildings and landmarks that followed the Civil War – but he is optimistic enough to hope that the time is approaching when the national taste will have improved sufficiently to check this process. And in the meantime at Mount Vernon he feels awe at the memory of Washington, invokes in the Capitol the American eagle as a symbol of the republican idealism, and writes one of the most eloquent and most moving pages to be found in the whole range of his work in celebration of the Concord bridge and the shot heard round the world. It is as if, after the many books which James had written in countries not native to him, under the strain of maintaining an attitude that should be rigorously international, yet addressing himself to an audience that rarely understood what he was trying to do and in general paid little attention to him – it is as if, after a couple of decades of this, his emotions had suddenly been given scope, his genius for expression liberated, as if his insight had been confronted with a field on which it could play without diffidence; and he produced in *The American Scene*, one of the very best books about modern America.

The point is that James's career – given his early experience of Europe – had inevitably been affected by the shift in American ambitions which occurred after the Civil War. It has been shown by Mr Van Wyck Brooks in his literary history of the United States how the post-Revolutionary American had been stimulated – much like the Russian of the first years of the Soviet régime – to lay the foundations for a new humanity, set free from the caste-barriers and the poverties of Europe, which should return to the mother-continent only to plunder her for elements of culture that might be made to serve the new aim; but how, with the growth of industry, the ascendancy of business ideals, the artists and the other intellectuals found it difficult to function at home and, discouraged with the United States, more and more took refuge in Europe. James explains, in *The American Scene*, that the residence abroad of Americans like himself, of small incomes and non-acquisitive tastes, had by this time become merely a matter of having found oneself excreted by a society with whose standards of expenditure one was not in a position to keep up, at the same time that one could not help feeling humiliated at being thrust by it below the salt. But though his maturity belonged to this second phase, he had grown up during the first – the brothers of his grandmother James had fought in the Revolution and been friends of Lafayette and Washington, and his James grandfather had come to America from Ireland and made a fortune of three million dollars – and he had never lost the democratic idealism, the conviction of having scored a triumph and shown the old world a wonder, that were characteristic of it. This appears at the beginning of James's career in the name of 'the American', Newman, and at the end in his magnificent phrase about Lincoln's 'mould-smashing mask'.

VI

But Henry James is a reporter, not a prophet. With less politics even than Flaubert, he can but chronicle the world as it passes, and in his picture the elements are mixed. In the Americans of Henry James's later novels (those written before his return) – the Milly Theales, the Lambert Strethers, the Maggie Ververs – he shows us all that was magnanimous, reviving, and warm in the Americans at the beginning of the new century along with all that was frustrated, sterile, excessively refined, depressing – all that they had in common with the Frédéric Moreaus and with the daughters of poor English parsons. Here they are with their ideals and their blights: Milly Theale, for example, quite real at the core of her cloudy integument, probably the best portrait in fiction of a rich New Yorker of the period. It is the period of the heyday of Sargent; but compare such figures of James's with the fashionable paintings of Sargent, truthful though these are in their way, and see with what profounder insight as well as with what superior delicacy Henry James has caught the moneyed distinction of the Americans of this race.

But between the first blooming and the second something tragic has happened to these characters. What has become of Christopher Newman? What has become of Isabel Archer? They are Lambert Strether and Milly Theale – the one worn out by Woollet, Mass., the other overburdened with money and dying for lack of love. Neither finds any fulfilment in Europe, neither ever gets his money's worth. Maggie Verver has her triumph in the end, but she, too, is much too rich for comfort. These people look wan and they are more at sea than the people of the earlier novels. They had been tumbled along or been ground in the sand by the surf of commercial success that has been running in the later part of the century, and in either case are very much the worse for it. It seems to me foolish to reproach Henry James for having neglected the industrial background. Like sex, we never get very close to it, but its effects are a part of his picture. James's tone is more often old-maidish than his sense of reality is feeble; and the changes in American life that have been going on during his absence are implied in these later books.

When he revisits the States at last, he is aroused to a new effort in fiction as well as to the reporting of *The American Scene*. The expatriate New Yorker of *The Jolly Corner* comes back to the old house on Fifth Avenue to confront the apparition of himself as he would have been if he had stayed and worked 'downtown'. 'Rigid and conscious, spectral yet human, a man of his own substance and stature waited there to measure himself with his power to dismay.' At first this *alter ego* covers its face with its hands; then it advances 'as for aggression, and he knew himself give ground. Then harder pressed still, sick with the force of his shock, and falling back as under the hot breath and the sensed passion of a life larger than his own, a rage of personality before which his own collapsed, he felt the whole vision turn to darkness and his very feet give way.' He faints.

Yet at contact with this new America which is extravagant at the same time as ugly, the old Balzac in James revives. I do not know why more has not been made in the recent discussion of James – especially by the critics of the Left, who are so certain that there is nothing in him – of the unfinished novel called *The Ivory Tower*. The work of James's all but final period has been 'poetic' rather than 'realistic'; but now he passes into a further phase in which the poetic treatment is applied to what is for James a new kind of realism. The fiction of his latest period is occupied in a special way with the forgotten, the poor, and the old, even – what has been rare in James – with the uncouth, the grotesque. It is perhaps the reflection of his own old age, his own lack of worldly success, the strange creature that he himself had become. This new vein had already appeared in the long short story *The Papers*, with its fantastically amusing picture of the sordid lives of journalists in London; and he later wrote *Fordham Castle*, in which he said he had tried to do something for the parents of the Daisy Millers whose children had left them behind – a curious if not very successful glimpse of the America of Sinclair Lewis; and *The Bench of Desolation*, the last story but one that he published, surely one of the most beautifully written and wonderfully developed short pieces in the whole range of James's work: a sort of prose poem of loneliness and poverty among the nondescript small shopkeepers and retired governesses of an English seaside resort.

But in the meantime the revelation of Newport, as it presented itself in the nineteen hundreds – so different from the Newport which James had described years ago in

An International Episode – stimulates him to something quite new: a kind of nightmare of the American *nouveaux riches*. Here his appetite for the varied forms of life, his old interest in social phenomena, seem brusquely to wake him up from reverie. The appearances of things become vivid again. To our amazement, there starts into colour and relief the America of the millionaires, at its crudest, corruptest, and phoniest: the immense amorphous mansions, complicated by queer equipment which seems neither to have been purchased by personal choice nor humanized by personal use; the old men of the Rockefeller-Frick generation, landed, with no tastes and no interests, amidst a limitless magnificence which dwarfs them; the silly or clumsy young people of the second generation with their dubious relationships, their enormous and meaningless parties, their touching longings and resolute strivings for an elegance and cultivation which they have no one to guide them in acquiring. The spectre of *The Jolly Corner* appeared to the expatriate American 'quite as one of those expanding fantastic images projected by the magic lantern of childhood'; and in somewhat the same way, for the reader of James, with the opening of *The Ivory Tower*, there emerges the picture of old Abner Gaw, a kind of monster from outside the known Jamesian world, sitting and rocking his foot and looking out on the sparkling Atlantic while he waits for his business partner to die. *The Ivory Tower*, in dealing with the newest rich, is comic and even homely; but it is also, like all this later work of Henry James, poetic in that highest sense that its characters and scenes and images shine out with the incandescence which shows them as symbols of phases through which the human soul has passed. The moral of the novel – which seems quite plain from the scenario left by James – is also of particular interest. The ivory tower itself, a fine piece of Chinese carving, is to represent, for the young American who has just returned from Europe and inherited his uncle's fortune, that independence of spirit, that private cultivation of sensations, and that leisure for literary work, which the money is to make possible for him; but it fatally contains, also, the letter in which Abner Gaw, out of vindictiveness towards the partner who has double-crossed him, has revealed all the swindles and perfidies by which the fortune has been created. So that the cosmopolitan nephew (he has always had a *little* money) is finally to be only too glad to give up the independence with the fortune.

Henry James dropped *The Ivory Tower* when the war broke out in 1914, because he felt it was too remote from the terrible contemporary happenings. These events seem to have presented themselves to James as simply a critical struggle between, on the one hand, French and English civilization and, on the other, German barbarity. He had believed in and had invoked rather vaguely the possible salutary effect for the world of an influential group of international élite made up of the kind of people with whom he associated and whom he liked to depict in his novels; but now he spoke of the past as 'the age of the mistake', the period when people had thought that the affairs of the world were sufficiently settled for such an élite to flourish. He was furiously nationalistic, or at least furiously pro-Ally. He railed against Woodrow Wilson for his delay in declaring war, and he applied in 1915, in a gesture of rejection and allegiance, to become a British subject. 'However British you may be, I am more British still!' he is said to have exclaimed to Edmund Gosse, when the process had been completed – something which, Gosse is supposed to have remarked, 'nobody wanted him to be'. He had hitherto refrained from this step, feeling, as we gather from *The American Scene*, some pride and some advantage in his status as a citizen of the United States. But he had been thrown off his balance again, had been swung from his poise of detachment, always a delicate thing to maintain and requiring special conditions. It never occurred to James that he had been, in *The Ivory Tower*, much closer to contemporary realities than he was when he threw up his hat and enlisted in a holy war on Germany; that the partnership of Betterman and Gaw was not typical merely of the United States but had its European counterparts – any more than it was present to him now that the class antagonisms of *The Princess Casamassima*, his response to the depression of the eighties, must inevitably appear again and that the events he was witnessing in Europe were partly due to that social system whose corruption he had been consciously chronicling, and were expediting the final collapse which he had earlier half-predicted.

But as Hyacinth Robinson had died of the class struggle, so Henry James died of the war. He was cremated, and a funeral service was held – on 3 March 1916 – at Chelsea Old Church in London; but his ashes, as he had directed, were brought to the United States and buried in the Cambridge cemetery beside his parents and sister and brother. One occasionally, however, finds references to him which assume that he was buried in England – just as one sometimes also finds references which assume that he was born in New England – so that even Henry James's death has been not without a suggestion of the equivocal.

The English had done him the honour, not long before he died, of awarding him the Order of Merit. But I do not think that anybody has yet done full justice to his genius as an international critic of manners, aesthetic values, and morals. The strength of that impartial intelligence of which his hesitating and teasing ambiguity sometimes represented a weakness had prompted him to find his bearings among social gravitational fields which must at the time have seemed almost as bewildering as the astronomical ones with which the physics of relativity were just beginning to deal. It had fortified him to meet and weather the indifference or ridicule of both the two English-speaking peoples to whom he had addressed himself and whose historian he had trained himself to be; and it had stimulated him, through more than half a hundred books, a long life of unwearying labour, to keep recreating himself as an artist and even to break new ground at seventy.

For Henry James *is* a first-rank writer in spite of certain obvious deficiencies. His work is incomplete as his experience was; but it is in no respect second-rate, and he can be judged only in company with the greatest. I have been occupied here with the elements that travail or contend or glow beneath the surface of his even fiction, and my argument has not given me occasion to insist, as ought to be done in any 'literary' discussion of James, on his classical equanimity in dealing with diverse forces, on his combination, equally classical, of hard realism with formal harmony. These are qualities – I have tried to describe them in writing about Pushkin – which have always been rather rare in American and English literature and of which the fiction of James is one of the truest examples.

*

1948. I have left my description of *The Turn of the Screw* mainly as I originally wrote it. In going over it again, however, it has struck me that I forced a point in trying to explain away the passage in which the housekeeper identifies, from the governess's description, the male apparition with Peter Quint. The recent publication of Henry James's note-books seems, besides, to make it quite plain that James's conscious intention, in *The Turn of the Screw*, was to write a *bona fide* ghost story; and it also becomes clear that the theme of youth feeding age was to have been the real subject of *The Sacred Fount*. I should today restate my thesis as follows:

At the time that James wrote these stories, his faith in himself had been somewhat shaken. Though he had summoned the whole force of his will and brought his whole mind to bear on writing plays, he had not made connexions with the theatre. The disastrous opening night of *Guy Domville* had occurred on 5 January 1895. On the evening of 10 January, we learn from an entry in the note-books, James had heard from Archbishop Benson the story that suggested *The Turn of the Screw*. On 23 January, he writes: 'I take up my *own* old pen again – the pen of all my old

unforgettable efforts and sacred struggles. To myself – today – I need say no more. Large and full and high the future still opens. It is now indeed that I may do the work of my life. And I will . . . I have only to face my problems.'
The Turn of the Screw was begun in the fall of 1897 (*The Spoils of Poynton* and *What Maisie Knew* had been written in between). Now, to fail as James had just done is to be made to doubt one's grasp of reality; and the doubts that some readers feel as to the soundness of the governess's story are, I believe, the reflection of James's doubts, communicated unconsciously by James himself (in sketching out his stories in his note-books – as for *The Friends of the Friends*, described below – he sometimes shifts over without a break from a first person which refers to himself to a first person which refers to the imaginary teller). An earlier story, *The Path of Duty*, published in 1884, is perhaps the most obvious example of James's interest in cases of self-deception and his trick of presenting them from their own points of view; and it is given a special relevance to the problem of *The Turn of the Screw* by the entry about it in the note-books. This entry is simply a notation of a curious piece of gossip which James had heard in London, with a discussion of the various ways in which it could be treated in fiction; but the story that James afterwards wrote depends for its effectiveness on an element which James does not mention there. The original anecdote is used, but it here gets another dimension from the attitude of the woman who is supposed to be telling it. This American lady in London is enamoured of an attractive nobleman in line for a desirable baronetcy, with whom she is on fairly close terms but who takes no serious interest in her. She therefore intervenes in a mischievous way, under the pretence of keeping him to the 'path of duty', to prevent him from marrying the woman he loves and induce him to marry one he doesn't – a situation in which everybody else is to be left as dissatisfied as she is. She has never admitted to herself her real motives for what she is doing, and they gradually dawn on the reader in the form of intermittent suspicions

like the suspicions that arise in one's mind in reading *The Turn of the Screw*. But in the case of *The Path of Duty*, we are quite clear as we finish the story, as to what role the narrator has actually played. She has written her account, we realize, though ostensibly to satisfy a friend who had been asking her about the episode, really as a veiled confession; and then she has decided to withhold it, ostensibly to shield the main actors, but really to shield herself. Here James, having noted down an anecdote, as he was also to do for *The Turn of the Screw* and had already done with the notion that was to be used in *The Sacred Fount*, has produced a psychological study for which the anecdote is only a pretext. Another story, *The Friends of the Friends*, the idea for which James first noted in the December of 1895 and which he immediately afterwards wrote, also offers a clue to the process which I believe was at work in *The Turn of the Screw*. *The Friends of the Friends* is a ghost story, which involves, like *The Marriages* and *The Path of Duty*, a mischievous intervention prompted by interested motives on the part of a woman narrator; and the ghost is presumably a product of this narrator's neurotic jealousy. *Maud-Evelyn*, a story written later and first published in 1900, though the first suggestion of it seems also to occur in the note-books of 1895, presents a young man who from interested motives lends himself to the spiritualistic self-deceptions of parents who have lost their daughter. One is led to conclude that, in *The Turn of the Screw*, not merely is the governess self-deceived, but that James is self-deceived about her.

A curious feature of these note-books is the tone that Henry James takes in collecting his materials and outlining his plots. It is not, as with the notes of most writers, as if James were sitting in the workshop of his mind, alone and with no consciousness of an audience, but exactly as if he were addressing a letter to a friend who took a keen interest in his work but with whom he is not sufficiently intimate to discuss his personal affairs. He calls himself *mon bon* and *caro mio* – 'Causons, causons, mon bon,' he will write – and speaks to himself with polite depreciation – referring to 'the narrator of the tale, as I may in courtesy call it'. But, though he talks to himself a good deal – and sometimes very excitedly and touchingly – about his relation to his work, his 'muse', he never notes down personal emotions in relation to anything else as possible subjects for fiction. One comes to the conclusion that Henry James, in a special and unusual way, was what is nowadays called an 'extrovert' – that is, he did not brood on himself and analyse his own reactions, as Stendhal, for example, did, but always dramatized his experience immediately in terms of imaginary people. One gets the impression here that James was not introspective. Nor are his characters really so. They register, as James himself registered, a certain order of perceptions and sensations; but they justify to some degree the objection of critics like Wells that his psychology is superficial – though it would be more correct to put it that, while his insight is not necessarily superficial, his 'psychologizing' tends to be so. What we are told is going on in the characters' heads is a sensitive reaction to surfaces which itself seems to take place on the surface. We do not often see them grappling with their problems in terms of concrete ambitions or of intimate relationships. What we see when we are supposed to look into their minds is something as much arranged by James to conceal, to mislead, and to create suspense as the actual events presented. These people, so far as the 'psychologizing' goes, are not intimate even with themselves. They talk to themselves about what they are doing and what is happening to them even a good deal less frankly than James talks to himself about them, and that is already with the perfect discretion of an after-dinner conversation between two gentlemanly diners-out. As Henry James gets further away – beginning with *What Maisie Knew* – from the realism of his earlier phases, his work – as Stephen Spender has said in connexion with *The Golden Bowl* – becomes all a sort of ruminative poem, which gives us not really a direct account of the internal workings of his characters, but rather James's reflective feelings, the flow of images set off in his mind, as he peeps not impolitely inside them. Not, however, that his sense of life – of personal developments and impacts – is not often profound and sure. The point is merely that it is not always so, and that the floor of the layer of consciousness that we are usually allowed to explore sometimes rings rather hollow. Where motivations are rarely revealed, we cannot always tell how much the author knows; and it is on this account that arguments occur – and not only in the case of *The Turn of the Screw* but also in that of *The Golden Bowl* – as to what is supposed to be happening in a given situation or as to what kind of personalities the characters are supposed to be. Carefully though, from one point of view, the point of view of technical machinery, Henry James always planned his novels, he seems sometimes to falter and grope in dealing with their human problems. The habits he imposed on himself in his attempt to write workable plays were unfortunate in this connexion. The unperformed comedies that he published in the two volumes of *Theatricals*, which are almost the only things he wrote that can really be called bad, show a truly appalling self-discipline in sterile and stale devices and artificial motivations. In the stage world of Henry James, young men are always prepared to marry, regardless of personal taste or even of close acquaintance, from an interest in a property or an inheritance, or because they have been told that they have compromised girls or simply because women have proposed to them; and an element of this false psychology was afterwards carried by James through the whole of his later fiction along with his stage technique. It is true that in this later fiction there is a good deal of illicit passion, as had not been the case in his plays; but his adulteries seem sometimes as arbitrary as the ridiculous engagements of *Theatricals*. They are not always really explained, we cannot always be sure they are really there, that the people have been to bed together. But, on the other hand, we sometimes feel the presence, lurking like 'the beast in the jungle', of other emotional factors with which the author himself does not always appear to have reckoned.

I once gave *The Turn of the Screw* to the Austrian novelist Franz Höllering to see what impression he would get of it. It did not occur to him that it was not a real ghost story, but he said to me, after he had read it: 'The man who wrote that was a *Kinderschander*'; and I remembered that in all James's work of this period – which extends from *The Other House* through *The Sacred Fount* – the favourite theme is the violation of innocence, with the victim in every case (though you have in *The Turn of the Screw* a boy as well as a girl) a young or a little girl. In *The Other House* a child is murdered; in *What Maisie Knew* and *The Awkward Age*, a child and a young virgin are played upon by forces of corruption which, though they do not destroy the girls' innocence, somewhat harm them or dislocate their emotions by creating abnormal relationships; in *The Turn of the Screw*, whichever way you take it, the little girl is either hurt or corrupted. (The candid and loyal young heroines of *The Spoils of Poynton* and *In the Cage*, though they can hardly be said to be violated, are both, in their respective ways, represented as shut out from something.) This, of course, in a sense, is an old theme for James: *Washington Square* and *The Portrait of a Lady* were studies in innocence betrayed. But there is something rather peculiar, during this relatively neurotic phase, in his interest in and handling of this subject. The real effectiveness of all these stories derives, not from the conventional pathos of a victim with whom we sympathize but from the excitement of the violation; and if we look back to Henry James's first novel, *Watch and Ward*, serialized when he was twenty-eight, we find a very queer little tale about a young man of twenty-six who becomes the guardian of a girl of ten and gradually falls in love with her but is for a long time debarred from marrying her, when she comes of age to marry, by a complication of scruples and misunderstandings. The relationship clearly connects itself with the relationship, in *The Awkward Age*, between Nanda and Mr Langdon, in which, also, the attitude of the pseudo-father is given a flavour of unavowed sex. We are not in a position to explain, on any basis of early experience, this preoccupation of James with immature girls who are objects of desire or defilement; but it seems clear what symbolic role they played from time to time in his work. He seems early to have 'polarized' with his brother William in an opposition of feminine and masculine. This appears in a significant anecdote which he tells in his autobiography about William's having left him once to go to play, as he said, with 'boys that curse and swear'; and in his description of his feeling from the first that William was 'occupying a place in the world to which I couldn't at all aspire – to any approach to which in truth I seem to myself ever conscious of having signally forfeited a title'; and one finds it in their correspondence and in everything one has heard of their relations. There was always in Henry James an innocent little girl whom he cherished and loved and protected and yet whom he later tried to violate, whom he even tried to kill. He must have felt particularly helpless, particularly unsuited for the battle with the world, particularly exposed to rude insult, after the failure of his dramatic career, when he retreated into his celibate solitude. The maiden innocent of his early novels comes to life again; but he now does not merely pity her, he does not merely adore her; in his impotence, his impatience with himself, he would like to destroy or rape her. The real dramatic and aesthetic values of the stories that he writes at this period are involved with an equivocal blending of this impulse and an instinct of self-pity. (The conception of *innocence excluded* is a reaction to the same situation: Fleda Vetch, in *The Spoils of Poynton*, misses marrying the man she loves and misses inheriting the spoils, which in any case go up in flames; the girl in the telegraph office finds that it is not she who is 'in the cage' but the dashing young captain whose amours she has fascinatedly watched from afar – just as James must have had to decide that the worldly success he had tried for was, after all, not worth having. So the innocents in certain of the other stories, too, are left with a moral advantage.) This is not in the least, on the critic's part, to pretend to reduce the dignity of these stories by reading into them the embarrassments of the author. They do contain, I believe, a certain subjective element which hardly appears to the same degree elsewhere in James's mature work; but he has expressed what he had to express – disappointments and dissatisfactions that were poignantly and not ignobly felt – with dramatic intensity and poetic colour. These are fairy-stories, but fairy-stories that trouble, that get a clear and luminous music out of chords very queerly combined. They are unique in literature, and their admirable style and form are not quite like anything else even in the work of James. In *The Wings of the Dove*, of course, which follows *The Awkward Age*, he is still occupied with violated innocence, but now his world is firm again on its base, and we are back on the international stage of *The Portrait of a Lady*. Milly Theale, though languishing and fatally ill, is a real and full-grown woman dealing with a practical conspiracy, not a tender little girl or *jeune fille* jeopardized by an ambiguous dream. *

* The immaturity of the heroines in James serves sometimes to provide one of his many pretexts for making it impossible for the heroes to marry them. The whole question of the motif of impotence in James has been discussed very suggestively and interestingly – though on the basis of an incomplete acquaintance with Henry James's work – in a paper called 'The Ghost of Henry James: A Study in Thematic Apperception' by Dr Saul Rosenzweig (*Character and Personality*, December 1943). Dr Rosenzweig suggests that the accident in which Henry James sprained his back at eighteen – 'a horrid even if an obscure hurt', as James himself calls it – and from which he suffered, sometimes acutely, all the rest of his life, may have been partly neurotic not only in its results but even in its origin – since it offers a strangely close parallel with the accident in which the elder Henry James had lost his leg – also in extinguishing a fire – at the age of thirteen. The son's accident had occurred, as he tells us himself, at the beginning of the Civil War and put it out of the question for him to answer Lincoln's first call for volunteers. Dr Rosenzweig has brought to light a very early story of James, the first he ever published: 'The Story of a Year', which appeared in the *Atlantic Monthly* in March 1865. Here you have a young man of the North who, just before going off to the war,

It is of course no longer true, as is implied in the above essay, that the stature and merits of James are not fully appreciated in the English-speaking world. Since the centenary of James's birth in 1943, he has been celebrated, interpreted, reprinted, on a scale which, I believe, is unprecedented for a classical American writer. There have contributed to this frantic enthusiasm perhaps a few rather doubtful elements. A novelist whose typical hero invariably decides not to act, who remains merely an intelligent onlooker, appeals for obvious reasons to a period when many

becomes engaged to a girl but makes her promise that, if he should die, she will forget him and marry someone else. She dreams, when he has gone, that she is walking in a wood with a man who calls her wife and that they find a dead man covered with wounds. They lift the corpse up to bury it, and it opens its eyes and says 'Amen'; they stamp down the dirt of the grave. The lover is actually wounded, lingers for some time between life and death, and then dies, leaving the fiancée to marry another man. Another factor in the story is the young man's mother, who comes between him and the girl, being unwilling to have him marry her and trying to prevent her seeing him after he has been brought home wounded – Henry James, it seems, was his mother's favourite child. Dr Rosenzweig might also have cited another early short story, *An Extraordinary Case* (1868), in which another returned soldier, suffering from an unspecified ailment, loses his girl to another man and dies.

One can agree with Dr Rosenzweig that a castration theme appears here – one recognizes it as the same that figures through the whole of James's work; but that work does not bear out the contention put forward by Dr Rosenzweig that James was to suffer all his life from unallayed feelings of guilt for not having taken part in the war. The only real pieces of evidence that Dr Rosenzweig is able to produce are the short story, *Owen Wingrave*, which deals with the deliberate pacifism of a young man from a military family and leaves the moral advantage all with the pacifist, who dies in the cause of peace; and Henry James's excitement at the beginning of World War I and his memoirs at this time of the Civil War. He must certainly be right, however, in assuming that well before the age when 'The Story of a Year' was written, a state of mind in which 'aggression and sexuality were repressed' had been 'established as a *modus vivendi*'. One of James's most curious symbols for his chronic inhibition occurs in a very early story called first *Théolinde*, then *Rose-Agathe*, in which a man falls in love with a dummy in a Parisian hairdresser's window and finally buys her and takes her home to live with. The wax dummy is cut off at the waist.

intellectuals, formerly romantic egoists or partisans of the political Left, have been resigning themselves to the role of observer or of passive participant in activities which cannot command their whole allegiance. The stock of Henry James has gone up in the same market as that of Kafka, and the recent apotheosis of him has sometimes been conducted as uncritically as the prayers and contemplations of the Kafka cult. At the same time, in a quite different way, he has profited from – or, at any rate, been publicized by – the national propaganda movement which has been advertising American civilization under the stimulus of our needs in the war and our emergence into the international world. The assumption seems to be that Henry James is our counterpart to Yeats, Proust, and Joyce, and he has been tacitly assigned to high place in the official American Dream along with 'Mr Jefferson', the *Gettysburg Address*, Paul Bunyan, the Covered Wagon, and Mom's Huckleberry Pie. He will doubtless be translated for the Japanese, who were fascinated before the war by the refinements of Paul Valéry and Proust.*

Yet we do well to be proud of him, and there are very good reasons for young people to read him straight through, as – incredible though it would have sounded at the time he was still alive – they seem more and more to be doing. Henry James stands out today as unique among our fiction writers of the nineteenth century in having devoted wholeheartedly to literature the full span of a long life and brought to it first-rate abilities. Beside James's half century of achievement, with its energy, continuity, and variety, the production of Hawthorne looks furtive and meagre and the work of Poe's brief years fragmentary. Alone among our novelists of the past, Henry James managed to master his art and to practise it on an impressive scale, to stand up to popular pressures so as not to break down or peter out, and to build up what the French call an *œuvre*.

* Since writing this, I have found in a book catalogue – along with a Japanese translation of *Ulysses* – a volume of James's short stories translated into Japanese (1924), and a Japanese book about James (1934).

John Jay Chapman

The Mute and the Open Strings

MR M. A. DE WOLFE HOWE has done an excellent job
with the letters and papers of the late John Jay Chapman.*
Mr Howe enjoyed the advantages of having known Chapman personally and of already being thoroughly at home in
the latter's period and circle.

One's only complaint about Mr Howe's book is that there
is not anywhere near enough of it. I understand that he was
induced by his publishers to cut down his original manuscript; and this seems to me to have been a mistake. Anybody
interested in Chapman at all would be able to read a book
twice as long as the present one. My own impression from
what is here published is that John Jay Chapman was probably the best letter-writer that we have ever had in this
country. And it seems to me a pity that Mr Howe did not
include the whole text of the autobiographical document
which Chapman prepared not long before his death,
instead of only selections from it. My hope and belief is,
in fact, that the future will be sufficiently interested in
Chapman to print and read his letters as eagerly as has been
done with Horace Walpole's – as well as to go back to his
published works as we have done to those of Thoreau.

Yet at the present time hardly one reader in a million has
heard of even the name of John Jay Chapman. His later
books have had no circulation, and most of his earlier ones
are out of print. How, then, is it possible to attach so much
importance to a writer who has been persistently ignored
by the historians of American literature and who has been
read by almost nobody, even during these last twenty years
when so much rummaging has been going on in the attic of

* *John Jay Chapman and His Letters.*

our literary history? How has it been possible thus for a writer who was at one time a conspicuous figure and who is still valued so highly by a few readers, to become completely invisible to the general reading public even while he was still living and writing?

This essay will attempt to answer that question, on which Mr Howe's biography has thrown a great deal of light.

I

Perhaps our most vivid impression as we read about Chapman in this book – especially through the first half of his life – is that we have encountered a personality who does not belong in his time and place and who by contrast makes us aware of the commonness, the provinciality, and the timidity of most of his contemporaries. 'Yes,' we say to ourselves in our amazement, 'people ought to be more like this!'

When John Jay Chapman was twenty-five and studying law at Harvard – it was the winter of 1886–7 – he made the acquaintance of the half-Italian niece of the Brimmer family of Boston: 'a swarthy, fiery large-eyed girl, who looked like the younger Sibyl of Michelangelo' and 'had the man-minded seriousness of women in classic myths, the regular brow, heavy dark hair, free gait of the temperament that lives in heroic thought and finds the world full of chimeras, of religious mysteries, sacrifice, purgation' – such a woman as had hardly existed outside the 'imagination of Aeschylus and the poets'.

'I had never abandoned my reading of Dante' – it would be a pity not to give it in his own words – 'and it somehow came about that I read Dante with Minna. There was a large airy room at the top of the old Athenaeum Library in Boston whose windows looked out on the church-yard. It was a bare and quiet place: no one ever came there. And during the winter we read Dante there together, and in the course of this she told me of her early life in Milan. There were five children, three of them boys, and there were tempestuous quarrels between the parents. I saw that it was from her mother that she had inherited her leonine temperament. The mother had been a fury. I could see this, though she did not say it ... The Dante readings moved gradually like a cloud between me and the law, between me and the rest of life. It was done with few words. I had come to see that she was in love with someone. It never occurred to me that she might be in love with me. An on-looker might have said, "You loved her for the tragedies of her childhood and she loved you that you did pity them."

'The case was simple, but the tension was blind and terrible. I was completely unaware that I was in love.'

But he did come to be aware that something was making her unhappy, and he decided that 'an acquaintance of hers, a friend in whom she had little interest', had been trifling with her affections. One evening at 'the most innocent kind of party that you can imagine at a country house', he suddenly, without conscious premeditation, in-vited the man outside and beat him.

'The next thing I remember is returning late at night to my room. At that time I was rooming alone in a desolate side-street in Cambridge. It was a small, dark, horrid little room. I sat down. There was a hard-coal fire burning brightly. I took off my coat and waistcoat, wrapped a pair of suspenders tightly on my left forearm above the wrist, plunged the left hand deep in the blaze and held it down with my right hand for some minutes. When I took it out, the charred knuckles and finger bones were exposed. I said to myself, "This will never do." I took an old coat, wrapped it about my left hand and arm, slipped my right arm into an overcoat, held the coat about me, and started for Boston in the horsecars. On arriving at the Massachusetts General Hospital I showed the trouble to a surgeon, was put under ether, and the next morning waked up without the hand and very calm in my spirits. Within a few days I was visited by the great alienist, Dr Reginald Heber Fitz, an extremely agreeable man. He asked me among other things whether I was insane. I said, "That is for you to find out." He reported me as sane. I took no interest in the scandal which my two atrocious acts must have occasioned.'

He knew now that he was in love with Minna and that it was he whom Minna loved. 'Do you know, Minna,' he wrote her, before they were married, in the summer of the same year, 'the one time in my life during which I lived was that twenty days of pain. I read *Henry Esmond*, Dickens' *Christmas Stories*, one morning – I never shall forget them – *Mr Barnes of New York*. Every word of it is glowing with life and love. There was fire in everything I touched – the fire of the activity of that part of me which was meant to be used, which got suppressed all my life till it broke. The depth of the intentions and remote unkempt wells of life and feeling. Browning I used to read anywhere. ... Somehow I have known the meaning of things, if not for long, and all the while I thought I need rest, I need sleep. You see life is an experiment. I had not the least idea but what [if] I met you all this would run the other way and the pain turn into pleasure. I thought I had opened life for ever – what matter if the entrance was through pain.'

And later, three years after they were married, he wrote her in an extraordinary love letter on one of his business trips to the West: 'It was not a waste desert in Colorado. It is not a waste time, for you are here and many lives packed into one life, and the green shoot out of the heart of the plant, springing up blossoms in the night, and many old things have put on immortality and lost things have come back knocking within, from before the time I was conceived in the womb, there were you, also. And what shall we say of the pain! it was false – and the rending, it was unnecessary. It was the breaking down of the dams that ought not to have been put up – but being up it was the sweeping away of them that the waters might flow together.'

They lived in New York, where he had been born. Chapman practised and hated law. He was, on the other hand, passionately interested in politics. He had been a member

of the City Reform Club, founded by Theodore Roosevelt
and others, almost from its beginning in 1882; and later
became president of the Good Government Club, which had
grown out of the City Reform Club. The Good Government Club had been founded by another Harvard man,
Edmond Kelly, for the purpose of fighting Tammany Hall.
When Kelly found out that it was impossible to recruit the
working-class to his movement, he gave it up and became a
socialist. But Chapman and another Harvard man assumed
the leadership of the Good Government movement, and
from 1895 through 1900 he had an odd and very interesting
career as a non-socialist political radical.

In the election of 1895, the 'Goo-Goo's', unable to agree
with the Republicans on a common ticket against Tammany, ran a campaign of their own and were defeated; and
in all this John Jay Chapman played a spirited and provoca-
tive part. He made speeches from the cart-tail in the streets
and created a great impression by getting down and man-
handling hecklers who were trying to break him up – he was
a man of formidable build – then going back and finishing
his speech and afterwards buying his opponents drinks; and
he was able, also, to upset the routine of such accepted
professional reformers as Joseph Choate and Godkin of the
Post. His announced policy at political dinners was 'to
say nothing that he would not regret'; and he is reported
to have been the only person who ever caused the venerable
and cultivated Choate to lose his urbanity in public –
by pointing out to him that the anti-Tammany organization
to which Mr Choate belonged had been guilty of a deal
with the enemy. John Jay Chapman did not understand
politics even as the political reformers did. He combined
the extreme exhilaration of hope with the utmost contempt
of compromise. He had at this period what the poet Yeats
calls 'the purity of a natural force', and he disturbed and
frightened people.

But he was presently to collide with another personality,
with whom he had supposed himself to be travelling, but

of whom he turned out to be crossing the path. In the autumn of 1898, John Jay Chapman was one of the leaders of a group of political Independents who wanted to nominate Theodore Roosevelt for the governorship of New York. Chapman had an interview with Roosevelt: the latter accepted the nomination and continued to affirm his willingness to be run by the Independents, even after the Republican Party had offered to nominate him, too. But, in the meantime, the Independents had drawn up a whole Independent ticket; and the Republican boss, Tom Platt, told Roosevelt that if he wanted the Republicans to run him, he would have to throw over the Independents – which Roosevelt immediately did. Chapman had been so unwary as to fail to extract a written promise from Roosevelt, because he had supposed a gentleman's word was enough. He had happened to start down to Oyster Bay to call on his supposed candidate just before the news of the defection broke in New York; and when he got there, he found there was no train back, so that he had to spend the evening with Roosevelt. It seems to have been a harrowing occasion, 'for I was not going home leaving any mist or misunderstandings in the air as to how the Good Government Club group viewed the situation. But I went further. I unloaded the philosophy of agitation upon Roosevelt and pictured him as the broken-backed half-good man, the successor of the doughface and Northern man with Southern principles of Civil War times, the trimmer who wouldn't break with his party and so, morally speaking, it ended by breaking him.'

Chapman knew very well what Roosevelt had promised him; and the incident gave him seriously to think. He observed that Roosevelt presently persuaded himself that he had never understood the original proposal; and that he thereafter became very vociferous over the damage done progressive movements by fanatics on their 'lunatic fringe'. Chapman had been publishing since March 1897 a review called the *Political Nursery* (originally, simply the *Nursery*), and he now used it to attack Roosevelt's subsequent activities and those of the reformist mayor, Seth Low, formerly a candidate of the Independents. It was the McKinley-Roosevelt era of American imperialist expansion, and Chapman fought the policy of the United States in Cuba and in the Philippines, as well as denounced the British in South Africa.

This review, which he carried on through January 1901, is one of the best written things of the kind which has ever been published anywhere. Chapman wrote most of it himself, and he dealt with philosophical and literary, as well as with political, subjects. Here he began the characteristic practice which William James described when he wrote of him: 'He just looks at things and tells the truth about them – a strange thing even to *try* to do, and he doesn't always succeed.' But he did succeed pretty often, and he is at his best during this early period. As I have not the files of the *Political Nursery* by me, I shall quote some portraits and comments from the letters of his later as well as of his earlier years.

Of James Russell Lowell, he wrote in 1896:

'I don't dislike the man. I think him a fine man, a little dandified and genteel perhaps, but still a good story character. His poetry is nothing but a fine talent, a fine ear, a fine facility – too much morality and an incredible deftness at imitating everybody from Milton down. I cannot read his poems with any comfort – but his early essays I still think the best things he ever did, witty, snappy, "smart" to a degree, and quite natural – they are the only things he ever did that were quite natural. In later life he got all barnacled with quotations and leisure. He pulls out pocket-books and gold snuff boxes and carbuncled cigarette-cases, and emerald eye-glasses, and curls and pomatums himself and looks in pocket looking glasses, and smoothes his Vandyke beard and is a literary fop – f-o-p, fop. Too much culture – over-nourished as Waddy Longfellow says – too many truffled essays and champagne odes and lobster sonnets, too much Spanish olives, potted proverbs – a gouty old cuss in his later essays. But in '54–'65 he wrote rapidly and most clearly. Belles Lettres is the devil after all. It spoils a man. His prefaces – sometimes very nice, in spirit – but his later prefaces are so expressive – O my! so expressive of hems and haws and creased literary trousers. I feel like running him in the belly and singing out Hulloo! old cockolorum.'

Of President Eliot of Harvard (1898):

'Read the essays of (Pres.) Eliot. There's no offence in them. Two by six. Everything in Massachusetts is deal boards. You can put every man in a box – Smug, Smug. He has a good word for poetry too. It's the Dodgedom of Culture. My God, how I hate it. He's the very highest type of a most limited and inspiring pork-chopism. My God, he is hopeful – calls his book *American Contributions to Civilization* – thinks we don't understand small parks and drainage – but will learn and are doing nicely. Has a chapter on "the pleasures of life". It's all one size. Every word in this work is the same size. The Puritans – the war – the problems of labour and capital – education – all excite the same emotion – i.e. that of a woodchuck eating a carrot.'

Of Eliot and J. Pierpont Morgan (1907):

'Pierpont Morgan is the actual apex as well as the type, of the commercial perversions of the era. The political corruption, etc., the power behind all ... Now then, at the dedication of the New Medical School, Eliot goes about in a cab with Pierpont, hangs laurel wreaths on his nose, and gives him his papal kiss. Now what I want to know is this – what has Eliot got to say to the young man entering business or politics who is about to be corrupted by Morgan and his class? How eloquently can Eliot present the case for honesty? Can he say anything that will reverberate through the chambers of that young man's brain more loudly than that kiss?

'If Eliot is a great man, I want a small man.'

Of Roosevelt and Wilson (1930):

'I have just read in type-writing a book about Roosevelt

– which ought to be called the Night Side of T.R.; for it is wholly malignant – and to that extent ineffective. But it's true. He was very nearly mad at times – and broke down his mind by his egotism and mendacity. I had a quarrel with him – political, and personal, and deadly. He was a great genius for handling a situation, and with men, in such a way as to get credit – but he was a damned scoundrel. His genius was to flash a light, put someone down a well, raise a howl to heaven about honesty, and move on to the next thing. Such a genius for publicity as never was – and our people being boy-minded and extremely stupid found him lovely. His feebleness of intellect appears in his writings – which are dull and bombastic – and I doubt whether he will go down as a great man. He's more like a figure out of Dumas. Wilson, a character more odious still, will go down to history as the father of the League of Nations. Drat him! His writings also are dull and he also had the power of hypnotizing men. They idolized him – even those who didn't like him – obeyed – worshipped.

'Apropos – aren't great men apt to be horrid?'

In 1898, he published a volume of literary papers called *Emerson and Other Essays*. In this collection and in the *Political Nursery*, he wrote a commentary on authors then popular – Stevenson, Kipling, Browning, etc. – of which in our day the acumen seems startling. I cannot remember any other American critic of that period – except, in his more specialized field and his more circumlocutionary way, Henry James – who had anything like the same sureness of judgement, the same freedom from current prejudices and sentimentalities. Chapman was then, as, it seems to me, he was to remain, much our best writer on literature of his generation – who made the Babbitts and the Mores and the Brownells, for all the more formidable rigour of their systems and the bulkier mass of their work, look like colonial schoolmasters.

It is worth while to rescue a passage from one of his more ephemeral papers – an article on Kipling in the *Political*

Nursery of April 1899 – for its statement of his organic ideal for literature:

'Permanent interest cannot attach to anything which does not consist, from rind to seeds, of instructive truth. A thing must be interesting from every point of view, as history, as poetry, as philosophy; good for a sick man, just the thing for Sunday morning. It must be true if read backwards, true literally and true as a parable, true in fragments and true as a whole. It must be valuable as a campaign document, and it must make you laugh or cry at any time, day or night. Lasting literature has got to be so very good as to fulfil all these conditions. Kipling's work does not do so since the time he began making money out of it.'

But the long study of Emerson had a special importance. It was something other than a mere essay on Emerson. It was rather an extension of Emerson, a re-creation of Emerson for a new generation, for it was really an expression – the first full expression – of Chapman's own point of view. And what Chapman got out of Emerson was something entirely different from the gentle and eupeptic personality – though that was a part of the real Emerson, too – of Van Wyck Brook's recent portrayals. What Chapman got out of Emerson was a sort of beneficent Nietzscheanism, as electrical as Nietzsche's but less rhetorical. It had seemed to him at college, Chapman wrote, 'as if Emerson were a younger brother of Shakespeare. . . . I was intoxicated with Emerson. He let loose something within me which made me in my own eyes as good as anyone else.' It was Emerson who had first made it possible for him to say to himself: 'After all, it is just as well that there should be *one* person like *me* in the world.' John Jay Chapman was thus a continuator of the individualist tradition of Emerson, which is also the tradition of Thoreau. (Chapman speaks of Thoreau less often, though it seems to me that he is in some ways even more closely akin to him.) He had carried this tradition to New York – for, in spite of the influence on his thought of Cambridge and Concord and Boston, he was distinctly to remain a

New Yorker; and in his hands it was to undergo here an interesting variation.

'As I look back over my past,' he writes, 'the figure of Emerson looms up in my mind as the first modern man, and the city of Boston as the first living civilization which I knew. New York is not a civilization; it is a railway station.' Yet the New Yorker, though beside the New Englanders, with their Concord flavour and colour, he may seem a little abstract and steely (as Henry James does, also, beside Hawthorne), is the man of a larger world. He was to bring against Emerson a new criticism. 'Our people are as thin-skinned as babies', he wrote in one of his lectures, 'and the Massachusetts crowd has never been criticized.' No one had ventured to stand up to Emerson on the issue of the sexual emotions since Walt Whitman had walked with him on Boston Common and, after listening to all his remonstrances against the *Children of Adam* section of *Leaves of Grass*, had replied that he couldn't answer Emerson's arguments, but that he felt sure of being right just the same. 'If an inhabitant of another planet', wrote Chapman, 'should visit the earth, he would receive, on the whole, a truer notion of human life by attending an Italian opera than he would by reading Emerson's volumes. He would learn from the Italian opera that there were two sexes; and this, after all, is probably the fact with which the education of such a stranger ought to begin. In a review of Emerson's personal character and opinions, we are thus led to see that his philosophy, which finds no room for the emotions, is a faithful exponent of his own and of the New England temperament, which distrusts and dreads the emotions. Regarded as a sole guide to life for a young person of strong conscience and undeveloped affections, his works might conceivably be even harmful because of their unexampled power of purely intellectual stimulation.'

And he was to take the Thoreauvian intransigence into society instead of into solitude. John Jay Chapman's attitude towards politics is to develop with a curious logic, which is set forth in two other remarkable books: *Causes and Consequences* (1898) and *Practical Agitation* (1900). *Causes and Consequences* is one of the most powerful tracts ever written on the debasement of our politics and government by unscrupulous business interests. It begins with a pungent fable about the gradual but complete domination of a small American town by a railroad which passes through it. This, says Chapman, when he has told his story, is the whole history of America since the Civil War. And he shows the results of this process in the general cultural life with a force which was not later surpassed by Mencken or Van Wyck Brooks:

'We have seen that the retailer in the small town could not afford to think clearly upon the political situation. But this was a mere instance, a sample of his mental attitude. He dare not face any question. He must shuffle, qualify, and defer. Here at last we have the great characteristic which covers our continent like a climate – intellectual dishonesty. This state of mind does not merely prevent a man having positive opinions. The American is incapable of taking a real interest in anything. The lack of passion in the American – noticeable in his books and in himself – comes from the same habitual mental distraction; for passion is concentration. Hence also the flippancy, superficiality, and easy humour for which we are noted. Nothing except the dollar is believed to be worthy the attention of a serious man. People are even ashamed of their tastes. Until recently, we thought it effeminate for a man to play on the piano. When a man takes a living interest in anything, we call him a "crank". There is an element of self-sacrifice in any honest intellectual work which we detect at once and score with contumely.

'It was not solely commercial interest that made the biographers of Lincoln so thrifty to extend and veneer their book. It was that they themselves did not, could not, take an interest in the truth about him. The second-rate quality of all our letters and verse is due to the same cause. The intellectual integrity is undermined. The literary man is concerned for what "will go", like the reformer who is half politician. The attention of everyone in the United States is on someone else's opinion, not on truth.'

What is one to do in such a world? The diagnosis of *Causes and Consequences* is followed by a programme of action in *Practical Agitation*; but Chapman's practical agitation is of a special and unexpected kind. As a result of his experience as a reformer, he has ceased to believe in the possibility of organized political reform under the American conditions of the time. One of the most amusing and searching passages of *Practical Agitation* describes the rapid absorption and the complete neutralization of a reform movement by the forces it has set out to correct. The commercial solidarity of society has rendered such crusading futile.

Once arrived at such a recognition, one might expect a man like Chapman to turn socialist; but his position on socialism is stated as follows:

'The function of Socialism is clear. It is a religious reaction going on in an age which thinks in terms of money. We are very nearly at the end of it, because we are very nearly at the end of the age. Some people believe they hate the wealth of the millionaire. They denounce corporations and trusts, as if these things hurt them. They strike at the symbol. What they really hate is the irresponsible rapacity which these things typify, and which nothing but moral forces will correct. In so far as people seek the cure in property-laws they are victims of the plague. The cure will come entirely from the other side; for as soon as the millionaires begin to exert and enjoy the enormous power for good which they possess, everybody will be glad they have the money.'

He does not, therefore, believe much in economics:

'The economic laws are valuable and suggestive, but they are founded on the belief that a man will pursue his own business interests exclusively. This is never entirely true even in trade, and the doctrines of the economists become more and more misleading when applied to fields of life where the money motive becomes incidental. The law of supply and demand does not govern the production of sonnets.'

But, 'when you see cruelty going on before you, you are put to the alternative of interposing to stop it, or of losing your sensibility'.

What then? Here is where Emerson comes in. 'If a soul', he wrote, 'be taken and crushed by democracy till it utter a cry, that cry will be Emerson'. And: 'The thing seems to me about this,' he wrote in a letter of this time – after finishing an essay on the *Social Results of Commercialism* – 'Emerson made coherent. It's all Emerson. I should have had neither the ideas reduced so clearly nor the public to understand them if it hadn't been for Emerson. I can't imagine what I should have been if it hadn't been for Emerson.' For he is thrown back on the individual conscience. Here is the situation with which the citizen finds himself confronted:

'Remember ... that there is no such thing as abstract truth. You must talk facts, you must name names, you must impute motives. You must say what is in your mind. It is the only means you have of cutting yourself free from the body of this death. Innuendo will not do. Nobody minds innuendo. We live and breathe nothing else. If you are not strong enough to face the issue in private life, do not dream that you can do anything for public affairs. This, of course, means fight, not tomorrow, but now. It is only in the course of conflict that anyone can come to understand the system, the habit of thought, the mental condition, out of which all our evils arise. The first difficulty is to see the evils clearly; and when we do see them it is like fighting an atmosphere to contend against them. They are so universal and omnipresent that you have no terms to name them by. You must burn a disinfectant.'

And one can take only individual action:

'You yourself cannot turn Niagara; but there is not a town in America where one single man cannot make his force felt against the whole torrent. He takes a stand on a practical matter. He takes action against some abuse.

What does this accomplish? Everything. How many people are there in your town? Well, every one of them gets a thrill that strikes deeper than any sermon he ever heard. He may howl, but he hears. The grocer's boy, for the first time in his life, believes that the whole outfit of morality has any place in the practical world.'

There can have been few codes of morality ever formulated so individualistic as John Jay Chapman's:

'If you want a compass at any moment in the midst of some difficult situation, you have only to say to yourself, "Life is larger than this little imbroglio. I shall follow my instinct." As you say this, your compass swings true. You may be surprised to find what course it points to. But what it tells you to do will be practical agitation.'

This code, with high courage and immense energy, he attempted to put into practice. These were intent and tumultuous years, during which he was shaken by many emotions. At the beginning of 1897, after the birth of their second son, his wife suddenly and unexpectedly died while he was reading to her aloud as she lay in bed. The next year he married his friend, Elizabeth Chanler. Through all this he had been speaking, writing, organizing, getting out his paper, practising law, and leading an active social life – while the immovable magnitude of the forces against him was gradually but inexorably becoming clear to him. 'My own family and connexions,' he wrote, 'being a lot of well-meaning bourgeois, are horrified at me. But I enjoy it.' Yet, 'Politics takes physique', he wrote at another time, 'and being odious takes physique. I feel like Atlas, lifting the entire universe. I hate this community and despise 'em – and fighting, fighting, fighting, fighting an atmospheric pressure gets tiresome.' When his friends expressed apprehension: 'As for insanity,' he replied, 'why, I was once examined for insanity by the two most distinguished physicians in Boston [at the time when he had burned off his hand]. It has no terrors. I talked to them like Plato.'

In the summer of 1900, he went out to attend a convention

in Indianapolis which nominated 'Gold Democrat' candidates to run against both McKinley and Bryan; and he worked hard to organize a 'National Party', the candidates proposed for which refused to run. That winter, after an attack of grippe, at the time when his wife was expecting a baby, he suddenly broke down in the midst of a speech in a small town in Pennsylvania. 'Too much will and self-will,' he wrote his mother.

He retreated to a darkened room. For a year he did not leave his bed, and when he was finally able to get up, remained for two or three years longer under the delusion that he was unable to walk without crutches. Turned in on his own blackness, the sight of a beautiful sunset or the interior of an Italian church, which he had been induced to come out to see, would excite him to the point of collapse.

II

The second half of John Jay Chapman's life is quite distinct from the first. In the August of 1903, one of his sons by his first wife Minna was drowned in an Austrian river; and the shock seems to have brought him to himself. He went back to the United States without his crutches.

He recovered, and thereafter for thirty years led the life of a well-to-do country squire at Barrytown on the Hudson. His second wife's family, the Chanlers, were among the most adventurous and gifted of that special race, the Hudson River gentry; and John Jay Chapman took his place in their world. Chapman's father had been president of the New York Stock Exchange, but had lost heavily in the panic of the seventies, so that John Jay had had partly to put himself through college by tutoring, and he seems to have had a certain amount of difficulty in supporting his family on his earnings from the law. In his youth he had had a variety of social experience which verged at moments on the picaresque. In the course of a trip to Europe after his graduation from Harvard, he had gone to visit an aunt who had married the German minister to Russia and had attended a ball at the Winter Palace, where he saw through the eyes of Tolstoy the Grand Dukes and 'the gorgeous ministers holding glittering staves' and the 'consoling duplicities' of the diplomats, and rescued a pair of toboggans which seemed about to become untied on a chute by throwing himself between them and holding them together while he was dragged on his belly to the bottom; and not long afterwards, when he had returned to America, he went to Canada and hired himself out as a farm-hand: he 'did chores, digged holes for posts, picked cherries on a ladder' till his 'head swam' and 'the landscape reeled', but was so bad at it that one farmer refused to pay him, and he finally came back to his family in such a condition of raggedness and shagginess that they were unable to recognize him; his whole exploit had netted him a dollar.

On the eve of his second marriage, he had been troubled by apprehensions at the prospect of being well-to-do. 'The first thing you know we'll be drowned in possessions,' he wrote at that time to Miss Chanler, 'and then by thinking of our horses' health. It is not so easy to keep the keen vision which an empty stomach lends, if you have footmen. I fear a footman. I tremble before a man with hot water. . . . Let's keep the New Testament open before us. The losing of wrath is to be feared. . . . If I become classed with men at ease about money, the Lord protect me. It is a steel corselet against the heart of mankind and the knowledge of life.' And there are indications in his later letters that he continued to shrink from allowing himself to be 'classed with men at ease about money.' 'I take rides on the buses – for 4d.,' he wrote a friend from London. 'You can go at the rate of 10 m. per hour for half an hour. These things recall London – and student days. The cheap things give one most pleasure – when one is old and rich like me.' And: 'The food of the rich is disgusting to me . . . messes. Last night I had to go to Childs and eat cornbeef hash and poached eggs, which pulled me round.'

Yet he is haunted by ideas of his affinities with royalty and aristocracy. 'I never saw children like them,' he wrote of his sons by his first wife. 'They are King's children in disguise, and I am a stepfather to them.' And, during a visit to an Italian noble, 'I am having some gold fringe put on my pants and I have assumed the title of Monsignore. It is amazing how easily gentility sits on me. I believe some people are just naturally swells – you know what I mean – and fit well in palaces and eat good food naturally and without effort. I remember the first royal palace I saw – seemed to me – gave me a feeling – just like the old homestead. I often think that Grandma Jones used to say, "the Chapmans were once Kings". Dear old Grandpa, with his old cotton socks, wouldn't he be proud if he could see me he-hawing and chaw-chawing with Roman princes!' His plays are full of princes and counts and kings. He had himself something of a kingly presence, especially adorned with the magnificent beard with which he had emerged from his illness. And it is impossible to escape the impression that the comfort and security of his later years did to some degree dull his responses and cut him off from the active world. He succumbed to the Hudson Valley in becoming one of its principal ornaments – to Dutchess County, with its cupolaed castles on their towering dark-wooded hills, which do their best to give work or give alms to the humble feudal villages on the riverbank, to the thunderstorms that seem to crack the firmament and the heavy and slumbrous summers, to the tradition of public responsibility which Hamilton Fish shares with Franklin D. Roosevelt, to the culture which, where it occurs, is likely to range so much more widely and to seem to have so much more authenticity than that of most wealthy communities in America, and to the naturalness and amiability which merge quietly and not unpleasantly with smugness – and all, as it were, walled-in from the rest of the United States and alone with the noble river.

The young John Jay Chapman had plunged into the thick of the conflicts of his time. *Emerson* and *Causes and Consequences* had been talked about and read, had had their influence. In both his political and his literary writing, he had dealt with matters of current interest. But now, in his second period, he seems to have withdrawn from contemporary life, and tends to confine himself to history and the classics. He seems almost to be talking to himself, he seems hardly to expect or hope for an audience; and so people cease to listen to him. The second half of Chapman's career must inevitably be surprising and depressing, though not entirely disappointing, to one who has been stirred by the first. Though he had been able to throw away his crutches, he was to remain, in a deeper sense, a crippled man all the rest of his life. Yet the alternative to survival on these terms would, one supposes, have been madness or death; and it is the proof of the authenticity of his genius that, throughout his long period when he is turned towards the past, when, as a rule, he emerges into the present to raise only trivial or unreal issues, he keeps his power not merely to charm but also sometimes to stimulate.

The Americans who graduated from college in the eighties had to contend with a world that broke most of them. One can see the situation very clearly if one compares the men of the eighties even with those of the seventies. In the seventies, the universities were still turning out admirable professional men, who had had the old classical education, a culture much wider than their profession, and the tradition of political idealism and public conscience which had presided at the founding of the Republic. The world which they had found when they got out had not yet become different enough from the world for which their education had fitted them so that they were not able, on the terms of that old education, to make for themselves positions of dignity in it. But by the later years of the eighties, the industrial and commercial development which followed the Civil War had reached a point where the old education was no longer an equipment for life. It had, in fact, become a troublesome handicap. The best of the men who had taken it seriously were launched on careers of tragic misunderstanding. They could no longer play the role in the professions of a trained and public-spirited caste: the new society did not recognize them. The rate of failure and insanity and suicide in some of the college 'classes' of the eighties shows an appalling demoralization.

Some set themselves to learn the new methods and choked their scruples and did their best to cash in; but John Jay Chapman – who had John Jay among his ancestors – was too honest, too fastidious, too proud, and too violently impulsive, for this. Others compromised shrewdly, like Roosevelt; but the merest suggestion of compromise seems at that period to have driven Chapman into a frenzy. Almost all were compelled to accept in some way the values of the world of business; but how little this was possible for Chapman is indicated in one of his late letters when he insists that, let people say what they please, business can never be a profession. (I have heard a college man of as late as the nineties, who had spent fifty years with an importing firm, tell of his feelings of humiliation when he first started in to work there at a time when the business men, on their side, were supposed to have no use for college graduates. By the second decade of our century, probably the majority of college students had no higher object, on graduating, than to qualify for selling bonds or to slip behind some desk in a family concern and present a well-brushed appearance; and the movement for business courses in the colleges and the talk of the university as a 'big business' were already well under way.)

Given the fineness of Chapman's equipment, the overpowering nature of his emotions, and the relentless clarity of his insight – and given the inescapable conviction of his superiority which made him, for all the ardour of his patriotism, talk about 'a soul crushed by democracy' – there was nothing for him to do but break. And the permanent psychological damage which he had inflicted upon himself by beating his head against the gilt of the Gilded Age was as much one of the scars of the heroism of his passionate and expiatory nature as the hand he had burnt off in his youth.

Let us see how he occupies himself. He begins by writing little plays for children – then, later, tries longer plays. *The Treason and Death of Benedict Arnold* (1910) is perhaps the best of these and has a certain personal interest – with its Coriolanian picture of a man of touchy pride and strong self-will driving through a perverse course of action, which will bring him, among his enemies, honour but no comfort and which will separate him for ever from the cause for which he has fought:

> They must pet me then,
> To show that loyal treason reaps reward.
> 'Twas policy, not liking for my face,
> That made King George so sweet.
> What in this world of savage Englishmen,
> Strange monsters that they are, have you and I
> Found of a country? Friends, good hearts and true;
> But alien as the mountains of the moon,
> More unrelated than the Polander,
> Are Englishmen to us. They are a race,
> A selfish, brawling family of hounds,
> Holding a secret contract on each fang,
> 'For us', 'for us', 'for us'. They'll fawn about;
> But when the prey's divided; – Keep away!
> I have some beef about me and bear up
> Against an insolence as basely set
> As mine own infamy; yet I have been
> Edged to the outer cliff. I have been weak,
> And played too much the lackey. What am I
> In this waste, empty, cruel, land of England,
> Save an old castaway, – a buccaneer, –
> The hull derelict Ambition, –
> Without a mast or spar, the rudder gone,
> A danger to mankind!

But, on the whole, as his biographer says, Chapman is unable to transmit to his characters his own power of self-dramatization. He shrank from and had little comprehension of the new dramatic forms of Ibsen and Shaw, as he shrank from the world they reflected. The companion of Shakespeare and Aeschylus, he followed their methods as a matter of course, with results which are not hopelessly academic only because he could not help getting some reality into everything that he wrote. His plays were mostly in verse; and his verse – he also made some translations from the Greeks and published a certain amount of miscellaneous poetry – is usually only effective when it approximates to the qualities of his prose. There are a few exceptions to this, such as his fine translations from Dante; but the poet that there undoubtedly was in Chapman – perhaps some Puritan heritage had its blighting effect there – found expression chiefly in preaching. As a moralist, John Jay Chapman is a highly successful artist; and it is mainly as a moralist now that he will continue to hold our attention.

With his illness, there emerges a new point of view – really a sort of rarefication of his earlier one. It was before the days of psychoanalysis, and he had been helped through his breakdown by 'faith healers'. In a peculiar and personal way, he now becomes religious. 'There was never anyone with more practical notions, or less under the belief that he was religious in his aims, than I,' he wrote to a friend in 1922 of his early political experience. 'I wanted to attack practical evils – find out about them anyway, affront and examine them, understand them – and I set out by experiment and analysis to deal with them as a workaday problem. And gradually under inspection and ratiocination they turned into spiritual things – mystical elements, and went back into the envelope of religious truth. Nothing else but religious truth was involved. It happened to me apropos of reform movements, to the next man in medicine, to the next in hygiene, in education, in literary work – (look at Winston Churchill). Surely all of us were toys in a shop, and were being turned by the same dynamo – we all approach more nearly all the time to a common frame of mind and temperament – a common sense of helplessness – we who were going to be so powerful and triumphant.' He had announced his new attitude in 1913 at the end of his book on William Lloyd Garrison: 'At first', he says, 'we desire to help vigorously, and we do all in our power to assist mankind. As time goes on, we perceive more and more clearly that the advancement of the world does not depend upon us, but that we, rather, are bound up in it, and can command no foothold of our own. At last we see that our very ambitions, desires, and hopes in the matter are a part of the Supernal Machinery moving through all things, and that our souls can be satisfied and our power exerted only in so far as we are taken up into that original motion, and merged in that primal power. Our minds thus dissolve under the grinding analysis of life, and leave behind nothing except God. Towards him we stand and look: and we, who started out with so many gifts for men, have nothing left in our satchel for mankind except a blessing.'

To one who, like the present writer, is fundamentally unsympathetic with all modern manifestations of religion, the books of John Jay Chapman on this subject – *Notes on Religion* (1922) and *Letters and Religion* (1924) – seem genuine and impressive in a way that most other such recent writings do not. There have been lately in fashion among literary people two main ways of being religious: one historical, philosophical, and ritualistic – the convert turns to the Catholic Church; the other through a substitute pseudo-religion, like that proposed by H. G. Wells. But in the flashes of revelation that were intermittently noted by Chapman, we seem to touch a live spiritual experience as we do not often do with these writers. It is, of course, intensely Protestant: it is Emersonianism again. We are not to look for direction to any established church; each is to trust his own instinct and to interpret the Scriptures for himself:

'Christianity accomplishes itself; and this not through a grand, frontal attack on humanity, but rather through the story and sayings of Christ which dart through the earth, pierce men's ears and heal them, run like elixirs through the languages and habits of men. They are couriers, arrows that live in the ether and need no inns or baiting-places between their flights. The sayings have inexhaustible meanings, and many depths of meaning which the comfortable people of the world cannot hope to fathom – meanings that lie in ambush in the texts, and enter men's hearts in the wake of grief. A man must have been disgraced and in jail to know many of them.' Yet the instincts of individuals are to unite in communion the whole of mankind. With the capacity for deep humility and the sympathy with American life which saved his sense of superiority from snobbery, he was able to interest himself in philanthropies and popular churches:

'I believe that if we could see the invisible church as it actually exists in the interlacing of all men in God and with each other through the force that makes them live, the alarm of those who are fostering religion for fear it will die out would appear ridiculous. Even the half-charlatan, half-illiterate American religious cults deserve our interest and respect.'

'The new American mysticism, for all its eccentricities, dropped an anchor for a generation that had been living in continuous flotation; and being at anchor, the waves of life began to play against the souls of that generation, and beat them into faith. The breakdown of the older ecclesiastical authorities proved a blessing. All the barriers, the interpretations, the shopworn catechisms, the churchy miasmas of many centuries, had been blown away, and the bare text of the New Testament began to convert a new generation and to bring them rest. The new faith was purest in the most humble, as has been the case with all Christian revivals.'

The later Chapman is a lesser Tolstoy, fighting out on his estate on the Hudson the same kind of long war with his conscience which Tolstoy fought at Yasnaya Polyana. And we feel about him somewhat as the contemporaries of Tolstoy seem to have felt about him: that, whatever his inconsistencies and his crusadings for mistaken causes, his spirit and example were a force of incalculable value.

'Truly', he wrote in one of his letters, 'it is the decay in the American brain that is the real danger, and in my narrow philosophy I see the only cure is self-expression, passion, feeling – spiritual reality of some sort. We're about dead spiritually – that's my illusion.' William James, the one of Chapman's contemporaries who probably appreciated him most, called him 'a profound moralist'. 'I have a notion', he once wrote James, 'that I could tell you what is the matter with pragmatism – if you would only stand still. A thing is not truth till it is so strongly believed in that the believer is convinced that its existence does not depend upon him. This cuts off the pragmatist from knowing what truth is.' And: 'It is utter nonsense,' he wrote another correspondent, 'this great passion and little passion – this upper clef and lower clef. All life is nothing but passion. From the great passion of love to the regard for a passing stranger is all one diapason, and is the same chord. The whole of it vibrates no matter where you touch it – tho' in different degrees.' His ideal of practical agitation has in his later phase subsided to this: 'I am saying things which will some day be thought of, rather than trying to get the attention of anyone.' 'It is an accident when I *do* right, but I *am* right,' he once declared.

This rightness was due to some influence which took possession of him and was stronger than he. We may be puzzled at first by the language in which he writes to Minna Timmins, his future wife, after the experience of burning off his hand: 'I do think there was something Promethean in it, in the capacity to yield.' What fire had Chapman snatched from Heaven? And is it Promethean to yield? He means that a divine revelation had caused him to mutilate himself – the revelation of his love for Minna, which was unable to break through into his consciousness and to assert its authority over him save by compelling him to recognize, and hence to punish himself for, his mistake. And he wrote later on to Miss Chanler: 'I . . . have broken and battered down the doors of silence once and for ever years ago, and go about the world escaped from that prison, I thank the powers of life.' Yet he must break out of prison again and again; and his language is always that of giving himself up to something that invades him from outside: 'I'll tell you my philosophy – that there's only one real joy in life . . . – the joy of casting at the world the stone of an unknown world.' His first love, his first wife and her children, with their fierce natures and their sudden or violent deaths, is itself like a power that seizes upon him, a current for which he acts as conductor and which will leave him partially shattered. And when it is not love, he calls it God.

Besides these religious *pensées*, Chapman publishes during this period several volumes of essays, literary, historical, and social, and some memoirs of New York and Boston. He perfects himself now as a writer: in these books, the 'style all splinters', of which William James wrote at the time of *Practical Agitation*, is hammered out into an instrument of perfect felicity, economy, limpidity, precision, and point. Some of his most beautiful prose is in his very latest writings. And he can still take our breath away by laying hold of the root of some subject, by thrusting through, with a brusqen direct gesture, all the familiar conventions and pretensious with which it has been enclosed.

In his relation to the literary classics, he was that almost unprecedented phenomenon, a highly intelligent and well-educated American who paid almost no attention to European criticism and scholarship. Well as he knew Europe, he was never afflicted with the nostalgia for it which seized so many of the cultivated Americans of his time. In his opinions on European culture, he was as naturally and uncompromisingly American as Walt Whitman or Mark Twain. The accepted apparatus of learning he either quarrelled with or disregarded – characterizing, for example, the taking-over of Greek literature by the mandarins of the English universities as an incident in the expansion of the British Empire.

To Chapman, the great writers of the past were neither a pantheon nor a vested interest. He approached them open-mindedly and boldly, very much as he did living persons who he thought might entertain or instruct him. Not that he judged them by contemporary standards; but he would go straight to them across the ages in the role of an independent traveller, who was willing to pay his toll to the people that kept the roads but wished to linger with them as little as possible. He sometimes committed blunders: he got the relationships mixed up in the *Antigone*, and he never grasped the simple enough principles which govern, in the *Divine Comedy*, the assignment of the souls to the different worlds – complaining that Dante's arrangements involved a good deal of injustice. 'You know,' he says in a letter, 'I've never known the literature of the subjects I wrote on. I never knew the Emerson literature – except Emerson himself.' But Chapman has at least always got there and had a good look at the man; and he can always tell you about him something that you have not heard before. To me, Chapman's flashlighting and spotlighting in his studies of the Greeks, Dante, Shakespeare, and Goethe (this last left unpublished at his death and unfortunately not yet published) are among the few real recent contributions to the knowledge of these familiar subjects. He cannot help bumping into aspects which, though they bulk very large in these authors, have so often been ignored or evaded that many people have never noticed they were there. He saw the basic barbarity of Greek tragedy, which he denounced Gilbert Murray for sentimentalizing; he saw the importance of the pederasty of Plato: Diotima, he writes, is 'an odious creature, being a man in disguise'; he saw, through all the Dante commentaries, how impossible it is to interpret Dante in terms of medieval theology.

Here are passages from some of the latest of these essays, which show the freshness of Chapman's mind in his sixties:

'Plato soothes and rests. He takes the mind off its troubles and supplies it with imaginative solutions for problems which do not press. To read him is a solace and to write commentaries on him is an entrancing and enduring preoccupation. He is the patron saint of those who sit in armchairs and speculate. His wealth of information, myth, and anecdote, the amenity and fluidity of his procedure, endear him to all book-lovers. He is enshrined in a civilization which will interest the world as long as intelligent men shall be born into it. Even the limitations and defects of the Athenians are stimulating. "Athens," we say, and surrender ourselves to romance. We sleep while awake; and if you point out that Plato deceives us by intellectual legerdemain which cheats the mind, nay, if you should prove it, this will make you no friends; for, as Mr Barnum discovered to his profit many centuries later, the public likes to be fooled. A vision of truth which does not call upon us to get out of our armchair – why, this is the desideratum of mankind.'

'Dante's frailty is the source of his power. Had he been truly a medieval theologian, or philosopher, or moralist, or historian, he would today be as dead as the rest of them ... [His philosophy] is full of whimsies and cobwebs, private significances and key-words; and there is no philosophic instrument of thought which he does not distort as he touches it – even as all poets do, and must do.' 'The conceptions of Greek mythology spring out of a Supermind which harmonizes the fantasies of childhood with the thought of mature age. They are embedded in the ganglia of the brain as music is: no explanation touches them. They defy analysis, and Dante himself fails to interpret them: his metaphysics will not stick to them.' 'To raise the question whether Dante was technically or virtually a heretic ... is to miss the human and important point of the whole question. Dante's attitude towards the Empire and the Papacy was that of a superautocrat who is above both of them, and holds a commission from on high to regulate the affairs of each.' 'The truth is that one must gather Dante's meanings, as one gathers the meanings of other men, by putting two and two together, not by drawing pictures of his Supposed Universe, and then hanging his phrases on them as on a Christmas Tree.' 'He had invented the *terza rima*, a form in which a continuous lyric can float and be indefinitely sustained upon the narrative below it.'

What a pity, one is moved to exclaim, that John Jay Chapman remained a dilettante! Yet 'dilettante' is not the proper word for one who worked at his writing so diligently and so seriously. And his literary essays, after all, are only a part of his general commentary, which possesses a sort of centre of its own, independent of the various subjects treated.

Aside from this purely literary activity, he carried on a

certain amount of agitation, sporadically and in behalf of a strange diversity of causes. His rejection of economics, his failure, when he had recognized political corruption as a mere by-product of the industrial-commercial system, to study the mechanics and the history of that system, had left him without bearings in the political world.

First of all, he went back to the Civil War – he was very proud of one of his grandmothers, who had been a prominent Abolitionist – and in his book on William Lloyd Garrison fought the battle of slavery all over again with a spirit that would have been employed more usefully in fighting the battle of labour. It was the period of the rise of Bill Haywood's Wobblies, of the growth of Eugene Debs's Socialist Party, of Lincoln Steffen's muck-raking movement.

On 13 August 1911, a Negro who had shot and killed a special officer of the Worth Brothers Steel Company in Coatesville, Pennsylvania, was burned alive by a mob under circumstances of special horror. Chapman, who was full of the Civil War, brooded upon this incident till he 'felt as if the whole country would be different if any one man did something in penance, and so I went to Coatesville and declared my intention of holding a prayer meeting to the various business men I could buttonhole'. He had difficulty in getting a hall, but finally, four days after the anniversary of the lynching, succeeded in finding a place to speak. The address he delivered was strange and moving. He said that, when he had read in the papers how 'hundreds of well-dressed American citizens' had stood by and watched the torture of the Negro, he had seemed to see into 'the unconscious soul' of America. And what he had seen there was death – 'the paralysis of the nerves about the heart in a people habitually and unconsciously given over to selfish aims'. They had 'stood like blighted things, like ghosts about Acheron, waiting for someone or something to determine their destiny for them.' It was the old wickedness, not yet purged, of the slave trade, and all America was to blame for it. They could but open their hearts to God and pray that new life might flow into them – The only persons who attended the meeting were an educated Negro woman from Boston and a stool pigeon sent by the police.

The World War, when it first broke out, aroused him to a new burst of agitation. He was in Europe in August 1914, and went immediately to Balfour, Haldane, and Sir Edward Grey, and told them that it was of vital importance, in order to elicit the sympathy of the world, that the Allies should declare their aims to be non-aggressive and announce their intention, in the event of their victory, of calling a world disarmament congress; and he seems to have been deceived by the intelligence and kindness with which these statesmen heard him out. Later, he went to Wilson and urged him to elicit such a declaration. He also published a book, *Deutschland über Alles* (1914), in which he pointed out the propaganda methods by which the Germans had been worked up to the war, and advised the United States to stay out. 'If America should enter the war, the world would lose the benevolence and commonsense which we now possess, and which is a strong factor in the whole situation. You and I would, in that case, become partisans, cruel, excited, and bent on immediate results.'

In the meantime, however, his son Victor, one of his children by his first wife, had, against his father's wishes, enlisted in the Foreign Legion and had later become one of the most daring pilots of the Lafayette Escadrille. He was killed – the first American aviator to die – on 23 June 1916; and his father now fell a victim to that war psychology which he had foreseen and dreaded for the country. Chapman was even betrayed temporarily into applauding his old enemy Roosevelt, whose pro-Ally bellowings and pawings of the ground were certainly no more to be taken seriously than the other Rooseveltian impostures which Chapman had so relentlessly exposed. Later, in 1920, when Siegfried Sassoon came to New York, and read his poems and made an anti-war speech at the Cosmopolitan Club, the former opponent of wartime fanaticism – who, no doubt, felt it a duty to speak for his dead son – got up and aroused consternation and hisses by denouncing what he characterized as a philosophy of fear and self-pity. The next day he tried to call on Sassoon and finally wrote him a letter: 'Sorry to miss you this morning. It was a suffering occasion last night. I think I suffered as much as you did. If you will do it, why, you must.' Had he remembered his early gospel of the value of the individual gesture and reflected that the young Sassoon had, after all, only been doing what he himself had done when, for example, at that political dinner in 1895, he had spoken out in a way that had made old Mr Choate turn pale?

The most wrongheaded of all his crusades, but the one to which he devoted most energy, was his attack on the Roman Catholic Church. He had received no doubt a terrifying impression of the bad influence of the Catholics in Boston; but he exaggerated its importance in the United States as a whole, and he had become, by 1925, so almost monomaniacally obsessed by it that it was thought best for him to go abroad to distract his mind from the subject and avoid another breakdown.* At one period he was inclined to believe – in spite of the admiration for Jewish culture which had caused him once to call himself a 'Hebraist' – that the Jews, also, were coming to be a sinister influence, and he even contributed a sonnet, anti-Catholic and anti-Semitic, to the organ of the Ku Klux Klan. ('The Jews', he had written in 1897, 'have in my experience more faith than the Christians. They have clever heads, better hearts, and more belief in the power of good every way. They gave to the world all the religion it has got and are themselves the most religious people in it. I work with them day and night and most of the time is spent in prying up some Christian to do a half day's work.')

For two years he and Mrs Chapman conducted a clubroom for young people in the Hell's Kitchen section of

---

* Since this was written, the Catholic Church has become in the United States a formidable pressure group, exercising the retrograde and repressive force that Chapman at that time ascribed to it.

New York. On one occasion, two boys whom he had put out, came back and blew kerosene in his beard and tried to set it afire. When they had failed, he handed them a handkerchief and told them to wipe themselves off.

Besides all this, he was continually agitating against the influence of big business at Harvard and harrying with scolding letters the Head Master of St Paul's School, as well as old friends in positions of prominence of whose activities he disapproved. One of his correspondents, Mr T. B. Wells, the editor of *Harper's Magazine*, was finally goaded to ask what Chapman himself had accomplished any more than 'a lot of other brilliant fellows who did not make full use of their talents' to give him the right to call everyone else to account over the way they handled their jobs. And it is true that one feels a touch of envy in his tone towards men like Shaw and Wells, even towards William James, whom he undoubtedly liked and admired – who were doing a kind of work that one would think he might have applauded. There is even an occasional accent of the ignorant and cutting Boston snootiness that he had disliked and ridiculed. As one goes through his later letters – as in reading his work of this period – one is made more and more uncomfortable by the feeling that one has been shut up in a chamber from which the air is being gradually withdrawn – shut in with a chafing spirit who, baffled of finding an outlet, is sometimes furious and sometimes faint. Then suddenly one recoils and stands outside the cell: one sees how Chapman's outlook has narrowed. One remembers all the things that have happened in the world of which there is almost no mention in these letters – almost the whole significant life of the time; and one realizes that Chapman's interests have come to be almost entirely confined to the horizons of his old Harvard circle. It is all Harvard College and St Paul's School, Porcellian Club and Tavern Club. He writes to Dr Drury of St Paul's and E. S. Martin of *Life* as if they were among the great moulders of thought of their age. We have the suspicion that even William James, as distinct from Wells and Shaw, is only admitted to the sphere of Chapman's interest because he, too, belongs to Harvard. It is the lost traveller's dream under the hill – the old conception of the caste of trained 'college men' who were to preside over the arts and professions. It is the same point of view – we had not recognized it at first – that seemed so fatuous, that became so unconsciously comic, in Owen Wister's memoirs of Roosevelt. Mr Wister, whose claim to celebrity consists in his having written novels, is wonderful when, after telling of his acquaintance with various personages of Philadelphia and Harvard of whom we have never heard, he says that, 'Huysmans (if I recall the right name) had recently published a novel, in which were described the rites of the Black Mass' – and he is even more wonderful when, after a life 'chiefly passed', as he says, 'among the Alexander Cassatts, the George Baers, and the Weir Mitchells' of Philadelphia, he goes West and discovers Coxey's army and the stoppage of trains due to the Pullman strike, and is obliged to spend two dreadful nights sleeping on the floor of a boat from San Pedro. But this failure of response to contemporary events, either artistic or economic is, in Chapman's case, simply depressing. Owen Wister thinks them still important, Olympians who dominate the world – Roosevelt and Henry Adams and Henry Cabot Lodge and the rest. John Jay Chapman has no illusions about them, but he has to go on nagging at them and abusing them. He does not seem to realize that they have all been either absorbed or left behind by a new world never contemplated by old Harvard. He himself – for all the piercing intuitions which still at moments strike through age and class – has been left behind by that world.

He believed in these later days that the society of the period after the war was on the eve of a great religious rewakening:

'Who shall say that this present era, when all the idols are broken, all the great traditions dead, and the fine arts have become mere wandering lights, while the mind of man seems to have passed into a tunnel of transition – who shall say that these apparent extinguishments and this twilight are not necessary? Our present incredulity as to all the explanations of life is very favourable to a direct vision of life itself. The floods have carried away our mills, and a thunderstorm has destroyed the wiring of our houses; but the powers of gravity and electricity are not abolished for a moment. The contrivances on which we had set so much store served but to obscure the phenomena. Like Job in the wreck of his homestead, we have been humbled. The war humbled that spirit which had ruled the nineteenth century. In scale the drama differed from the Book of Job, but in plot it was similar.

'In the meantime, though the arts have lost their message, religion stalks in upon us. The auld wives' tales about prayer and healing, which during many centuries had been regarded as ecstatic parables, are now taken literally: we live in them. This tunnel into which the age is running is one of the clairvoyant periods of history in which men are seen as trees walking. The actual world does not disappear, nor is it relegated to a life to come, or disparaged, or condemned as evil. It remains perfectly real, and yet visibly penetrated by the rays of an inner universe which are at play everywhere.'

One used to see him, during those years, in New York, in company a figure of a distinction almost exotic for the United States, with his fine manners, his sensitive intelligence, his clothes with their attractive suggestion of the elegance of another era, his almost Jove-like beard and brow, his deep and genial laugh; or for a moment under a quite different aspect, when one had happened to meet him in the street: walking alone, head drooping and brooding, with his muffler around his neck, in his face dreadful darkness and sadness and fear, as if he were staring into some lidless abyss.

He died, after an operation, on 4 November 1933. He had loved music, and when he was a student at Harvard had had what he described as 'an obsession, a sort of self-willed mania for learning to play the violin, for which I had no talent'. He had worked at it two years, but his fellow students had discouraged him by throwing coal scuttles at his door and hanging alarm-clocks outside his windows. After his father's financial failure, he wrote home, 'I shall sell the violin: it's no half-way business.' But at the time he was recovering from his breakdown, he had taken up the study of harmony and tried to compose a little. Now two days before his death, writes Mrs Chapman, he kept murmuring, 'A soldier lay dying, a soldier lay dying.' 'I bent over him to catch the words, and he repeated the first four lines of "A soldier of the Legion lay dying in Algiers", adding, *But there is lack of nothing here*," in a voice of deep feeling.' But later, when semi-conscious, he began saying, 'plucking at my fingers, "I want to take it away, I want to take it away!" "What?" I asked. "The pillow?" "No," he said. "The mute, the mute. I want to play on the open strings."'

Bernard Shaw at Eighty

TIME has shifted our point of view on Bernard Shaw, yet he is still worth our contemplation. Let us cast a look back over his career.

George Bernard Shaw was born in Dublin, 26 July 1856, the son of shabby-genteel parents who had connexions with the Irish nobility. The elder Shaw became an alcoholic, and the boy had to go to work as a clerk at the age of fifteen. Mrs Shaw finally left her husband and went to London, where she made a living by teaching music. Her son came to live with her when he was twenty and wrote novels which he was unable to sell and picked up through journalism such money as he could. He remained with his mother till he was forty-two.

In the fall of 1882 he happened to attend a lecture on land nationalization delivered by Henry George in London. The result was a revelation: 'It flashed on me', he writes, 'that "the conflict between religion and science" ... the overthrow of the Bible, the higher education of women, Mill on Liberty, and all the rest of the storm that raged around Darwin, Tyndall, Huxley, Spencer, and the rest, on which I had brought myself up intellectually, was a mere middle-class business .... The importance of the economic basis dawned on me.' He read George's *Progress and Poverty* – then someone told him to read *Das Kapital*. 'Karl Marx', he once said, 'made a man of me.'

The result of the depression of the eighties was a revival of socialist agitation. Bernard Shaw became a socialist and spoke in halls, on street corners, in Hyde Park. The 'insurrectionism' of the period reached a climax in the 'Bloody Sunday' of November 1887, when the socialists, at the head of a working-class demonstration, invaded Trafalgar Square and were routed by the police. After this, business revived and took up the slack of unemployment, and the agitation quieted down.

In the meantime Shaw had attached himself to the socialist statistician, Sidney Webb, and with others they had founded the Fabian Society, which had 'agreed to give up the delightful ease of revolutionary heroics and take to the hard work of practical reform on ordinary parliamentary lines'. Webb was a civil servant with a post in the colonial office and later a member of the London County Council; Shaw became a vestryman, then a borough councillor. The Fabians continued to treat Marx with respect, but the polite and reasonable criticism to which they subjected him was designed to discredit some of his main assumptions. Marx had asserted that the value of commodities was derived from the labour which had gone to produce them; and the Fabians, by elaborating a counter-theory that made value depend on demand, shifted the emphasis from the working class to the 'consumer'. They also repudiated the class war, showed that it would never occur. Socialist nationalization was to be accomplished by a corps of experts who should 'permeate' government and business, quietly invading Whitehall and setting up state departments which, unassisted by the action of the masses, should put socialist ideas into effect. Shaw boasted that the Fabians had made socialism respectable.

This variation of Marxism in England was natural to the place and time. A period of prosperity during the seventies had deflated the Chartist agitation (I am indebted to Mr Mark Starr for a Marxist analysis of Fabian Marxism); and it was not until the eighties, when British commercial domination was being challenged by the United States and Germany, that the dangers of the capitalist system began to become generally plain. But now attention was principally directed towards the evils of competition. The development of large-scale industry was eliminating competition and making municipal ownership seem desirable, not only to the lower layers of the middle class, but even to private enterprise itself, which benefited from good housing and cheap tram-lines. The professional middle class were in a position to see the value of nationalization, and the working class had not yet discovered that for them there was not very much difference between being exploited by a private employer and being exploited by a government that was controlled by the propertied classes. The Fabians looked no further than their reforms.

In Bernard Shaw's case, this compromise Marxism played in with the elements of his character and influenced its subsequent development. Coming to London, as he has recently told us, with a conviction of his own superiority and a snobbish family tradition, but with no money and no social experience, Shaw was himself one of the dispossessed, and the socialist criticism of the class system based on property strongly recommended itself to him. Yet at the same time that in all good faith he was working to destroy that system, there is apparent in his career a tendency in the inverse direction to this. At the same time that he was spurred by a moral need to work for a future society consistent with his sense of justice, he was spurred, also, by a social need to vindicate his rightful position in the society in which he lived. He has told us that his father's bad habits had caused his family to be dropped socially in Dublin and that when he first came to London he was so shy that he would not accept dinner invitations and would 'sometimes walk up and down the Embankment for twenty minutes or more before venturing to knock at the door' of a house to which he had been asked. He goes on to say, 'The house and its artistic atmosphere were most congenial to me; and I liked all the Lawsons; but I had not mastered the art of society at that time and could not bear making an inartistic exhibition of myself; so I soon ceased to plague them.' There has always been thus in Shaw a certain amount of social snobbery mixed up with his intellectual snobbery.

The confusion produced in his thought by these two

conflicting tendencies is curiously illustrated in a passage from his autobiographical preface to the collected edition of his works: 'Finding one's place may be made very puzzling', he writes, 'by the fact that there is no place in ordinary society for extraordinary individuals. For the worldly wiseman, with common ambitions, the matter is simple enough: money, title, precedence, a seat in parliament, a portfolio in the cabinet, will mean success both to him and to his circle. But what about people like St Francis and St Clare? Of what use to them are the means to live the life of the country house and the West End mansion? They have literally no business in them, and must necessarily cut an unhappy and ridiculous figure there. They have to make a society of Franciscans and Poor Clares for themselves before they can work or live socially. It is true that those who are called saints are not saintly all the time and in everything. In eating and drinking, lodging and sleeping, chatting and playing: in short, in everything but working out their destiny as saints, what is good enough for a ploughman is good enough for a poet, a philosopher, a saint, or a higher mathematician. But Hodge's work is not good enough for Newton, nor Falstaff's conversation holy enough for Shelley. Christ adapted himself so amicably to the fashionable life of his time in his leisure that he was reproached for being a gluttonous man and a winebibber, and for frequenting frivolous and worthless sets. But he did not work where he feasted, nor flatter the Pharisees, nor ask the Romans to buy him with a sinecure. He knew when he was being entertained, well treated, lionized: not an unpleasant adventure for once in a way; and he did not quarrel with the people who were so nice to him. Besides, to sample society is part of a prophet's business: he must sample the governing class above all, because his inborn knowledge of human nature will not explain the anomalies produced in it by Capitalism and Sacerdotalism. But he can never feel at home in it.'

But which is true: that the St Francis or the St Clare can't 'live socially' till they have 'made a society of Franciscans and Poor Clares' or that 'in eating and drinking, lodging and sleeping, chatting and playing', 'what is good enough for a ploughman is good enough for a saint'? And as for Shaw's description of Christ, it evokes an incongruous picture: what one sees is the preacher of the Sermon on the Mount very much pleased with himself on the beach at the Riviera or playing Santa Claus at Lady Astor's Christmas party.

And other influences, from his early education, came to deflect the straight line of his socialism.

The escapades of the romantic hero, from Childe Harold through Don César de Bazan, with his ' *Tant pis! C'est moi!,*' to Siegfried, had been a protest against the meanness and dullness of the commercial bourgeois world; but this revolt was itself merely a further phase of the tradition of individual assertion which, deriving from the Protestant conscience, had produced the anarchic individualism of the competitive commercial system. The romantic, like the old-fashioned capitalist, proclaimed the power of the personal will in defiance of society and God.

William Archer tells us that the first time he ever saw Shaw, the latter was sitting in the British Museum studying alternately the French translation of *Das Kapital* and the score of *Tristan und Isolde*. When Shaw first came before the public, he fell instinctively into dramatizing himself as a semi-romantic character – and this in spite of the fact that he was managing to figure at the same time as the arch-enemy and blasphemer of romanticism. The impulse to satirize romanticism implies, as in the case of Flaubert, a strong predisposition towards it; and the exploded romantic, Captain Brassbound, is offset by the Devil's Disciple. It is true that Shaw's conscious intention was to ridicule and shame his audience out of exclusive preoccupation with the emotions of their personal lives – especially, with romantic love – and to interest them in the problems of society. Here is the fine and well-known passage from *Man and Superman*, in which he defends what he calls the 'artist-philosophers' against the 'mere artists': 'This is the true joy in life, the being used for a purpose recognized by yourself as a mighty one; the being thoroughly worn out before you are thrown on the scrap heap; the being a force of Nature instead of a feverish selfish little clod of ailments and grievances complaining that the world will not devote itself to making you happy.' Yet is this not, too, a kind of romanticism – romanticism *par excellence*? The ego has now, to be sure, identified itself with a force of nature, but this simply makes the ego seem godlike. There is nothing to guarantee that it will respect either the feelings or the interests of others. The ideal artist-philosopher of Bernard Shaw has always a strong social conscience, and his heroes are likely to be philosopher-statesmen or social prophets or saviours of society; but there is nothing to guarantee that they shall be, in the socialist sense, genuine popular leaders, deriving their power from, as well as guiding, the dispossessed: they may be simply despot-heroes – as Shaw's Julius Caesar actually is – acting in the right of their own superiority and giving people what they know to be good for them.

And finally, of course, Bernard Shaw was not only a political prophet struggling for socialist ideas, but an artist trying to realize himself through art. There was a poet in Shaw, still partly suppressed, or at any rate terribly overtaxed, by the round of political meetings, the functions of vestryman and borough councillor, and the years of theatre-going and weekly article-writing about the theatre, which he had come to judge almost exclusively in terms of the sort of thing that he wanted to do himself. His own plays he had been writing in notebooks while travelling on the tops of buses between one engagement and another. Now in 1898, when he was forty-two, he had what seems to have been a general collapse as the result of a bad fall and a serious injury to his foot. When he recovered, he married an Irish lady, well-to-do but belonging like Shaw to the general 'advanced' movement, who gave him for apparently the first time in his life a comfortable place to live and took the most excellent care of him. Thereafter, he was able to give up the journalism on which he had depended for a living and to devote all his best energies to his plays. He remained a public man, but he spoke no more at dockers' strikes.

By 1905 he was writing *Major Barbara*, in which the type of Christian sainthood, an aristocratic Salvation Army worker, is confronted with a self-made munitions manufacturer, the type of successful capitalism; and ending the play with an alliance between them. In his preface, he made out a ringing case for the man who recognizes poverty as the worst of all the evils and consequently the worst of all the sins, and who saves himself from it at any cost. *Major Barbara* contains one of the best expositions of the capitalist point of view ever written. Bernard Shaw, like his hero, Andrew Undershaft, had come by that time to know what it was to make one's way in capitalist society and to occupy a position of power. He had himself become the type of the critic, who, by scolding the bourgeoisie, makes good with it and becomes one of its idols. He was gradually, for all the scandal of his début, turning into a dependable member of the British propertied classes; and he was to end as an esteemed public figure in a country where an aristocratic governing class was still able to contribute to public life a certain distinction and glamour.

II

The real Shaw has thus never been the single-minded crusader that people at one time used to think him. Except for a limited period during the eighties and early nineties – when he wrote his only straight socialist plays, *Widowers' Houses* and *Mrs Warren's Profession* – he has never really been a practising socialist. And I am inclined to believe that the future will exactly reverse the opinion which his contemporaries have usually had of him. It used always to be said of Shaw that he was primarily not an artist, but a promulgator of certain ideas. The truth is, I think, that he is a considerable artist, but that his ideas – that is, his social philosophy proper – have always been confused and uncertain. As he has grown older and as the world has been shaken out of the pattern to which he had adapted his attitudes, the inadequacy of those attitudes has been exposed.

One is struck, as one goes through the volumes of the collected edition of Shaw, which includes a good deal of his journalism, by the fact that, though his writing on musical and theatrical and literary subjects remains remarkably fresh, the pieces on public affairs and on social questions in general prove very much less satisfactory than one had remembered their seeming when they first came out. There are passages of admirable exposition and passages of wonderful eloquence – some of which, such as the peroration to *The Intelligent Woman's Guide to Socialism and Capitalism*, will probably always stand among the classics of socialist literature. But the political writing of Shaw does not drive you into taking up a position as the greatest socialist writing does: indeed, before he has finished – and he is likely to go on talking too long – he has often seemed to compromise the points which you had imagined he was trying to make, and has produced, with much earnestness and emphasis, an impression rather blurred by rhetoric. Both his intelligence and his sense of justice have prevented him from assailing the capitalist system with such intolerant resentment and unscrupulous methods as Voltaire trained on the Church. With Voltaire, it *is* the crusader that counts: with Shaw, it is the dramatic poet.

The volume which covers the wartime exposes Bernard Shaw's contradictions in a particularly striking manner. Though he was perfectly familiar with the Marxist theory of capitalist expansion and aggression, and had expounded it on many occasions, he had always been liable to fits of admiration for the exploits of the British Empire. Irishman though he was, he had never been an Irish patriot; and, critical though he was of the English, he had in *John Bull's*

Other Island – which was written for but declined by the Abbey Theatre – backed them against the Irish on account of what he regarded as their superior enterprise and practicality. And though he denounced the Denshawai massacre in Egypt, he supported the British against the Boers at the time of the South African war, because the Boers represented for him a backward civilization and the British a progressive one. When the civilizing forces of the various nations had finally collided in 1914, it was Lenin, the revolutionary exile, not Shaw, the successful British citizen, who wrote *Imperialism: The Last Stage of Capitalism*.

What Bernard Shaw did write was *Common Sense About the War*, which, although it raised a terrible outcry in the fall of 1914 on the part of certain elements of the British public who thought that Shaw ought to be put in the Tower, seems today rather a double-facing document. Shaw, to be sure, makes a certain amount of effort still to keep before the minds of his readers the socialist interpretation of the War. 'Will you', he writes, 'now at last believe, O stupid British, German, and French patriots, what the Socialists have been telling you for so many years: that your Union Jacks and tricolours and Imperial Eagles ("where the carcase is, there will the eagles be gathered") are only toys to keep you amused, and that there are only two real flags in the world henceforth: the red flag of Democratic Socialism and the black flag of Capitalism, the flag of God and the flag of Mammon? What earthly or heavenly good is done when Tom Fool shoots Hans Narr? The plain fact is that if we leave our capital to be dealt with according to the sefishness of the private man he will send it where wages are low and workers enslaved and docile: that is, as many thousand miles as possible from the Trade Unions and Trade Union rates and parliamentary Labour parties of civilization; and Germany, at his sordid behest, will plunge the world into war for the sake of disgracing herself with a few rubber plantations, poetically described by her orators and journalists as "a place in the sun". When you do what the Socialists tell you by keeping your capital jealously under national control and reserving your shrapnel for the wasters who not only shirk their share of the industrial service of their country, but intend that their children and children's children shall be idle wasters like themselves, you will find that not a farthing of our capital will go abroad as long as there is a British slum to be cleared and rebuilt or a hungry, ragged, and ignorant British child to be fed, clothed, and educated.'

This sounds spirited enough by itself, yet the burden of *Common Sense About the War* is that the war must be supported and vigorously prosecuted. Shaw afterwards visited and wrote about the front at the invitation of Sir Douglas Haig and even did some work for the propaganda department of the government. In his discussion of compulsory military service in *Common Sense About the War*, he defends his position as follows: 'In my own case, the question of conscientious objection did not arise: I was past military age. I did not counsel others to object, and should not have objected myself if I had been liable to serve: for intensely as I loathed the war, and free as I was from any illusion as to its character, and from the patriotic urge (patriotism in my native country taking the form of an implacable hostility to England), I knew that when war is once let loose, and it becomes a question of kill or be killed, there is no stopping to argue about it: one must just stand by one's neighbours and take a hand with the rest. If England had adopted me, as some of my critics alleged in their attempts to convict me of gross ingratitude, I could have pleaded that she must take the consequences without claiming any return; but as I had practically adopted England by thrusting myself and my opinions on her in the face of every possible rebuff, it was for me to take the consequences, which certainly included an obligation to help my reluctant ward in her extremity as far as my means allowed.'

Frank Harris, in his book about Shaw, reproached him for supporting the war; and Shaw retorted in a postscript that

Harris 'could not stop to ask himself the first question ... of the intellectually honest judicious critic, "What else could I have done had it been my own case?"' Yet surely there were other courses open to a man of Shaw's opinions. He could have expressed his disapproval and shut up, as John Morley and others did. But it is impossible for Shaw to shut up, and he went on talking incessantly through the whole four years of slaughter. Much of what he had to say was intelligent, and it required some courage to say it. Compared with most of the British writers, he seemed at the time to an American remarkably cool and sagacious. The atmosphere was feverish with panic and stupefying with the fumes of propaganda, and Shaw did do something to clear the air for a discussion of the origin and aims of the war. But when we reread what he wrote today, he looks a little foolish. The old socialist has gone down into the mêlée and sacrificed something of his moral dignity: we hear him remonstrating, scolding, exhorting, making fun of the politicians, and at the same time lending a hand to the government, pleading for the conscientious objectors and at the same time 'joy-riding at the front' – and doing everything with equal cocksureness.

Before the Peace Conference, he had great hopes of Wilson. Before the Washington Disarmament Conference, he was cynical. Later, he spoke a kind word for the League of Nations. And in the meantime the Russian Revolution had set him off on a different tack. He would alternately lecture Lenin and Trotsky on the futility of what they were trying to do and applaud them for succeeding in doing it: he was alternately a middle-class socialist using Fabianism against the Marxists and a Marxist using Lenin and Trotsky against the British governing class. (It is interesting to note that Lenin characterized him as 'a good man fallen among Fabians', and that Trotsky, of whom Shaw wrote enthusiastically as 'the Prince of Pamphleteers', expressed the wish, apropos of his own exclusion from England, that 'the Fabian fluid that ran in [Bernard Shaw's] veins might have been strengthened by even so much as five per cent of the blood of Jonathan Swift'. It is amusing to see Trotsky's indignation in his *Where Is Britain Going?* over Shaw's cavalier suggestion that Marx had been superseded by H. G. Wells's *Outline of History*: Trotsky had gone to the trouble of procuring and looking into Wells.)

In his political utterances since the war, it is hardly too much to say that Bernard Shaw has behaved like a jackass. In the autumn of 1927, he was staying in Italy on the Lago Maggiore and throwing bouquets at Mussolini. It was his old admiration for the romantic hero, his old idealization – which was as likely to be set off by an imperialist as a Marxist theme – of the practical Caesarean statesman who makes people stand around. Mussolini had, according to Shaw, 'achieved a dictatorship in a great modern state without a single advantage, social, official, or academic, to assist him, after marching to Rome with a force of Black Shirts which a single disciplined regiment backed by a competent government could have routed at any moment. . . . After the war the government of Italy' had been 'so feeble that silly Syndicalists were seizing factories, and fanatical devotees of that curious attempt at a new Catholic church called the Third International were preaching a *coup d'état* and a Crusade in all directions, and imagining that this sort of thing was Socialism and Communism. Mussolini, without any of Napoleon's prestige, has done for Italy what Napoleon did for France, except that for the Duc d'Enghien you must read Matteotti.' When Gaetano Salvemini reminded Shaw that, so far from being 'without a single advantage', Mussolini had had behind him 'the money of the banks, the big industrialists, and the landowners', and that his Black Shirts had been 'equipped with rifles, bombs, machine-guns, and motor-lorries by the military authorities, and assured of impunity by the police and the magistracy, while their adversaries were disarmed and severely punished if they attempted resistance', Shaw's rebuttal was almost unbelievable: Why, he demanded, had

Mussolini been able to command the support of the army officers and capitalists 'instead of Signors Salvemini, Giolitti, Turati, Matteotti, and their friends, in spite of the fact that he was farther to the Left in his political opinions than any of them? The answer, as it seems to me, is that he combined with extreme opinions the knowledge that the first duty of any Government, no matter what its opinions are, is to carry on, and make its citizens carry on, liberty or no liberty, democracy or no democracy, socialism or no socialism, capitalism or no capitalism. Until Salvemini and his friends convince Italy that they understand this necessity as well as Mussolini does they will never shake his hold on the situation. To rail at him as Shelley railed at Castlereagh and Eldon, Marx at Napoleon III and Thiers, Kautsky at Lenin, is to play the amusing but inglorious part of Thersites.' Now a dramatist in his capacity of dramatist may make out a very interesting case for a Castlereagh or a Napoleon III; but why should Shaw in his capacity as a political writer take the part of such politicians against their philosophical opponents? He is himself of the company of Shelley and Marx – the company of the poets and prophets; and railing at the Castlereaghs and Napoleons – of which Shaw himself has done plenty on occasion – is by no means the least valuable of their functions. The analogy between these other cases and Kautsky complaining of Lenin is certainly a silly and dishonest one.

That spring he had finished a long treatise – *The Intelligent Woman's Guide* – in which he had made a more comprehensive effort than he had ever done in his socialist days in the eighties to analyse capitalist society and to argue the case for socialism. Perhaps the book should have been written in the eighties. Ramsay MacDonald and Sidney Webb had come to power with the Labour Government in 1924, and MacDonald had not yet definitely sold out; and the whole story is repeated in general in the familiar Fabian terms – to which Shaw, without Fabian sanction, had added equality of income as a prime item of his socialist programme. Through many pages of swift exposition, perhaps Shaw's most precise and limpid writing, which, together with the magnificent close, give the book an enduring value, he makes his way to conclusions that perplex us in proportion as the reasoning becomes more fine-spun, and that do not seem finally to land us in any very realistic relation to the England of after the war. 'A series of properly prepared nationalizations may not only be understood and voted for by people who would be quite shocked if they were called Socialists, but would fit in perfectly with the habits of the masses who take their bread as it comes and never think about anything of a public nature.' And in the meantime the road to socialism remains for a good part of the way – through 'nationalizations, expropriative taxation, and all the constructive political machinery' – identical with the road to state capitalism. So that Lenin, says Shaw, had been quite in the wrong when he had denounced the methods of the Fabians as state capitalism.

But Lenin had been aware of the psychological pitfalls in the approach of the Fabians towards socialism – pitfalls which no amount of lucid explanation was able to get them over and which Shaw continued to stumble into himself. From the moment that you propose to benefit people from the point of view of imposing upon them what is best for them rather than of showing them the way to what they ought to have and awaiting the moment when they will know that they must have it, what is to prevent your slipping – the post-Lenin period in Russia has proved it as much as the Ramsay MacDonald Labour Government – into imposing upon the people something which will benefit you yourself?

I shall not here pursue the story of the subsequent career of the Fabians, as I want to show further on how it was reflected in Bernard Shaw's later plays. But I will note here that in 1931 he visited Soviet Russia in company with the Tory Lady Astor and with the Liberal Marquess of Lothian, had an audience with Stalin, at which, as he said, they treated Stalin like 'a friendly emperor', and, on his return, began loudly endorsing Russia and especially scolding the United States for not following the Soviet example. Later, in his *Preface on Bosses* in his volume of plays of 1936, he was back praising Mussolini again and even throwing a few kind words to Hitler, whom he described as 'not a stupid German' (did Bernard Shaw prefer a crazy Austrian?) and whose persecution of the Jews he characterized considerately as 'a craze, a complex, a bee in his bonnet, a hole in his armour, a hitch in his statesmanship, one of those lesions which sometimes prove fatal.' Of the systematic persecution by the Nazis of Communists, Socialists, and Pacifists, of everybody – including critics and artists – who belonged to Bernard Shaw's own camp, he had nothing whatever to say save to mention it and minimize it in passing as 'plundering raids and *coups d'état* against inconvenient Liberals or Marxists'. At the time of the Ethiopian War, he came out strongly for Mussolini on the same grounds on which he had formerly defended the behaviour of the British in South Africa, and insisted that the League of Nations, on behalf of which in 1928 he had written a Fabian pamphlet, should never have tried to interfere.

Thus in this period of disastrous dictatorships, when it was very important for a socialist to keep clear in the eyes of the public the difference between the backing and aims of Lenin and the backing and aims of Mussolini, Bernard Shaw has done a good deal to confuse them and, parliamentary socialist though he claims to be, to exalt the ideal of the dictator. When the socialist dictatorship of Lenin gave way to the despotism of Stalin, Shaw did not seem to know the difference, but applauded the suppression of the old Leninists, on the ground that most professional revolutionists ought to be shot the morning after the revolution, and, on the principle that the socially harmful had to be got out of the way, gave his blessing to the Russian concentration camps, with their millions of political prisoners.

All this he has handled, of course, with his marvellous cleverness and style. Analysing everybody perpetually, he is a great master of the smoke-screen against criticism. It is done partly by sheer personal hypnotism and Irish gift of gab. Before you arrive at any book of Bernard Shaw's — from *What I Really Wrote About the War* to his correspondence with Ellen Terry — you have almost invariably been told what to think of it in a preface by which Shaw has protected himself against your possible perception of his weakness. If you submit to his spell, you will allow him to manipulate the lights in such a way that, by the time the curtain goes up, you find Shaw looking noble in the centre of the stage with everything else left in semi-obscurity, and yourself with your discriminatory powers in a temporary state of suspension, under the illusion that you must either accept or reject him. (Of late the exhibitionistic vanity which seemed dashing in his early days when he was assailing the philistines with such spirit has come to be tiresome and even repellent — as, for example, when his comment on the death of one of his distinguished contemporaries takes the form of the irrelevant reflection, 'I'll be dead very soon myself!')

But there has been also an odd kind of trickery involved in the whole of Bernard Shaw's career. It depends on a technique which he has mastered of functioning on three distinct planes and of shifting from one to another. His air of certainty, his moralist's tone, his well-drilled sentences, his regular emphasis, all go to create an impression of straightforwardness. But actually the mind of Shaw is always fluctuating between various emotions which give rise to various points of view.

The mechanics seem to be somewhat as follows: At the bottom of Shaw is a commonsense sphere of practical considerations; above this is a plane of socialism, of the anticipated reorganization of society in the interest of ideal values; and above this, a poet-philosopher's ether from which he commands a longer view of life *sub specie aeternitatis* and where the poet allows himself many doubts which neither the socialist nor the bourgeois citizen can admit. Shaw has never really taken up his residence for any great length of time on any one of these three planes of thinking. The socialist, for example, denounces war; but when England actually goes to war, the respectable householder backs her. The moralist denounces marriage; but the conventional married man always advises young people to get married. The socialist takes sword in hand to battle for a sounder society based on a redistribution of income; and the long-view philosopher-poet comes to sap the socialist's faith with misgivings as to the capacity for intellect and virtue of the material of common humanity as contrasted with philosopher-poets. The poet gets a good way above the earth in the ecstasy of imaginative vision; but the socialist reminds him that it is the duty of art to teach a useful social lesson, and the householder damps the fires of both by admonishing them that the young people in the audience oughtn't to be told anything that will get them into trouble. The result is that reading Shaw is like looking through a pair of field glasses of which the focus is always equally sharp and clear but the range may be changed without warning.

So adroit are Shaw's transitions that we are usually unaware of what has happened; and when we have come to be conscious of them, we wonder how much Shaw is aware. It is curious to go back over his work and see him juggling with his various impersonations: the socialist, the fascist, the saint, the shrewd businessman, the world genius, the human being, the clever journalist who knows how to be politic, the popular speaker who knows how to be tactful. It is quite as if they were the characters in a comedy, each of whom he can pick up where he has dropped him and have him go on with his part.

III

But comedies are best presented in the theatre; and in the theatre Shaw's conflicts of impulse, his intellectual flexibility, and his genius for legerdemain – all the qualities that have had the effect of weakening his work as a publicist – have contributed to his success as an artist.

One of the prime errors of recent radical criticism has been the assumption that great novels and plays must necessarily be written by people who have everything clear in their minds. People who have everything clear in their minds, who are not capable of identifying themselves imaginatively with, who do not actually embody in themselves, contrary emotions and points of view, do not write novels or plays at all – do not, at any rate, write good ones. And – given genius – the more violent the contraries, the greater the works of art.

Let us consider Shaw as an artist.

Bernard Shaw's great role in the theatre has been to exploit the full possibilities of a type of English comedy which had first been given its characteristic form during the seventies of the nineteenth century in the comedies of W. S. Gilbert. The comedy of the Restoration, which had culminated in Congreve, had been the product of an aristocratic society, which depended for its ironic effects on the contrast between artificial social conventions and natural animal instincts, between fine manners and fine intelligence, on the one hand, and the crudest carnal appetites, on the other. The comedy of the nineteenth century – setting aside Oscar Wilde – depended on the contrast between the respectable conventions of a pious middle-class society and the mean practical realities behind them, between the pretension to high moral principles and the cold complacency which underlay it. As with the dramatists of the Restoration, it was always the pursuit of pleasure that emerged from behind the formalities, so, in the comedies of Gilbert which preceded his Savoy operas and of which the most famous and successful was *Engaged* (1877), it is always the greed for money that extrudes from behind the screen of noble words and discreet behaviour. 'Dear papa,' says the Victorian young lady in one of the scenes of *Engaged*, when she has just heard of the failure of a bank in which the fortune of her fiancé was invested, 'I am very sorry to disappoint you, but unless your tom-tit is very much mistaken, the Indestructible was registered under the Joint Stock Companies Act of '62 and in that case the stockholders are jointly and severally liable to the whole extent of their available capital. Poor little Minnie don't pretend to have a business head; but she is not quite such a little donkey as that, dear papa!' The characters of Gilbert's comedies, who talk the language of Victorian fiction, are never for a moment betrayed by emotion into allowing themselves to be diverted from the main chance; and the young men are perfectly ready, not from appetite but from sheer indifference, to make equally passionate professions to any number of young ladies at the same time. It is not far from the Symperson family and Cheviot Hill of *Engaged* to Shaw's *The Philanderer* and *Widowers' Houses*.

But neither Gilbert nor Dickens nor Samuel Butler – those two other great satirists of the money-minded English, to whom, also, Shaw is indebted – could teach him to analyse society in terms of economic motivation or to understand and criticize the profit system. This he learned to do from Karl Marx, whose work during his English residence, the period when *Das Kapital* was written, was itself of course a product of and an ironical protest against English nineteenth-century civilization. Bernard Shaw thus brought something quite new into English imaginative literature. His study of economics had served him, as he said, for his plays as the study of anatomy had served Michelangelo. And with economic insight and training he joined literary qualities of a kind that had never yet appeared in combination with them – qualities, in fact, that, since the century before, had been absent from English literature entirely.

The Irish of Bernard Shaw's period enjoyed, in the field of literature, certain special advantages over the English, due to the fact that, since Irish society was still mainly in the pre-industrial stage, they were closer to eighteenth-century standards. If we compare Shaw, Yeats, and Joyce to, say, Galsworthy, Wells, and Bennett, we are struck at once by the extent to which these latter writers have suffered from their submergence in the commercial world. In their worst phases of sentimentality and philistinism, there is almost nothing to choose between them and the frankly trashy popular novelist; whereas the Irish have preserved for English literature classical qualities of hardness and elegance.

Bernard Shaw has had the further advantage of a musical education. 'Do not suppose for a moment', he writes, 'that I learnt my art from English men of letters. True, they showed me how to handle English words; but if I had known no more than that, my works would never have crossed the Channel. My masters were the masters of a universal language; they were, to go from summit to summit, Bach, Handel, Haydn, Mozart, Beethoven, and Wagner. . . . For their sakes, Germany stands consecrated as the Holy Land of the capitalistic age.' Einstein has said that Shaw's plays remind him of Mozart's music: every word has its place in the development. And if we allow for some nineteenth-century prolixity, we can see in Shaw's dramatic work a logic and grace, a formal precision, like that of the eighteenth-century composers.

Take *The Apple Cart*, for example. The fact that Shaw is here working exclusively with economic and political materials has caused its art to be insufficiently appreciated. If it had been a sentimental comedy by Molnar, the critics would have applauded its deftness; yet Shaw is a finer artist than any of the Molnars or Schnitzlers. The first act of *The Apple Cart* is an exercise in the scoring for small orchestra at which Shaw is particularly skilful. After what he has himself called the overture before the curtain of the conversation between the two secretaries, in which the music of King Magnus is foreshadowed, the urbane and intelligent King and the 'bull-roarer Boanerges' play a duet against one another. Then the King plays a single instrument against the whole nine of the cabinet. The themes emerge: the King's disinterestedness and the labour government's sordid self-interest. The development is lively: the music is tossed from one instrument to another, with, to use the old cliché, a combination of inevitableness and surprise. Finally, the King's theme gets a full and splendid statement in the long speech in which he declares his principles: 'I stand for the great abstractions: for conscience and virtue; for the eternal against the expedient; for the evolutionary appetite against the day's gluttony,' etc. This silver voice of the King lifts the movement to a poignant climax; and now a dramatic reversal carries the climax further and rounds out and balances the harmony. Unexpectedly, one of the brasses of the ministry takes up the theme of the King and repeats it more passionately and loudly: 'Just so! . . . Listen to me, sir,' bursts out the Powermistress, 'and judge whether I have not reason to feel everything you have just said to the very marrow of my bones. Here am I, the Powermistress Royal. I have to organize and administer all the motor power in the country for the good of the country. I have to harness the winds and the tides, the oils and the coal seams.' And she launches into an extraordinary tirade in which the idea of political disinterestedness is taken out of the realm of elegant abstraction in which it has hitherto remained with the King and reiterated in terms of engineering: 'every little sewing machine in the Hebrides, every dentist's drill in Shetland, every carpet sweeper in Margate', etc. This ends on crashing chords, but immediately the music of the cabinet snarlingly reasserts itself. The act ends on the light note of the secretaries.

This music is a music of ideas – or rather, perhaps, it is a music of moralities. Bernard Shaw is a writer of the same kind as Plato. There are not many such writers in literature – the *Drames philosophiques* of Renan would supply another example – and they are likely to puzzle the critics. Shaw, like Plato, repudiates as a dangerous form of drunkenness the indulgence in literature for its own sake; but, like Plato, he then proceeds, not simply to expound a useful morality, but himself to indulge in an art in which moralities are used as the motifs. It is partly on this account, certainly, that Bernard Shaw has been underrated as an artist. Whether people admire or dislike him, whether they find his plays didactically boring or morally stimulating, they fail to take account of the fact that it is the enchantment of a highly accomplished art which has brought them to and kept them in the playhouse. It is an art that has even had the power to preserve such pieces as *Getting Married*, of which the 1908 heresies already seemed out of date twenty or thirty years later but of which the symphonic development still remains brilliant and fresh. So far from being relentlessly didactic, Shaw's mind has reflected in all its complexity the intellectual life of his time; and his great achievement is to have reflected it with remarkable fidelity. He has *not* imposed a cogent system, but he has worked out a vivid picture. It is, to be sure, not a passive picture, like that of Santayana or Proust: it is a picture in which action plays a prominent part. But it does not play a consistent part: the dynamic principle in Shaw is made to animate a variety of forces.

Let us see what these forces are and to what purpose they interact.

IV

What are the real themes of Bernard Shaw's plays?

He has not been a socialist dramatist in the sense that, say, Upton Sinclair has been a socialist novelist. His economics have served him, it is true, as anatomy served Michelangelo; but to say that is to give as little idea of what kind of characters he creates and what his plays are about as it would of the figures of the sculptor to say that they were produced by an artist who understood the skeleton and the muscles. It is quite wrong to assume, as has sometimes been done, that the possession of the social-economic intelligence must imply that the writer who has it writes tracts for social reform.

Shaw is himself partly responsible for this assumption. In his early days, when he *was* a social reformer, he wrote books about Wagner and Ibsen which introduced them to the English-speaking public as primarily social reformers, too. There is of course a social revolutionist, a man of 1848, in

Wagner, and a critic of bourgeois institutions in Ibsen. But Bernard Shaw, in his brilliant little books, by emphasizing these aspects of their work at the expense of everything else, seriously misrepresents them. He appreciates Siegfried and Brunhilde in their heroic and rebellious phases; but Wagner's tragedies of love he pooh-poohs; and it is sometimes just when Ibsen is at his strongest – as in *Brand* or *Rosmersholm* – that Bernard Shaw is least satisfactory on him, because the tragic spirit of Ibsen does not fit into Shaw's preconception. In Ibsen's case, Shaw is particularly misleading, because Ibsen disclaimed again and again any social-reforming intentions. His great theme, characteristic though it is of nineteenth-century society, is not a doctrine of social salvation: it is the conflict between one's duty to society as a unit in the social organism and the individual's duty to himself. Ibsen treats his theme over and over but in a number of different ways, sometimes emphasizing the validity of social claims as opposed to the will of the individual (*Little Eyolf*), sometimes showing them as unjustified and oppressive (*Ghosts*); sometimes showing the individual undone by self-indulgence or perverse self-assertion (*Peer Gynt* and *Brand*), sometimes showing him as noble and sympathetic (the hero and heroine of *Rosmersholm*); sometimes dramatizing the two poles of conduct in the career of a single individual, like Dr Stockman in *An Enemy of the People*, who begins by trying to save society but who later, when society turns against him, is driven back into an individualistic vindication of the social conscience itself with the realization that 'the strongest man is he who stands most alone'. But the conflict is always serious; and it usually ends in disaster. Rarely – *A Doll's House* is the principal example – does it result in a liberation. Ibsen is hardly ever a social philosopher: he goes no further than the conflict itself.

Now is there any such basic theme in Bernard Shaw? Has he been creating a false impression not only about Ibsen but also about himself? Certainly the prefaces he prefixes to his plays do not really explain them any more than *The Quintessence of Ibsenism* really explains Ibsen.

The principal pattern which recurs in Bernard Shaw – aside from the duel between male and female, which seems to me of much less importance – is the polar opposition between the type of the saint and the type of the successful practical man. This conflict, when it is present in his other writing, has a blurring, a demoralizing effect, as in the passage on Saint Francis *et al.* which I quoted at the beginning of this essay; but it is the principle of life of his plays. We find it in its clearest presentation in the opposition between Father Keegan and Tom Broadbent in *John Bull's Other Island* and between Major Barbara and Undershaft – where the moral scales are pretty evenly weighted and where the actual predominance of the practical man, far from carrying ominous implications, produces a certain effect of reassurance: this was apparently the period – when Bernard Shaw had outgrown his early battles and struggles and before the war had come to disturb him – of his most comfortable and self-confident exercise of powers which had fully matured. But these opposites have also a tendency to dissociate themselves from one another and to feature themselves sometimes, not correlatively, but alternatively in successive plays. In *The Devil's Disciple* and *The Shewing-up of Blanco Posnet*, the heroes are dashing fellows who have melodramatic flashes of saintliness; their opponents are made comic or base. *Caesar and Cleopatra* is a play that glorifies the practical man; *Androcles and the Lion* is a play that glorifies the saint. So is *Saint Joan*, with the difference that here the worldly antagonists of the saint are presented as intelligent and effective.

Certainly it is this theme of the saint and the world which has inspired those scenes of Shaw's plays which are most moving and most real on the stage – which are able to shock us for the moment, as even the 'Life Force' passages hardly do, out of the amiable and objective attention which has been induced by the bright play of the intelligence. It is the moment when Major Barbara, brought at last to the realization of the power of the capitalist's money and of her own weakness when she hasn't it to back her, is left alone on the stage with the unregenerate bums whose souls she has been trying to save; the moment when Androcles is sent into the arena with the lion; the moment in the emptied courtroom when Joan has been taken out to be burned and the Bishop and the Earl of Warwick are trying each to pin the responsibility on the other. It is the scene in *Heartbreak House* between Captain Shotover and Hector, when they give voice to their common antagonism towards the forces that seem to have them at their mercy: 'We must win powers of life and death over them. . . . There is enmity between our seed and their seed. They know it and act on it, strangling our souls. They believe in themselves. When we believe in ourselves, we shall kill them. . . . We kill the better half of ourselves every day to propitiate them.' It is the scene in *Back to Methuselah* when the Elderly Gentleman declares to the Oracle: 'They have gone back to lie about your answer [the political delegation with whom he has come]. I cannot go with them. I cannot live among people to whom nothing is real!' – and when she shows him her face and strikes him dead.

But now let us note – for the light they throw on Bernard Shaw in his various phases – the upshots of these several situations. In *Major Barbara*, the Christian saint, the man of learning, and the industrial superman form an alliance from which much is to be hoped. In *Androcles and the Lion*, written in 1913, in Shaw's amusing but least earnest middle period, just before the war, Androcles and the lion form an alliance, too, of which something is also to be hoped, but go out arm in arm after a harlequinade on the level of a Christmas pantomime. In *Heartbreak House*, which was begun in 1913 and not finished till 1916, the declaration of war by the unworldlings takes place in the midst of confusion and does not lead to any action on their part.

In *Back to Methuselah*, of the post-war period, the Elderly

Gentleman is blasted by the Oracle in a strange scene the implications of which we must stop to examine a moment. The fate of the Elderly Gentleman is evidently intended by Shaw to have some sort of application to himself: though a member of a backward community in which people have not yet achieved the Methuselah-span of life, he differs from his fellows at least in this: that he finds he cannot bear any longer to live among people to whom nothing is real. So the Oracle shrivels him up with her glance.

But what is this supposed to mean? What *is* this higher wisdom which the Elderly Gentleman cannot contemplate and live? So far as the reader is concerned, the revelation of the Oracle is a blank. The old system of Bernard Shaw, which was plausible enough to pass before the war, has just taken a terrible blow, and its grotesque and gruesome efforts to pull itself together and function give the effect of an umbrella, wrecked in a storm, which, when the owner tries to open it up, shows several long ribs of steel sticking out. The Life Force of the man and woman in *Man and Superman* no longer leads either to human procreation or to social-revolutionary activity. The Life Force has been finally detached from socialism altogether. In the *Intelligent Woman's Guide*, Shaw will reject the Marxist dialectic as a false religion of social salvation; but the Life Force is also a religious idea, which we have always supposed in the past to be directed towards social betterment, and now, in *Back to Methuselah*, we find that it has misfired with socialism. Socialism has come and gone; the planet has been laid waste by wars; the ordinary people have all perished, and there is nobody left on earth but a race of selected supermen. And now the race of superior human beings, which was invoked in *Man and Superman* as the prime indispensable condition for any kind of progress whatever but which was regarded by Shaw at that time as producible through eugenic breeding, has taken here a most unearthly turn. It has always been through the superman idea that Shaw has found it possible to escape from the implications of his socialism; and he now no longer even imagines that the superior being can be created by human idealism through human science. The superior beings of *Back to Methuselah* are people who live for ever; but they have achieved this superiority through an unconscious act of the will. When they have achieved it, what the Life Force turns out to have had in store for them is the mastery of abstruse branches of knowledge and the extra-uterine development of embryos. Beyond this, there is still to be attained the liberation of the spirit from the flesh, existence as a 'whirl-pool in pure force'. 'And for what may be beyond, the eye-sight of Lilith is too short. It is enough that there is a beyond.'

Humanity, in *Back to Methuselah*, has dropped out for the moment altogether. The long-livers of the period of progress contemporary with the Elderly Gentleman are not the more 'complete' human beings, with lives richer and better rounded, which Marx and Engels and Lenin imagined for the 'classless society': they are Shavian super-prigs who say the cutting and dampening things which the people have always said in Shaw's plays but who have been abstracted here from the well-observed social setting in which Shaw has always hitherto presented them. And the beings of the later epoch are young people playing in an Arcadia and ancients immersed in cogitations, alike – both cogitations and Arcadia – of the bleakest and most desolating descrip-tion. There is in *Back to Methuselah* nothing burning or touching, and there is nothing genuinely thrilling except the cry of the Elderly Gentleman; and that, for all the pretence of revelation, is answered by a simple extinction.

In the *Tragedy of an Elderly Gentleman*, the Elderly Gentle-man is frightened, but his tragedy is not a real tragedy. *Saint Joan* (1924) is an even more frightened play, and, soft-ened though it is by the historical perspective into which Shaw manages to throw it through his epilogue, it was the first genuine tragedy that Shaw had written. The horror of *Back to Methuselah* is a lunar horror; the horror of *Saint Joan* is human. The saint is suppressed by the practical man; and even when she comes back to earth, though all those

who exploited or destroyed her are now obliged to acknowledge her holiness, none wants her to remain among them:
each would do the same thing again. Only the soldier who
had handed her the cross at the stake is willing to accept her
now, but he is only a poor helpless clown condemned to the
dungeon of the flesh.

v

Back to Methuselah is a flight into the future; *Saint Joan* is a
flight into the past. But with *Heartbreak House* Bernard Shaw
had already begun a series of plays in which he was to deal
with the post-war world and his own relation to it in terms
of contemporary England – a section of his work which, it
seems to me, has had too little appreciation or comprehension.

Heartbreak House has the same sort of setting and more or
less the same form as such Shavian conversations as *Getting
Married* and *Misalliance*; but it is really something new for
Shaw. There is no diagram of social relations, no tying-up
of threads at the end. *Heartbreak House*, Shaw says in his
preface, is 'cultured leisured Europe before the War'; but
the play, he told Archibald Henderson, 'began with an
atmosphere and does not contain a word that was foreseen
before it was written', and it is the only one of his plays
which he has persistently refused to explain. 'How should
I know?' he replied, when he was asked by his actors what
it meant. 'I am only the author.' Heartbreak House, built
like a ship, with its old drunken and half-crazy master, the
retired adventurer Captain Shotover, is cultured and
leisured England; but the characters are no longer pinned
down and examined as social specimens: in an atmosphere
heavily charged, through a progression of contacts and
collisions, they give out thunder and lightning like storm-
clouds. Brooding frustrations and disillusions, childlike
hurts and furious resentments, which have dropped the old
Shavian masks, rush suddenly into an utterance which for
the moment has burst out of the old rationalistic wit. For

once, where Bernard Shaw has so often reduced historical myths to the sharp focus of contemporary satire, he now raises contemporary figures to the heroic proportions of myth. – An air-raid brings down the final curtain: Heartbreak House has at last been split wide. The capitalist Mangan gets killed, and there is a suggestion that they may all be the better for it.

But in 1924 the Labour Party came to power, with Ramsay MacDonald as Prime Minister. MacDonald had been a member of the Executive Committee of the Fabian Society, and he brought with him two other Fabians, Sidney Webb and Sydney Oliver, who took the portfolios of Minister of Labour and Secretary of State for India. When MacDonald was re-elected in 1929, he was accompanied by no less than twenty Fabians, of whom eight were cabinet members. The Fabians had now achieved the aim which was to have been the condition for the success of their ideas: they had 'interpenetrated' the government. But in the meantime the competition of the British Empire with the German had culminated in a four years' war; and in England of after the war, with the top manhood of her society slaughtered and the lower classes laid off from their wartime jobs, and with English commercial domination further damaged by the United States, the influence of the Fabians could do little to bridge over the abyss which had been blasted between the extremes of the British class society. The best measures of the Labour Government were able to accomplish no more than just to keep the unemployed alive; and when the capitalists began to feel the pinch, they openly took over control. Ramsay MacDonald, in 1931, became Prime Minister in a Nationalist government and cleared his socialists out of office.

At the moment of the second accession of the Labour Party to power, Shaw had written *The Apple Cart*, in which MacDonald is caricatured as Proteus, the Prime Minister of a labour government. This government is represented as really controlled by Breakages, Limited, a great monopoly which opposes industrial progress for the reason that it has an interest in perpetuating the inferior and less durable machinery that requires more frequent repairs. But one finds in *The Apple Cart* no comment on the Fabianism, which, after all, has been partly responsible for Proteus: the blame is laid at the door, not of that socialism by interpenetration which has ended by itself being interpenetrated, but of something which Shaw calls 'democracy'; and what is opposed to the corrupt socialism of Proteus is not socialism of a more thoroughgoing kind, but the super-constitutional-monarch, King Magnus. Again, Shaw has given the slip to his problems through recourse to the cult of the superior person.

Yet in 1931, after the final collapse of the Labour Government, Bernard Shaw visited Russia and, by applauding the Soviet system, incurred unpopularity in England for the first time since the war. In the same year, he wrote *Too True to Be Good*, a curious 'political extravaganza', in which he turns back upon and criticizes his own career. Here the theme of the bourgeois radical of the eighties, disillusioned with himself under stress of the disasters of the twentieth century, is treated in the same vein, with the same kind of idealist poetry, now grown frankly elegiac and despairing, which Shaw had opened in *Heartbreak House* and which had made the real beauty of *The Apple Cart*.

A rich young English girl of the upper middle class is languishing with an imaginary illness in a gloomy Victorian chamber, fussed over by a Victorian mother. Into this sickroom erupt two rebels: a young preacher and a former chambermaid, who is an illegitimate child of the aristocracy. The chambermaid has been masquerading as the heiress's trained nurse, and she and the preacher have a plot to steal the heiress's pearl necklace. The girl comes to from her megrims and puts up an unexpected struggle. The preacher becomes interested in his victim and says that he has always wondered why she does not steal the necklace herself. Why doesn't she take it and go and do what she pleases, instead of staying home with her mother, moping and fancying herself sick? Why doesn't she let him and his accomplice sell the necklace for her, taking 25 per cent of the price apiece and giving her the other 50? The girl enthusiastically agrees, and while she is getting dressed to go with them, the preacher jumps up on the bed and delivers one of those live-your-own-life sermons with which Shaw, in the nineties, made his first success. Then he is off – in the excitement of his rhetoric, at first forgetting the necklace, which the heiress has to remind him they need.

All three sail away together to an imaginary Balkan country reminiscent of *Arms and the Man*, where they are able to do whatever they like but where their revolt turns out to lead to nothing and eventually to bore them to death. Shaw has evidently put into *Too True to be Good* a sort of recapitulation of his earlier themes, the shams of bourgeois society: the capitalistic doctor of *The Doctor's Dilemma* is as much a fraud as ever; the pompous British military officer, though retaining an air of authority, has practically ceased even to pretend to be anything other than a fraud and is quite willing to leave the command to a private (drawn from Lawrence of Arabia), if he can only be left in peace with his water-colours; the old-fashioned materialist-atheist who is also the most rigorous of moralists, of the type of Roebuck Ramsden in *Man and Superman*, has lived through into a world where his morality has no power to prevent his son's turning thief, etc. Finally everyone except the preacher sets out for the 'Union of Sensible Republics'.

The preacher is left alone on the shore, abandoned between two worlds. He had come too late for the old and too early for the new. He had had the courage once to steal a necklace but he hadn't carried through his idea. He had given it back to the owner and they had made common cause together: the liberated bourgeois girl had gotten 50 per cent of the price, the radicals only 25 apiece. In this last scene, the darkness comes, the clouds gather; the morale of the preacher breaks down. He can only go on explaining and exhorting, whether or not he has anything to say. A keen wind is blowing in, and it may be the breath of life, but it is too fierce for him to bear.

This, Shaw tells us, is a political fable; and now he is to return to politics proper. In *On the Rocks* (1933), he appears to drive himself into a corner as he has never before done and then comes out with a political position which still manages to be somewhat equivocal.

The first act shows a liberal Prime Minister, hard beset during a period of depression. Pall Mall and Trafalgar Square are full of excited crowds. The Prime Minister, on the verge of a breakdown, can think of nothing to do except to call out the police against them, but he is dissuaded by the Police Commissioner himself and finally induced to go away for a rest. He has just been visited by a labour delegation who have impressed him with the importance of Marxism, and he takes volumes of Marx and Lenin away with him.

When the curtain goes up on the second act, the Prime Minister has read Marx and Lenin; but the effect upon him is unexpected. He has gained an insight into economic motivation, an understanding of the technique of making use of it; but he has not been converted to socialism: he has worked out, on the contrary, an exceedingly clever scheme for preserving the capitalist state through a programme, essentially fascist, of partial nationalization and taxation of unearned incomes. He will conciliate the various social groups which would normally be antagonistic by promising a concession to each. The plan seems bidding fair to succeed when it runs aground on Sir Dexter Rightside, the Liberal Prime Minister's Tory colleague in a coalition National Government. Sir Dexter represents the blind conservatism which sticks to the *status quo* through sheer obstinacy and inability to imagine anything else: he threatens to put coloured shirts on 'fifty thousand patriotic young Londoners' and to call them into the streets against the proposed programme of the government. The Prime Minister has to give up his attempt, but he is now forced to face his situation: 'Do you think I didn't know', he confesses to his wife, 'in the days of my great speeches and my roaring popularity, that I was only whitewashing the slums? I couldn't help knowing as well as any of those damned Socialists that though the West End of London was chockful of money and nice people all calling one another by their Christian names, the lives of millions of people whose labour was keeping the whole show going were not worth living; but I was able to put it out of my mind because I thought it couldn't be helped and I was doing the best that could be done. I know better now! I know that it can be helped, and how it can be helped. And rather than go back to the old whitewashing job, I'd seize you tight around the waist and make a hole in the river with you.... Why don't I lead the revolt against it all? Because I'm not the man for the job, darling.... And I shall hate the man who will carry it through for his cruelty and the desolation he will bring on us and our like.'

The shouting of the crowd and the crash of glass is suddenly heard outside. The people have broken into Downing Street. The police begin to club them and ride them down. The people sing, 'England, arise!'

Sir Arthur Chavender's more or less liberal fascism has been defeated by the reactionary fascism of his Tory colleague in the National Government, with whom he is indissolubly united. (There is no question any longer of the superior man: King Magnus has disappeared from the scene.) There is a third point of view, opposed to both, but this, also, sounds rather fascist. Old Hipney, the disillusioned labour veteran, who speaks for the dissatisfied classes, seems to be looking for a Man on Horseback, too: 'Adult suffrage: that was what was to save us all. My God! It delivered us into the hands of our spoilers and oppressors, bound hand and foot by our own folly and ignorance. It took the heart out of old Hipney; and now I'm for any Napoleon or Mussolini or Lenin or Chavender that has the stuff in him to take both the people and the spoilers and oppressors by the scruffs of their silly necks and just sling them into the way they should go with as many kicks as may be needful to make a thorough job of it.' But Chavender declines the job and the people begin throwing bricks.

The conclusion we are apparently to draw is that parliamentary fascism must fail; and that we may then get either a Lenin or a Mussolini. Is this also a final confession of the failure of Fabianism, which depended on parliament, too?

In any case, at the end of this play, we have come in a sense to the end of Shaw. With the eruption of the uprising, we should be plunged into a situation which could no longer be appropriately handled by the characteristic methods of his comedy. He is still splendid when he is showing the bewilderment of the liberal governing-class prime minister: it is surprising how he is still able to summon his old flickering and piercing wit, his old skill at juggling points of view, to illuminate a new social situation – how quick and skilful he is at describing a new social type: the communist viscount, with his brutal language, which shocks his proletarian allies. But with the shouts and the broken glass, we are made to take account of the fact that Shaw's comedy, for all its greater freedom in dealing with social conditions, is almost as much dependent on a cultivated and stable society as the comedy of Molière, who had his place in the royal dining-room and depended on Louis's favour for the permission to produce his plays. Shaw, as much as Molière, must speak the same language as his audience; he must observe the same conventions of manners. And further than *On the Rocks* – in depicting the realities of the present – we feel that he cannot go.

Then we realize that, after a detour of the better part of half a century, of almost the whole of his artistic career, Shaw has only returned to that Bloody Sunday of 1887 when the Socialists had headed a demonstration and been driven away by the police; and we remember, apropos of Molière, that the most celebrated of British dramatists for a long time found it impossible to get a theatre in London for *On the Rocks*.

Shaw's most recent pieces are weaker. *The Simpleton of the Unexpected Isles* (1934) is the only play of the author's which has ever struck me as silly. In it, the Day of Judgement comes to the British Empire, and the privilege of surviving on earth is made to depend upon social utility. But, by setting up a purely theocratic tribunal, Shaw deprives this scene of social point: the principle of selection is so general that it might be applied by the fascists as readily as by the socialists, at the same time that the policy of wholesale extinction seems inspired by an admiration for the repressive tactics of both. The play ends with a salute to the unknown future, which, like the vision of infinity of *Back to Methuselah*, seems perfectly directionless. *The Millionairess* (1936) makes a farce out of the notion that a natural boss, deprived of adventitious authority, will inevitably gravitate again to a position where he can bully and control people, and sounds as if it had been suggested by the later phases of Stalin.

Here it cannot be denied that Bernard Shaw begins to show signs of old age. As the pace of his mind slackens and the texture of his work grows looser, the contradictory impulses and principles which have hitherto provided him with drama begin to show gaping rifts. In his *Preface on Bosses* to *The Millionairess*, he talks about 'beginning a Reformation well to the left of Russia', but composes the panegyric on Mussolini, with the respectful compliments to Hitler, to which I have already referred.

Yet the openings – the prologue to *The Simpleton*, with its skit on the decay of the British Empire and the knockabout domestic agonies of the first act or two of *The Millionairess* – still explode their comic situations with something of the old energy and wit; and the one-acter, *The Six of Calais*, though it does not crackle quite with the old spark, is not so very far inferior to such an earlier trifle as *How He Lied to Her Husband*. It is interesting to note – what bears out the idea that Shaw is at his best as an artist – that the last thing he is to lose, apparently, is his gift for pure comic invention, which has survived, not much dimmed, though we may tire of it, since the days of *You Never Can Tell*.

And he has also maintained his integrity as a reporter of the processes at work in his time – in regard to which his point of view has never been doctrinaire but always based on observation and feeling. He has not acted a straight role as a socialist; a lot of his writing on public affairs has been nonsense. But his plays down to the very end have been a truthful and continually developing chronicle of a soul in relation to society. Professionally as well as physically – he has just turned eighty-one as I write – he is outliving all the rest of his generation.

Nor can it be said that the confusions of his politics have invalidated his social criticism. Of his educative and stimulative influence it is not necessary today to speak. The very methods we use to check him have partly been learned in his school.

Marxism and Literature

LET us begin with Marx and Engels. What was the role assigned to literature and art in the system of Dialectical Materialism? This role was much less cut-and-dried than is nowadays often supposed. Marx and Engels conceived the forms of human society in any given country and epoch as growing out of the methods of production which prevailed at that place and time; and out of the relations involved in the social forms arose a 'superstructure' of higher activities such as politics, law, religion, philosophy, literature, and art. These activities were not, as is sometimes assumed, wholly explicable in terms of economics. They showed the mould, in ways direct or indirect, of the social configuration below them, but each was working to get away from its roots in the social classes and to constitute a professional group, with its own discipline and its own standards of value, which cut across class lines. These departments 'all react upon one another and upon the economic base. It is not the case that the economic situation is the sole active cause and everything else only a passive effect. But there is a reciprocal interaction within a fundamental economic necessity, which in the last instance always asserts itself' (Engels to Hans Starkenburg, 25 January 1894). So that the art of a great artistic period may reach a point of vitality and vision where it can influence the life of the period down to its very economic foundations. Simply, it must cease to flourish with the social system which made it possible by providing the artist with training and leisure, even though the artist himself may have been working for the destruction of that system.

Marx and Engels, unlike some of their followers, never attempted to furnish social-economic formulas by which the validity of works of art might be tested. They had grown up in the sunset of Goethe before the great age of German literature was over, and they had both set out in their youth to be poets; they responded to imaginative work, first of all, on its artistic merits. They could ridicule a trashy writer like Eugène Sue for what they regarded as his *petit bourgeois* remedies for the miseries of contemporary society (*The Holy Family*); they could become bitter about Ferdinand Freiligrath, who had deserted the Communist League and turned nationalist in 1870 (Marx to Engels, 22 August 1870). And Marx could even make similar jibes at Heine when he thought that the latter had stooped to truckling to the authorities or when he read the expressions of piety in his will (Marx to Engels, 21 December 1866 and 8 May 1856). But Marx's daughter tells us that her father loved Heine 'as much as his work and was very indulgent of his political shortcomings. He used to say that the poets were originals, who must be allowed to go their own way, and that one shouldn't apply to them the same standards as to ordinary people.' It was not characteristic of Marx and Engels to judge literature – that is, literature of power and distinction – in terms of its purely political tendencies. In fact, Engels always warned the socialist novelists against the dangers of *Tendenz-Literatur* (Engels to Minna Kautsky, 26 November 1885; and to Margaret Harkness, April 1888). In writing to Minna Kautsky about one of her novels, he tells her that the personalities of her hero and heroine had been dissolved in the principles they represent. 'You evidently', he says, 'felt the need of publicly taking sides in this book, of proclaiming your opinions to the world. . . . But I believe that the tendency should arise from the situation and the action themselves without being explicitly formulated, and that the poet is not under the obligation to furnish the reader with a ready-made historical solution for the future of the conflict which he describes.' When Ferdinand Lassalle sent Marx and Engels his poetic tragedy, *Franz von Sickingen*, and invited them to criticize it, Marx replied that, 'setting aside any purely critical attitude towards the work', it had on a first reading affected him powerfully – characteristically adding that upon persons of a more emotional nature it would doubtless produce an even stronger effect; and Engels wrote that he had read it twice and had been moved by it so profoundly that he had been obliged to lay it aside in order to arrive at any critical perspective. It was only after pulling themselves together and making some purely literary observations that they were able to proceed to discuss, from their special historical point of view, the period with which the drama dealt and to show how Lassalle's own political position had led him to mistake the role of his hero. Aeschylus Marx loved for his grandeur and for the defiance of Zeus by Prometheus; Goethe they both immensely admired: Engels wrote of him as a 'colossal' and 'universal' genius whose career had been marred by an admixture in his character of the philistine and the courtier (*German Socialism in Verse and Prose*); Shakespeare Marx knew by heart and was extremely fond of quoting, but never – despite the long, learned, and ridiculous essays which have appeared in the Soviet magazine, *International Literature* – attempted to draw from his plays any general social moral. So far, indeed, was Marx from having worked out a systematic explanation of the relation of the art to social arrangements that he could assert, apropos of Greek art, in his *Introduction to the Critique of Political Economy*, that 'certain periods of highest development of art stand in no direct connexion with the general development of society nor with the material basis and the skeleton structure of its organization'.

With Marx and Engels there is not yet any tendency to specialize art as a 'weapon'. They were both too much under the influence of the ideal of the many-sided man of the Renaissance, of the 'complete' man, who, like Leonardo, had been painter, mathematician, and engineer, or, like Machiavelli, poet, historian, and strategist, before the division of labour had had the effect of splitting up human nature and limiting everyone to some single function (Engels' preface to his *Dialectic and Nature*). But with Lenin we come to a Marxist who is specialized himself as an organizer and fighter. Like most Russians, Lenin was sensitive to music; but Gorky tells us that on one occasion, after listening to Beethoven's Appassionata Sonata and exclaiming that he 'would like to listen to it every day: it is marvellous superhuman music – I always think with pride ... what marvellous things human beings can do', he screwed up his eyes and smiled sadly and added: 'But I can't listen to music too often. It affects your nerves, makes you want to say stupid, nice things, and stroke the heads of people who could create such beauty while living in this vile hell. And now you mustn't stroke anyone's head – you might get your hand bitten off.' Yet he was fond of fiction, poetry, and the theatre, and by no means doctrinaire in his tastes. Krupskaya tells how, on a visit to a Youth Commune, he asked the young people, ' "What do you read? Do you read Pushkin?" "Oh, no!" someone blurted out. "He was a bourgeois. Mayakovsky for us." Ilyitch smiled. "I think Pushkin is better." ' Gorky says that one day he found Lenin with *War and Peace* lying on the table: ' "Yes, Tolstoy. I wanted to read over the scene of the hunt, then remembered that I had to write a comrade. Absolutely no time for reading." ... Smiling and screwing up his eyes, he stretched himself deliciously in his armchair and, lowering his voice, added quickly, "What a colossus, eh? What a marvellously developed brain! Here's an artist for you, sir. And do you know something still more amazing? You couldn't find a genuine *muzhik* in literature till this count came upon the scene." ' In his very acute essays on Tolstoy, he deals with him much as Engels deals with Goethe – with tremendous admiration for Tolstoy's genius, but with an analysis of his non-resistance and mysticism in terms not, it is interesting to note, of the psychology of the landed nobility, but of the patriarchal peasantry with whom Tolstoy had identified himself. And Lenin's attitude toward Gorky was much like that of Marx towards Heine. He suggests in one of his letters that Gorky would be helpful as a journalist on the side of the

Bolsheviks, but adds that he mustn't be bothered if he is busy writing a book.

Trotsky is a literary man as Lenin never was, and he published in 1924 a most remarkable little study called *Literature and Revolution*. In this book he tried to illuminate the problems which were arising for Russian writers with the new society of the Revolution. And he was obliged to come to grips with a question with which Marx and Engels had not been much concerned – the question of what Mr James T. Farrell in his book, *A Note on Literary Criticism*, one of the few sensible recent writings on this subject, calls 'the carry-over value' of literature. Marx had assumed the value of Shakespeare and the Greeks and more or less left it at that. But what, the writers in Russia were now asking, was to be the value of the literature and art of the ages of barbarism and oppression in the dawn of socialist freedom? What in particular was to be the status of the culture of that bourgeois society from which socialism had just emerged and of which it still bore the unforgotten scars? Would there be a new proletarian literature, with new language, new style, new form, to give expression to the emotions and ideas of the new proletarian dictatorship? There had been in Russia a group called the Proletcult, which aimed at monopolizing the control of Soviet literature; but Lenin had discouraged and opposed it, insisting that proletarian culture was not something which could be produced synthetically and by official dictation of policy, but only by natural evolution as a 'development of those reserves of knowledge which society worked for under the oppression of capitalism, of the landlords, of the officials'. Now, in *Literature and Revolution*, Trotsky asserted that 'such terms as "proletarian literature" and "proletarian culture" are dangerous, because they erroneously compress the culture of the future into the narrow limits of the present day.' In a position to observe from his Marxist point of view the effects on a national literature of the dispossession of a dominant class, he was able to see the unexpected ways in which the presentments of life of the novelists, the feelings and images of the poets, the standards themselves of the critics, were turning out to be determined by their attitudes towards the social-economic crises. But he did not believe in a proletarian culture which would displace the bourgeois one. The bourgeois literature of the French Revolution had ripened under the old regime; but the illiterate proletariat and peasantry of Russia had had no chance to produce a culture, nor would there be time for them to do so in the future, because the proletarian dictatorship was not to last: it was to be only a transition phase and to lead the way to 'a culture which is above classes and which will be the first truly human culture'. In the meantime, the new socialist literature would grow directly out of that which had already been produced during the domination of the bourgeoisie. Communism, Trotsky said, had as yet no artistic culture; it had only a political culture.

All this seems to us reasonable enough. But, reasonable and cultured as Trotsky is, ready as he is to admit that 'one cannot always go by the principles of Marxism in deciding whether to accept or reject a work of art', that such a work 'should be judged in the first place by its own law – that is, by the law of art', there is none the less in the whole situation something which is alien to us. We are not accustomed, in our quarter of the world, either to having the government attempt to control literature and art or to having literary and artistic movements try to identify themselves with the government. Yet Russia, since the Revolution, has had a whole series of cultural groups which have attempted to dominate literature either with or without the authority of the government; and Trotsky himself, in his official position, even in combating these tendencies, cannot avoid passing censure and pinning ribbons. Sympathizers with the Soviet regime used to assume that this state of affairs was inseparable from the realization of socialism: that its evils would be easily outgrown and that in any case it was a great thing to have the government take so lively an interest in culture. I believe that this view was mistaken. Under the Tsar, imaginative literature in Russia played a role which was probably different from any role it had ever played in the life of any other nation. Political and social criticism, pursued and driven underground by the censorship, was forced to incorporate itself in the dramatic imagery of fiction. This was certainly one of the principal reasons for the greatness during the nineteenth century of the Russian theatre and novel, for the mastery by the Russian writers – from Pushkin's time to Tolstoy's – of the art of implication. In the fifties and sixties, the stories of Turgenev, which seem mild enough to us today, were capable of exciting the most passionate controversies – and even, in the case of *A Sportsman's Sketches*, causing the dismissal of the censor who had passed it – because each was regarded as a political message. Ever since the Revolution, literature and politics in Russia have remained inextricable. But after the Revolution the intelligentsia themselves were in power; and it became plain that in the altered situation the identification of literature with politics was liable to terrible abuses. Lenin and Trotsky, Lunacharsky and Gorky, worked sincerely to keep literature free; but they had at the same time, from the years of the Tsardom, a keen sense of the possibility of art as an instrument of propaganda. Lenin took a special interest in the moving pictures from the propaganda point of view; and the first Soviet films, by Eisenstein and Pudovkin, were masterpieces of implication, as the old novels and plays had been. But Lenin died; Trotsky was exiled; Lunacharsky died. The administration of Stalin, unliterary and uncultivated himself, slipped into depending more and more on literature as a means of manipulating a people of whom, before the Revolution, 70 or 80 per cent had been illiterate and who could hardly be expected to be critical of what they read. Gorky seems to have exerted what influence he could in the direction of liberalism: to him was due, no doubt, the liquidation of RAPP, the latest device for the monopoly of culture, and the opening of the Soviet canon to the best contemporary foreign writing and the classics. But though this made possible more freedom of form and a wider range of reading, it could not, under the dictatorship of Stalin, either stimulate or release a living literature. Where no political opposition was possible, there was possible no political criticism; and in Russia political questions involve vitally the fate of society. What reality can there be for the Russians, the most socially-minded writers on earth, in a freedom purely 'aesthetic'? Even the fine melodramatic themes of the post-revolutionary cinema and theatre, with their real emotion and moral conviction, have been replaced by simple trash not very far removed from Hollywood, or by dramatized exemplifications of the latest 'directive' of Stalin which open the night after the speech that has announced the directive. The recent damning of the music of Shostakovich on the ground that the commissars were unable to hum it seems a withdrawal from the liberal position. And it is probable that the death of Gorky, as well as the imprisonment of Bukharin and Radek, have removed the last brakes from a precipitate descent, in the artistic as well as the political field, into a nightmare of informing and repression. The practice of deliberate falsification of social and political history which began at the time of the Stalin-Trotsky crisis and which has now attained proportions so fantastic that the government does not seem to hesitate to pass the sponge every month or so over everything that the people have previously been told and to present them with a new and contradictory version of their history, their duty, and the characters and careers of their leaders – this practice cannot fail in the end to corrupt every department of intellectual life, till the serious, the humane, the clear-seeking must simply, if they can, remain silent.

Thus Marxism in Russia for the moment has run itself into a blind alley – or rather, it has been put down a well. The Soviets seem hardly at the present time to have retained even the Marxist political culture, even in its cruder forms

– so that we are relieved from the authority of Russia as we are deprived of her inspiration. To what conclusions shall we come, then, at this time of day, about Marxism and literature – basing our views not even necessarily upon texts from the Marxist Fathers, but upon ordinary common sense? Well, first of all, that we can go even further than Trotsky in one of the dicta I have quoted above and declare that Marxism by itself can tell us nothing whatever about the goodness or badness of a work of art. A man may be an excellent Marxist, but if he lacks imagination and taste he will be unable to make the choice between a good and an inferior book both of which are ideologically unexceptionable. What Marxism *can* do, however, is throw a great deal of light on the origins and social significance of works of art. The study of literature in its relation to society is as old as Herder – and even Vico. Coleridge had flashes of insight into the connexion between literary and social phenomena, as when he saw the Greek state in the Greek sentence and the individualism of the English in the short separate statements of Chaucer's Prologue. But the great bourgeois master of this kind of criticism was Taine, with his *race* and *moment* and *milieu*; yet Taine, for all his scientific professions, responded artistically to literary art, and responded so vividly that his summings-up of writers and recreations of periods sometimes rival or surpass their subjects. Marx and Engels further deepened this study of literature in relation to its social background by demonstrating for the first time inescapably the importance of economic systems. But if Marx and Engels and Lenin and Trotsky are worth listening to on the subject of books, it is not merely because they created Marxism, but also because they were capable of literary appreciation.

Yet the man who tries to apply Marxist principles without real understanding of literature is liable to go horribly wrong. For one thing, it is usually true in works of the highest order that the purport is not a simple message, but a complex vision of things, which itself is not explicit but implicit; and the reader who does not grasp them artistically, but is merely looking for simple social morals, is certain to be hopelessly confused. Especially will he be confused if the author *does* draw an explicit moral which is the opposite of or has nothing to do with his real purport. Friedrich Engels, in the letter to Margaret Harkness already referred to above, in warning her that the more the novelist allows his political ideas to 'remain hidden, the better it is for the work of art', says that Balzac, with his reactionary opinions, is worth a thousand of Zola, with all his democratic ones. (Balzac was one of the great literary admirations of both Engels and Marx, the latter of whom had planned to write a book on him.) Engels points out that Balzac himself was, or believed himself to be, a legitimist engaged in deploring the decline of high society; but that actually 'his irony is never more bitter, his satire never more trenchant, than when he is showing us these aristocrats . . . for whom he felt so profound a sympathy', and that 'the only men of whom he speaks with undissimulated admiration are his most determined political adversaries, the republican heroes of the Cloître-Saint-Merri, the men who at that period (1830–36) truly represented the popular masses'. Nor does it matter necessarily in a work of art whether the characters are shown engaged in a conflict which illustrates the larger conflicts of society or in one which from that point of view is trivial. In art – it is quite obvious in music, but it is also true in literature – a sort of law of moral interchangeability prevails: we may transpose the actions and the sentiments that move us into terms of whatever we do or are ourselves. Real genius of moral insight is a motor which will start any engine. When Proust, in his wonderful chapter on the death of the novelist Bergotte, speaks of those moral obligations which impose themselves in spite of everything and which seem to come through to humanity from some source outside its wretched self (obligations 'invisible only to fools – and are they really to them?'), he is describing a kind of duty which he felt only in connexion with the literary work which he performed in his dark and fetid room; yet he speaks for every moral, aesthetic, or intellectual passion which holds the expediencies of the world in contempt. And the hero of Thornton Wilder's *Heaven's My Destination*, the travelling salesman who tries to save souls in the smoking car and writes Bible texts on hotel blotters, is something more than a symptom of Thornton Wilder's religious tendencies: he is the type of all saints who begin absurdly; and Wilder's story would be as true of the socialist Upton Sinclair as of the Christian George Brush. Nor does it necessarily matter, for the moral effect of a work of literature, whether the forces of bravery or virtue with which we identify ourselves are victorious or vanquished in the end. In Hemingway's story *The Undefeated*, the old bull-fighter who figures as the hero is actually humiliated and killed, but his courage has itself been a victory. It is true, as I. Kashkin, the Soviet critic, has said, that Hemingway has written much about decadence, but in order to write tellingly about death you have to have the principle of life, and those that have it will make it felt in spite of everything.

The Leftist critic with no literary competence is always trying to measure works of literature by tests which have no validity in that field. And one of his favourite occupations is giving specific directions and working out diagrams for the construction of ideal Marxist books. Such formulas are of course perfectly futile. The rules observed in any given school of art become apparent, not before but after, the actual works of art have been produced. As we were reminded by Burton Rascoe at the time of the Humanist controversy, the aesthetic laws involved in Greek tragedy were not formulated by Aristotle until at least half a century after Euripides and Sophocles were dead. And the behaviour of the Marxist critics has been precisely like that of the Humanists. The Humanists knew down to the last comma what they wanted a work of literature to be, but they never – with the possible exception, when pressed, of *The Bridge of San Luis Rey*, about which they had, however, hesitations – were able to find any contemporary work which fitted their specifications. The Marxists did just the same thing. In an article called *The Crisis in Criticism* in the *New Masses* of February 1933, Granville Hicks drew up a list of requirements which the ideal Marxist work of literature must meet. The primary function of such a work, he asserted, must be to 'lead the proletarian reader to recognize his role in the class struggle' – and it must therefore (1) 'directly or indirectly show the effects of the class struggle'; (2) 'the author must be able to make the reader feel that he is participating in the lives described'; and, finally, (3) the author's point of view must 'be that of the vanguard of the proletariat; he should be, or should try to make himself, a member of the proletariat'. This formula, he says, 'gives us . . . a standard by which to recognize the perfect Marxian novel' – and adds 'no novel as yet written perfectly conforms to our demands'. But the doctrine of 'socialist realism' promulgated at the Soviet Writers' Congress of August 1934 was only an attempt on a larger scale to legislate masterpieces into existence – a kind of attempt which always indicates sterility on the part of those who engage in it, and which always actually works, if it has any effect at all, to legislate existing good literature *out* of existence and to discourage the production of any more. The prescribers for the literature of the future usually cherish some great figure of the past whom they regard as having fulfilled their conditions and whom they are always bringing forward to demonstrate the inferiority of the literature of the present. As there has never existed a great writer who really had anything in common with these critics' conception of literature, they are obliged to provide imaginary versions of what their ideal great writers are like. The Humanists had Sophocles and Shakespeare; the socialist realists had Tolstoy. Yet it is certain that if Tolstoy had had to live up to the objectives and prohibitions which the socialist realists proposed he could never have written a chapter; and that if Babbitt and More had been able to enforce against Shakespeare their moral and aesthetic injunctions he would never have written a line. The misrepresentation of Sophocles, which has involved even a tampering with his text in the interests not merely of Humanism but of academic classicism in general, has been one of the scandalous absurdities of scholarship. The Communist critical movement in America, which had for its chief spokesman Mr Hicks, tended to identify their ideal with the work of John Dos Passos. In order to make this possible, it was necessary to invent an imaginary Dos Passos. This ideal Dos Passos was a Communist, who wrote stories about the proletariat, at a time when the real Dos Passos was engaged in bringing out a long novel about the effects of the capitalist system on the American middle class and had announced himself – in the *New Republic* in 1930 – politically a 'middle-class liberal'. The ideal Dos Passos was something like Gorky without the moustache – Gorky, in the meantime, having himself undergone some transmogrification at the hands of Soviet publicity – and this myth was maintained until the Communist critics were finally compelled to repudiate it, not because they had acquired new light on Dos Passos, the novelist and dramatist, but because of his attitude towards events in Russia.

The object of these formulas for the future, as may be seen from the above quotations from Mr Hicks, is to make of art an effective instrument in the class struggle. And we must deal with the dogma that 'art is a weapon'. It is true that art may be a weapon; but in the case of some of the greatest works of art, some of those which have the longest carry-over value, it is difficult to see that any important part of this value is due to their direct functioning as weapons. The *Divine Comedy*, in its political aspect, is a weapon for Henry of Luxemburg, whom Dante – with his medieval internationalism and his lack of sympathy for the nationalistic instincts which were impelling the Italians of his time to get away from the Austrian emperors – was so passionately eager to impose on his countrymen. Today we may say with Carducci that we would as soon see the crown of his 'good Frederick' rolling in Olona vale: 'Jove perishes; the poet's hymn remains.' And, though Shakespeare's *Henry IV* and *Henry V* are weapons for Elizabethan imperialism, their real centre is not Prince Hal but Falstaff; and Falstaff is the father of *Hamlet* and of all Shakespeare's tragic heroes, who, if they illustrate any social moral – the moral, perhaps, that Renaissance princes, supreme in their little worlds, may go to pieces in all kinds of terrible ways for lack of a larger social organism to restrain them – do so evidently without Shakespeare's being aware of it. If these works may be spoken of as weapons at all, they are weapons in the more general struggle of modern European man emerging from the Middle Ages and striving to understand his world and himself – a function for which 'weapon' is hardly the right word. The truth is that there is short-range and long-range literature. Long-range literature attempts to sum up wide areas and long periods of human experience, or to extract from them general laws; short-range literature preaches and pamphleteers with the view to an immediate effect. A good deal of the recent confusion of our writers in the Leftist camp has been due to their not understanding, or being unable to make up their minds, whether they are aiming at long-range or short-range writing.

This brings us to the question of what sort of periods are most favourable for works of art. One finds an assumption on the Left that revolutionary or pre-revolutionary periods are apt to produce new and vital forms of literature. This, of course, is very far from the truth in the case of periods of actual revolution. The more highly developed forms of literature require leisure and a certain amount of stability; and during a period of revolution the writer is usually deprived of both. The literature of the French Revolution consisted of the orations of Danton, the journalism of Camille Desmoulins, and the few political poems that André Chénier had a chance to write before he was guillotined. The literature of the Russian Revolution was the political writing of Lenin and Trotsky, and Alexander Blok's poem, *The Twelve*, almost the last fruit of his genius before it was nipped by the wind of the storm. As for pre-revolutionary periods in which the new forces are fermenting, they *may* be great periods for literature – as the eighteenth century was in France and the nineteenth century in Russia (though here there was a decadence after 1905). But the conditions that make possible the masterpieces are apparently not produced by the impending revolutions, but by the phenomenon of literary technique, already highly developed, in the hands of a writer who has had the support of long-enduring institutions. He may reflect an age of transition, but it will not necessarily be true that his face is set squarely in the direction of the future. The germs of the Renaissance are in Dante and the longing for a better world in Virgil, but neither Dante nor Virgil can in any real sense be described as a revolutionary writer: they sum up or write elegies for ages that are passing. The social organisms that give structure to their thought – the Roman Empire and the Catholic Church – are already showing signs of decay. It is impossible, therefore, to identify the highest creative work in art with the most active moments of creative social change. The writer who is seriously intent on producing long-range works of literature should, from the point of view of his own special personal interests, thank his stars if there is no violent revolution going on in his own country in his time. He may disapprove of the society he is writing about, but if it were disrupted by an actual upheaval he would probably not be able to write.

But what about 'proletarian literature' as an accompaniment of the social revolution? In the earlier days of the Communist régime in Russia, one used to hear about Russian authors who, in the effort to eliminate from their writings any vestige of the bourgeois point of view, had reduced their vocabulary and syntax to what they regarded as an A B C of essentials – with the result of becoming more unintelligible to the proletarian audience at whom they were aiming than if they had been Symbolist poets. (Indeed, the futurist poet Mayakovsky has since that time become a part of the Soviet canon.) Later on, as I have said, Soviet culture followed the road that Trotsky recommended: it began building again on the classics and on the bourgeois culture of other countries and on able revolutionary Russian writers who had learned their trade before the Revolution. 'Soviet publishers' – I quote from the Russian edition of *International Literature*, issue 2 of 1936 – 'are bringing out Hemingway and Proust not merely in order to demonstrate "bourgeois decay". Every genuine work of art – and such are the productions of Hemingway and Proust – enriches the reader's knowledge of life and heightens his aesthetic sensibility and his emotional culture – in a word, it figures, in the broad sense, as a factor of educational value. Liberated socialist humanity inherits all that is beautiful, elevating, and sustaining in the culture of previous ages.' The truth is that the talk in Soviet Russia about proletarian literature and art has resulted from the persistence of the same situation which led Tolstoy under the old régime to put on the muzhik's blouse and to go in for carpentry, cobbling, and ploughing: the difficulty experienced by an educated minority, who were only about 20 per cent of the people, in getting in touch with the illiterate majority. In America the situation is quite different. The percentage of illiterates in this country is only something like 4 per cent; and there is relatively little difficulty of communication between different social groups. Our development away from England, and from the old world generally, in this respect – in the direction of the democratization of our idiom – is demonstrated clearly in H. L. Mencken's *The American Language*; and if it is a question of either the use for high literature of the language of the people or the expression of the dignity and importance of the ordinary man, the country which has produced *Leaves of Grass* and *Huckleberry Finn* has certainly nothing to learn from Russia. We had created during our pioneering period a literature of the common man's escape, not only from feudal Europe, but also from bourgeois society, many years before the Russian masses were beginning to write their names. There has been a section of our recent American literature of the last fifteen years or so – the period of the boom and the depression – which has dealt with our industrial and rural life from the point of view of the factory hand and the poor farmer under conditions which were forcing him to fight for his life, and this has been called proletarian literature; but it has been accompanied by books on the white-collar worker, the storekeeper, the well-to-do merchant, the scientist, and the millionaire in situations equally disastrous or degrading. And this whole movement of critical and imaginative writing – though with some stimulus, certainly, from Russia – had come quite naturally out of our literature of the past. It is curious to observe that one of the best of the recent strike novels, *The Land of Plenty* by Robert Cantwell, himself a Westerner and a former mill worker, owes a good deal to Henry James.

Yet when all these things have been said, all the questions have not been answered. All that has been said has been said of the past; and Marxism is something new in the world: it is a philosophical system which leads directly to programmes of action. Has there ever appeared before in literature such a phenomenon as M. André Malraux, who alternates between attempts, sometimes brilliant, to write long-range fiction on revolutionary themes, and exploits of aviation for the cause of revolution in Spain? Here creative political action and the more complex kind of imaginative writing have united at least to the extent that they have arisen from the same vision of history and have been included in the career of one man. The Marxist vision of Lenin – Vincent Sheean has said it first – has in its completeness and its compelling force a good deal in common with the vision of Dante; but, partly realized by Lenin during his lifetime and still potent for some years after his death, it was a creation, not of literary art, but of actual social engineering. It is society itself, says Trotsky, which under communism becomes the work of art. The first attempts at this art will be inexpert and they will have refractory material to work with; and the philosophy of the Marxist dialectic involves idealistic and mythological elements which have led too often to social religion rather than to social art. Yet the human imagination has already come to conceive the possibility of re-creating human society; and how can we doubt that, as it acquires the power, it must emerge from what will seem by comparison the revolutionary 'underground' of art as we have always known it up to now and deal with the materials of actual life in ways which we cannot now even foresee? This is to speak in terms of centuries, of ages; but, in practising and prizing literature, we must not be unaware of the first efforts of the human spirit to transcend literature itself.

Morose Ben Jonson

WHEN Swinburne published his study of Ben Jonson hardly sixty years ago, he indignantly called attention to the fact that English scholarship, which had shown such devotion to the texts of the Greek and Latin classics, should never, in two centuries and a half, have produced a decent edition of so important an English writer. That complaint can no longer be made – though the definitive edition of Jonson by C. H. Herford and Percy and Evelyn Simpson, brought out by the Oxford University Press, has been slow in appearing and is not yet complete. The first two volumes were published in 1925, and the eighth has only just come out. This, containing Jonson's poems and prose, is the last instalment of the text of Jonson, but it is to be followed by two volumes of commentaries, which ought to be particularly valuable, since no writer is more full of allusions, both topical and learned, than Jonson, and his work has never been properly annotated. There has not appeared, from this point of view and from that of clearing up the text, a serious edition of Jonson since that of William Gifford in 1816. This new one is a model of scholarship, handsomely printed and interestingly illustrated – in some cases, with hitherto unpublished drawings made by Inigo Jones for the décors and costumes of Jonson's masques.

Except, however, for the first two volumes, which assemble biographical materials and contain historical and critical essays on Jonson's various works, the Herford-Simpson edition is not especially to be recommended to the ordinary non-scholarly reader who may want to make the acquaintance of Jonson. It presents the original text with the seventeenth-century punctuation and spelling and with no glossary and no notes except textual ones. The books are, besides, expensive, and the earlier volumes are now hard to get – so the approach to this beetling author remains, as it has always been, rather forbidding and fraught with asperities. The best reprinting of the Gifford edition is also expensive and out of print. The three volumes of selections in the Mermaid Series are full of perplexing misprints, which drop out words or substitute wrong ones, and equipped with inadequate notes that turn up often on the wrong pages. The two volumes in the Everyman's Series include only Jonson's plays, and they are printed in a small dense type that makes them uncomfortable reading; there is a glossary, but it is incomplete. The only breach that I know in the hedge that seems to have sprung up around Jonson, as if his editors had somehow been influenced by their bristling and opaque subject, has been made by Mr Harry Levin in his *Selected Works of Ben Jonson* (published by Random House). Here, in a clear readable text of his own and with a brilliant introduction, Mr Levin has got together most of the best of Jonson for a compact and well-printed volume. There is an obstacle, though, even here, for he has furnished no notes and no glossary, and with Jonson, the explanation of a literary reference or the key to a phrase of slang is often absolutely indispensable for the understanding of a passage.

But it is not merely that Jonson's text itself has been a little hard to get at. It is rather that lack of demand has not stimulated popular editions. *Volpone* can still hold an audience – though it took a German adaptation to bring it back into fashion; and *The Alchemist* has been recently done both in New York and in London; but, among a thousand people, say, who have some knowledge and love of Shakespeare, and even some taste for Webster and Marlowe, I doubt whether you could find half a dozen who have any enthusiasm for Jonson or who have seriously read his plays. T. S. Eliot, admitting the long neglect into which Ben Jonson's work had fallen, put up, in *The Sacred Wood*, a strong plea for Jonson as an artist, and thus made a respect for this poet *de rigueur* in literary circles. But one's impression is that what people have read has been, not Jonson, but

Eliot's essay. The dramatist himself, a great master for the age that followed his own, is still for ours mostly a celebrated name, whose writings are left unexplored. What I want to do here is to attack the problem of Jonson's unpopularity from what I believe to be a new point of view, and to show that his failure as a drawing attraction, in either the theatre or the study, is bound up in a peculiar way with his difficulties as an artist.

It is a fault of Eliot's essay, so expert in its appreciation of the best-woven passages of Jonson's verse, that it minimizes his glaring defects. If you read it without reading Jonson, you will get a most plausible picture of a special kind of great writer, but this picture is not exactly Jonson. What is suppressed is all that Bernard Shaw meant when, telling off the Elizabethan dramatists, he characterized Ben Jonson as a 'brutish pedant'; and, in grappling with Jonson's short-comings, we cannot perhaps do better than begin by facing squarely those qualities which made it impossible for Shaw – who admired, though he patronized, Shakespeare – to take seriously the comic writer who had, up to Shaw's own appearance, achieved the greatest reputation in English dramatic literature. The point is that Shakespeare, like Shaw, however much they differ in their philosophies, has an immense range, social and moral, in understanding a variety of people. To an intelligent and sensitive man of any school of thought, Shakespeare appears sensitive and in-telligent. But Ben Jonson, after Shakespeare, seems neither. Though he attempts a variety of characters, they all boil down to a few motivations, recognizable as the motivations of Jonson himself and rarely transformed into artistic creations. Shakespeare expands himself, breeds his cells as organic beings, till he has so lost himself in the world he has made that we can hardly recompose his personality. Jonson merely splits himself up and sets the pieces – he is to this extent a dramatist – in conflict with one another; but we have merely to put these pieces together to get Jonson, with little left over. In the theatre, he aims at several styles, as he tries for a multiplicity of characters, but the variety here, too, is mainly a mere technical matter of metrics and vocabulary, where Shakespeare can summon voices that seem to come from real human throats.

Jonson also lacks natural invention, and his theatre has little organic life. His plots are incoherent and clumsy; his juxtapositions of elements are too often like the 'mechanical mixtures' of chemistry that produce no molecular reactions. His chief artifices for making something happen are to introduce his characters in impossible disguises and to have them play incredible practical jokes. Nor has he any sense of movement or proportion: almost everything goes on too long, and while it continues, it does not develop. Nor is his taste in other matters reliable. His puns, as Dryden complained, are sometimes of a stunning stupidity; and when he is dirty, he is, unlike Shakespeare, sometimes disgusting to such a degree that he makes one sympathetic with the Puritans in their efforts to clean up the theatre. His reading of Greek and Latin, for all the boasting he does about it, has served him very insufficiently for the refinement and ordering of his work, and usually appears in his plays as either an alien and obstructive element or, when more skilfully managed, as a padding to give the effect of a dignity and weight which he cannot supply himself. He is much better when he lets himself go in a vein that is completely unclassical.

It is surely, then, misleading for Eliot to talk of Jonson's 'polished surface', to call him a 'great creative mind', who 'created his own world', and not to warn you of the crudities and aridities, the uncertainty of artistic intention and the flat-footed dramatic incompetence, that you will run into when you set out to read him. None of his plays, with the exception of *The Alchemist*, really quite comes off as a whole. The three others of the best four of his comedies, though they all suffer from the faults I have mentioned, have elements of genuine humour and passages of admirable writing. But the story of *The Silent Woman* is revolting in its forced barbarity (Jonson's murderous practical jokes have their only analogue in literature in the booby-traps of Rudyard Kipling); *Volpone*, which reaches at moments a kind of heroic magnificence in exploiting its sordid and cruel themes, suffers, also, though somewhat less, from being based upon practical joking, and it is badly let down at the end by an improbable conventional conclusion; and, as for *Bartholomew Fair*, with some terribly funny scenes and a rich pageant of London low-life, there is in it so much too much of everything that the whole thing becomes rather a wallow of which the Pig-Woman and her pigs are all too truly the symbol. Contrast it with Hogarth's *Southwark Fair* (the product, to be sure, of a more disciplined age), equally confused and crowded, but so much better composed, so much sharper and firmer in outline. With *The Alchemist*, Jonson did ring the bell. This comedy is concentrated and well-constructed. There is no element of false morality to blur Jonson's acrid relish of the confidence games of his rogues: the cynicism is carried right through. The verse, which invests with style, which raises to distinction and glitter till it gives a ring almost like poetry, the slang of the underworld and the jargon of its various chicaneries, is an original achievement of Jonson's, which is only sustained in this one play. And, though there are one or two laboured devices, the invention is more resourceful and the dialogue more spontaneous than in any of Jonson's other comedies. Yet this play, one of the funniest in English, is not really an example of high comedy as either a play of Molière's or a play of Aristophanes' is. Ben Jonson is not enough of a critic – that is, he has not enough intelligence – for either Molière's kind of interest in character and human relations or Aristophanes' kind of interest in institutions and points of view. *The Alchemist* is a picaresque farce, fundamentally not different from the Marx brothers. And it shows Jonson's poverty of themes that, when he had earlier attempted a tragedy, he should have arrived at a similar story. *Sejanus*, which takes us to the Roman Senate and inside the court of Tiberius, is also a chronicle of the intrigues of rogues who begin by working together but later sell each other out.

This is too off-hand a summary of Jonson's work, but I want to get at him in another way.

Ben Jonson seems an obvious example of a psychological type which has been described by Freud and designated by a technical name, *anal erotic*, which has sometimes misled the layman as to what it was meant to imply. Let me introduce it simply by quoting from the account of it in a handbook of psychoanalysis, *The Structure and Meaning of Psychoanalysis* by William Healy, A. F. Bronner, and A. M. Bowers. The three main characteristics of this type are here paraphrased from Freud as follows: ' (a) orderliness . . . in an over-accentuated form, pedantry; (b) parsimony, which may become avarice; (c) obstinacy, which may become defiance and perhaps also include irascibility and vindictiveness.' Now, Jonson had all these qualities. He was a pedant, whose cult of the classics had little connexion with his special kind of genius. There is something of the 'compulsive', in the neurotic sense, about his constant citing of precedents and his working into the speeches of his plays passages, sometimes not translated, from the Greek and Latin authors (though it was common for the Elizabethans to stick in scraps from Seneca or Ovid), as if they were charms against failure. That he always did fear failure is evident; and the arrogance, irritability, and stubbornness which are also characteristic of this Freudian type have obviously, in Jonson's case, their origin in a constant anxiety as to the adequacy of his powers. The more he defies his audience, vindicates himself against his critics (though at the same time he puts himself to special pains to propitiate the vulgar with vulgarity and to impress the learned with learning), in his innumerable prologues, inductions, interludes between the acts, epilogues, dramatic postscripts, and apologies added to the printed texts – the more he protests and explains, declaims at unconscionable length his indifference to and scorn of his detractors, the more we feel that he is unquiet, not confident. He is offsetting his internal doubts by demonstrations of self-assertion.

The hoarding and withholding instinct which is the third of the key traits of this type Jonson also displays to a high degree. This tendency is supposed to be based on an attitude towards the excretory processes acquired in early childhood. Such people, according to Freud, have an impulse to collect and accumulate; they feel that doing so gives them strength and helps them to resist the pressures that their elders are bringing to bear on them. Sometimes they simply concentrate on storing up; sometimes they expend in sudden bursts. They are likely to have a strong interest in food both from the deglutitionary and the excretory points of view; but the getting and laying by of money or of some other kind of possession which may or may not seem valuable to others is likely to substitute itself for the infantile preoccupation with the contents of the alimentary tract. Now, Jonson certainly exemplified this tendency, and he exhibited it in a variety of ways. His learning is a form of hoarding; and allied to it is his habit of collecting words. He liked to get up the special jargons of the various trades and professions and unload them in bulk on the public – sometimes with amusing results, as in the case of the alchemical and astrological patter reeled off by the crooks of *The Alchemist*, and even of the technique of behaviour of the courtiers in *Cynthia's Revels*, but more often, as with the list of cosmetics recommended by Wittipol in *The Devil Is an Ass* and, to my taste, with the legal Latin of the divorce scene in *The Silent Woman*, providing some of his most tedious moments. The point is that Ben Jonson depends on the exhibition of stored-away knowledge to compel admiration by itself. And the hoarding and withholding of money is the whole subject of that strange play *Volpone*. Volpone is not an ordinary miser: he is a Venetian 'magnifico', whose satisfaction in his store of gold is derived not merely from gloating alone but also, and more excitingly, from stimulating others to desire it, to hope to inherit it from him, and then frustrating them with the gratuitous cruelty which has been noted as one of the features of the aggressive side of this Freudian type. The practical jokes in Jonson have usually this sadistic character, and the people who perpetrate them are usually trying either to get something for themselves or to keep someone else from getting something. The many kinds of frauds and sharpers – from pickpockets to promoters – who figure in Jonson's plays as prominently as the practical jokers are occupied with similar aims; and Subtle and Face, in *The Alchemist*, lurk closeted, like Volpone, in a sombre house, where they are hoarding their cleverness, too, and plotting their victims' undoing.

I am not qualified to 'analyse' Jonson in the light of this Freudian conception, and I have no interest in trying to fit him into any formulation of it. I am not even sure that the relation between the workings of the alimentary tract and the other phenomena of personality is, as Freud assumes, a relation of cause and effect; but I am sure that Freud has here really seized upon a nexus of human traits that are involved with one another and has isolated a recognizable type, and it seems to me to leap to the eyes that Jonson belongs to this type. I shall fill in the rest of my picture with the special characteristics of Jonson, which are consistent with the textbook description and which in some cases strikingly illustrate it.

Ben Jonson's enjoyment of tavern life and his great reputation for wit have created, among those who do not read him, an entirely erroneous impression of high spirits and joviality; but his portraits show rather the face of a man who habitually worries, who is sensitive and holds himself aloof, not yielding himself to intimate fellowship. In many of his plays there figures an unsociable and embittered personage who sometimes represents virtue and censors the other characters, but is in other cases presented by Jonson as a thoroughly disagreeable person and the butt of deserved persecution.

Such, in the second of these categories, are Macilente in *Every Man Out of His Humour*, Morose in *The Silent Woman*, Surly in *The Alchemist*, and Wasp in *Bartholomew Fair*. The most conspicuous of these is Morose, and Jonson's treatment of him is particularly significant. The dramatist, on a visit to the country, had encountered a local character who gave him an idea for a play. This was a man who had a morbid aversion to noise. Now, Jonson seems never to have inquired the reason, never to have tried to imagine what the life of such a man would be really like; nor could he ever have been conscious of what it was in himself that impelled him to feel so vivid an interest in him. According to his usual custom, he simply put him on the stage as a 'humour', an eccentric with an irrational horror of any kind of sound except that of his own voice, who lives in a room with a double wall and the windows 'close shut and caulked' in a street too narrow for traffic, and who, declaring that 'all discourses but mine own' seem to him 'harsh impertinent, and irksome', makes his servants communicate with him by signs. And the only way that Jonson can find to exploit the possibilities of this neurotic is to make him the agonized victim of a group of ferocious young men, who hunt him in his burrow like a badger, and trick him into marrying a 'silent woman', who, immediately after the ceremony – while her sponsors raise a hideous racket – opens fire on him with a frenzy of chatter, and turns out in the end to be a boy in disguise. But Morose himself is cruel through meanness: he has merited the worst he can suffer. He has wanted to disinherit his nephew, and has consigned him, in a venomous outburst, to the direst humiliation and poverty. Through Morose and through the characters like him, Ben Jonson is tormenting himself for what is negative and recessive in his nature. In *Volpone*, the withholder is punished only after he has had his fling at the delight of tormenting others. Miserliness, unsociability, a self-sufficient and systematic spite – these are among Jonson's dominant themes: all the impulses that grasp and deny. In the final scene of *Cynthia's Revels*,

the last play of Jonson's first period, he makes Cynthia
rhetorically demand:

> When has Diana, like an envious wretch,
> That glitters only to his soothed self,
> Denying to the world the precious use
> Of hoarded wealth, withheld her friendly aid?

Yet Cynthia is Diana, and Diana is a virgin queen, who has
herself forbidden love to her court; and the attitude which
she is here repudiating is to supply almost all the subjects
for the rest of Jonson's plays, among them all of his best.
In these four lines, you have the whole thing in the words
that come to his pen: envy, denial, hoarding, withholding.
The first of these is very important. (Envy then meant hatred
and spite as well as jealousy of what others have, but I am
dealing with it here in its modern sense, which is usually the
sense of Jonson.) In several of the earlier plays, it has been
one of the chief motivations. In those you have had, on the
one hand, the worthy and accomplished scholar – Horace
of *The Poetaster*, Crites of *Cynthia's Revels* – who is envied by
lesser men; and, on the other hand, the poor and exacerbated
wit – Macilente in *Every Man Out of His Humour* – who envies
lesser men. But both are aspects of the same personality;
both are identified with Jonson himself. Whether the injury
done the superior man consists of being slandered by fools
or by the fools' being better off than he, it is the only fulfilment of the play that he is granted his just revenge, and he
scores off his victims with a cruelty almost equal to that of
Volpone frustrating his mercenary friends.

With this, there is no love in Jonson's plays to set against
these negative values. The references to seduction, frequent
though they are, in both his plays and his personal poems,
suggest nothing but the coldest of appetites, and often
show more gratification at the idea of cuckolding a husband
than at that of enjoying a woman. In the plays, two sexual
types recur, neither of whom finds any satisfaction in sex.
Jonson said of his wife, from whom he separated, that she had

been 'a shrew, yet honest'; and the only women in his plays that have even a semblance of life are shrews of the most pitiless breed. The typical wife in Jonson is always ready to doublecross her husband, and she does not want to allow him a moment of self-confidence or tranquillity: whatever the man does must be wrong; yet she may cherish at the same time an illusion that there waits for her somewhere a lover who can give her what she desires and deserves, and the appearance of a tenth-rate courtier may be enough to turn her head. The recurrent male type is a man who is insanely jealous of his wife but, paradoxically, is willing to prostitute her. The rival of the obsessive jealousy is always an obsessive greed either for money, as in the case of Corvino of *Volpone*, or, as in the case of Fitzdottrel of *The Devil Is an Ass*, for some other material advantage which the husband will enjoy by himself: Fitzdottrel likes to dress up and be seen on public occasions, but he never takes his wife with him. We may suspect, reading Jonson today, a connexion between the impotence of these husbands to spend any real love on their wives and their fears that they are going to lose them. We may reflect that the self-centred husband might produce the shrewish wife, or that, living with a shrewish wife, a man might grow more self-centred, if he did not, as usually happens with the unfortunate husbands of Jonson's plays, become totally demoralized. But Jonson had nothing of Shakespeare's grasp of organic human character or situation. It is interesting to contrast these bitches with the heroine of *The Taming of the Shrew*. Katharina's bad temper with men is accompanied by a deep conviction that no man can really want to marry her: it is a defiant assertion of self-respect. And so the jealousy of Othello (if not of Leontes) is explained by his consciousness, as a Moor in Venice, living among cleverer people who feel his colour as a bar to close fellowship, of being at a disadvantage with the race to which his wife belongs. Whereas Jonson's two depressing stock figures do not afford very much insight into the causes of the traits they exemplify. Turning up again and again with a monotony of which Shakespeare was incapable, they obviously represent phenomena which Jonson has known at first hand and on which he cannot help dwelling: two more aspects of that negative soul that he is impelled to caricature. Yet sometimes, with his special experience, he can make them reveal themselves – as in the self-torturing Proustian soliloquies of Kiteley in *Every Man in His Humour* – in a way that strips off the skin to show, not what is in the depths, but what is just below the surface.

Jonson's positive ideal of womanhood may be summed up in the well-known lyric that begins, '*Have you seen but a bright lily grow, Before rude hands have touched it?,*' and ends '*O so white! O so soft! O so sweet is she!*' It is something quite remote and unreal which he is unable – when he tries, which is seldom, as in the Celia of *Volpone* – to bring to life in his plays, and, though the poems inspired by it are neat and agreeable enough, they have no human tenderness in them, let alone human passion. The touches in Jonson's poetry that come closest to lyric feeling are invariably evocations of coldness: '*Like melting snow upon a craggy hill . . . Since nature's pride is now a withered daffodil*', or '*Except Love's fires the virtue have To fright the frost out of the grave*', (from a poem in which the same stanza begins with the incredibly prosaic couplet: '*As in a ruin, we it call One thing to be blown up or fall . . .*'). And we may cite from the masque called *The Vision of Delight* the lines that remained in the memory of Joyce's Stephen Dedalus: '*I was not wearier where I lay By frozen Tithon's side tonight*' . . . ; as well as the passage from the prose *Discoveries* which Saintsbury selected for praise: '*What a deal of cold business doth a man misspend the better part of life in! – in scattering compliments, tendering visits, gathering and venting news, following feasts and plays, making a little winter-love in a dark corner.*' At the end of *Cynthia's Revels*, Cupid tries to shoot Cynthia's courtiers and make them fall in love with one another, but he finds that his bow is powerless: they have been drinking from the fount of Self-Love, in which Narcissus admired himself, and they are impervious to his shafts. When Diana is told of his presence, she sends him packing at once. Few lovers are united by Jonson. Is there indeed a case in all his work? And in Jonson's latest plays, the heroines undergo a transformation that makes Cynthia seem relatively human. The Lady Pecunia of *The Staple of News*, surrounded by her female retinue, Mortgage, Statute, Band, and Wax, is simply a figure in a financial allegory; and so is Mistress Steel, the Magnetic Lady. Both are heiresses, kept close by guardians and sought by baffled suitors. The feminine principle here has been turned by the instinct for hoarding into something metallic, unyielding. The woman has lost all her womanhood: she is literally the hoarded coin. This evidently appeared to Ben Jonson a perfectly natural pleasantry, but it is quite enough to account for the failure, in his time, of these pieces, and for the distaste that we feel for them today.

To these stock characters of Jonson's theatre should be added another that evidently derives from the playwright's social situation as well as from his psychology of hoarding. Ben Jonson, from his own account, was the son of a Scotch gentleman who had possessed some little fortune, but who had been thrown into prison, presumably for his Protestant leanings, in the reign of Bloody Mary, and had had his property confiscated. He died before Ben was born, and Ben's mother married a master bricklayer. Young Ben went to Westminster school, under the patronage of one of the masters, whose attention had been attracted by the boy's exceptional abilities, and may have started in at Cambridge on a scholarship; but he was obliged, apparently through poverty, to give up his studies there, and was set to learn the bricklayer's trade, which he loathed and from which he escaped by enlisting to fight in Flanders. Now, one of Jonson's favourite clowns, who varies little from play to play, is a young heir who is an utter numbskull and who, just having come into his money, begins throwing it away by the handful and soon finds himself fleeced by sharpers. This figure, too, in a different way from the envied or the envious man, is obviously the creation of Jonson's own envy, stimulated, no doubt, from two sources – first, the grievance of the man of good birth unjustly deprived of his patrimony, and, second, the sulky resentment of the man who can only withhold against the man who can freely lavish.

Jonson's hardships and uncertainty in his earlier years – when he can never have known anything but poverty – must have spurred him to desperate efforts to ballast and buttress himself. (For, as I have said, I do not necessarily accept the view of Freud that the training of the excretory functions must precede the development of other traits which exhibit resistance through hoarding, though it seems certain that, in personalities like Jonson's, these various traits are related.) He had acquired classical learning where he could not acquire money; and it was to remain for him a reservoir of strength, a basis of social position, to which he was to go on adding all his life. But his habit of saving and holding back – did his Scotch ancestry figure here, too? – had an unfortunate effect on his work, as well as on his personal relations, in that it made it very difficult for him fully to exploit his talents. It is not that the audiences of Jonson's day, the readers who have come to him since, have been unwilling to give themselves to his talents, but that his talents, authentic though they were, have not given themselves to us – or rather, that they were able to give themselves for only a limited period and then only at the expense of much effort. Ben Jonson, at his best, writes brilliantly; he has a genuine dramatic imagination. But it is hard for him to pump up his powers to work that will display their capacities. His addiction to wine – 'drink', Drummond said, 'is one of the elements in which he liveth' – was, I believe, bound up with the problem of getting himself to the point of high-pressure creative activity. He explained the strength of *Volpone* on the basis of its having been written at the time when he had just received a gift of ten dozen of sack; asserted that a passage in *Cataline* had suffered from having been composed when he was drinking watered wine; and apologized for the weakness of his later plays on the ground that he and his 'boys' – by which he meant his drinking companions – had been getting bad wine at their tavern. This shows that he drank while he was writing; and it is possible that liquor, though effective in helping him to keep up his high vein, may also have been to blame for the badness of some of his work. There are at times a peculiar coarseness in the texture of Jonson's writing, a strained falseness in his comic ideas, which, intolerable to a sober mind, may very well have seemed inspired to a constipated writer well primed with sack.

What Jonson was aiming at – from *Cynthia's Revels*, say – was a majesty and splendour of art which should rival the classics he venerated and the work of his more dashing contemporaries, with their rhetoric, colour, and spirit. But it is hard to be noble and grand with material so negative, so sour, as that which Jonson's experience had given him. To write in blank verse that is also poetry of the imbecile ambitions and the sordid swindles which furnish the whole subject of *The Alchemist* was a feat that even Ben Jonson was never to achieve but once. When he attempts a Roman tragedy, as in *Cataline* or *Sejanus*, his Romans are mostly the envious rogues, the merciless prigs, and the treacherous sluts with whom we are familiar in his comedies, and they make a more unpleasant impression for not being humorously treated. When Jonson attempts Renaissance splendour, he always gives it an element of the factitious as well as an element of the vulgar, which, as Mr Levin says, have the effect of making it look ridiculous. The dreams of Sir Epicure Mammon bring a kind of hard glow to the writing, but his banquets and his beds and his mirrors are imaginary like the gold that is to buy them: they never get on to the stage as does the 'alchemist's' fusty lair. And with *Volpone*, the great difficulty is that the mean motivations of the characters have no intimate connexion with the background, the house of a rich Venetian. Volpone is simply another of Jonson's hateful and stingy men, who behaves as if he were envious of others, without being provided by Jonson with any real reason for envy. The magnificence of Jonson's grandees, like the purity of his women, is a value that is always unreal and that can never make a satisfactory counterweight to a poverty and a squalour that are actual and vividly rendered. One has to go to the later French naturalists who were influenced by both Flaubert and Zola to find anything comparable to the poetry which Jonson was able to extract from all the cheap and dirty aspects of London: the 'poor spoonful of dead wine, with flies in't'; the gingerbread made of 'stale bread, rotten eggs, musty ginger, and dead honey'; the rogue out of luck,

> at Pie Corner,
> Taking your meal of steam in, from cooks' stalls,
> Where, like the father of hunger, you did walk
> Piteously costive, with your pinched horn-nose,
> And your complexion of the Roman wash
> Stuck full of black and melancholic worms,
> Like powder-corns shot at th' artillery-yard;

the theatre pick-ups, 'lean playhouse poultry,' as described by fat Ursula of the pig-roasting booth, 'that has the bony rump sticking out like the ace of spades or the point of a partizan, that every rib of 'em is like the tooth of a saw; or will so grate 'em [their customers] with their hips and shoulders as – take 'em altogether – they were as good lie with a hurdle'. It is the peculiar beauty of *The Alchemist* that the visions of splendour here are all, frankly, complete illusion created out of sordid materials by rogues in the minds of dupes. The poor stupid whore Doll has to impersonate the Queen of Faery and a great lady in romantic circumstances. A more humane writer might have extracted some pathos from this; but Jonson does get an aesthetic effect that is quite close to the Flaubertian chagrin.

But, in *Volpone*, where real gold is involved, we are never allowed to see it. The German adaptation of this play made by Stefan Zweig and done here by the Theatre Guild, which has also been used as a basis for the current French film, is an improvement on Jonson's original in one very important respect. It shows us what we want to see, what, subconsciously, we have come to demand: the spending, the liberation of Volpone's withheld gold – when Mosca, to everyone's relief, finally flings it about the stage in fistfuls. But Ben Jonson cannot squander his gold, his gold which he has never possessed; he can only squander excrement. Karl Abraham, one of the psychologists quoted in the book referred to above, 'cites, in proof of the close association between sadistic and anal impulses instances in his experiences with neurotics when an explosive bowel evacuation has been a substitute for a discharge of anger or rage, or has accompanied it'. Certainly Jonson seems to explode in this fashion. The directness with which he gives way to the impulse is probably another cause of his chronic unpopularity. The climax of *The Poetaster* is the administering of emetic pills, the effects of which take, in this case, the form of a poetic joke. The comic high point of *The Alchemist* comes with the locking of one of the characters in a privy, where he will be overcome by the smell. The whole malodorous side of Jonson was given its fullest and most literal expression in the poem called *The Famous Voyage* which was too much for even Gifford and Swinburne, in which he recounts a nocturnal expedition made by two London blades in a wherry through the roofed-over tunnel of Fleet Ditch, which was the sewer for the public privies above it. A hardly less literal letting-go is the whole play of *Bartholomew Fair*, which followed the more pretentious work (from *Sejanus* through *Catiline*) that we have just been discussing. It is Ben Jonson's least strained and inhibited play, and one of his most successful. He drops verse for colloquial prose; he forgets about classical precedents. He dumps out upon his central group of characters, for the most part pusillanimous examples of the lower middle class, puritan parsons and petty officials, with, of course, a young spendthrift from the country, what must have been a lifetime's accumulation of the billingsgate and gutter practices of the pickpockets, booth-keepers, peddlers, pimps, ballad-singers, and professional brawlers of the Elizabethan underworld. This comedy, novel in its day, anticipates both Hogarth and Dickens; but Jonson's impulse to degrade his objects is something not shared by either. Hogarth and Dickens both, for all their appetite for rank vulgarity, are better-humoured and more fastidious. The flood of abusive language let loose by the infuriated Pig-Woman, well-written and funny though it is, is outpouring for outpouring's sake: it effects no dramatic move and has in itself no rhetorical development; and the even more filthy travesty of Marlowe's *Hero and Leander* in terms of bankside muck has an ugliness which makes one suspect that Jonson took an ugly delight in defiling a beautiful poem which he could not hope to rival. Yet we cannot but succumb – in certain scenes, at least – to the humour of *Bartholomew Fair*. The tumult of Ursula's booth and her devotion to her roasting pigs, the monumental pocket-picking episode that moves to its foreseen conclusion almost with the inevitability of tragedy – these somehow create more sympathy (always for the characters outside the law) than anything else in Jonson's plays.

And Ben Jonson is somehow a great man of letters, if he is not often a great artist. His very failure to make the best of his gifts had the result of his leaving a body of work full of hints – unrealized ambitions, undeveloped beginnings – which later writers were able to exploit in a way that it was hardly possible for them to do with the work of Shakespeare, which *was* realized, consummate, complete. The most astonishing variety of writers owe quite different kinds of debts to Jonson. It is as if they had found means to deliver, in viable forms of art, the genius that Jonson had had to withhold. Gifford was certainly right in supposing that Milton owed something to such passages as the opening of

Volpone, in which the hoarder invokes his gold. The whole comedy of Congreve and Wycherley seems to have grown out of the cynical men-about-town, with their bravura-pieces of wit, in *The Silent Woman*; and Swift must have picked up from Jonson, not only the title of *A Tale of a Tub*, but also the style and tone of his series of poems to Stella, which are so much like certain of those in Jonson's series, *A Celebration of Charis*, as well as his general vein of morosely humorous realism, exemplified in *The Lady's Dressing Room* and *A Description of a City Shower*. The comedy of humours eventually led to the one-idea characters of Peacock, which led, later, to those of Aldous Huxley; and it must have contributed to the novels of Dickens, who loved to act Bobadil in *Every Man in His Humour*. Though Tennyson was under the impression that he himself had invented the stanza-form that he made famous in *In Memoriam*, it had already been used by Jonson in his *Elegy* (xxii of *Underwoods*), the tone of which is quite close to Tennyson in his elegiac vein, and in the second of the choruses to *Catiline*, which suggests such weightier use of the metre as one finds in the dedication to Queen Victoria or in the dedication of *Demeter* to Lord Dufferin. And there are touches in Lewis Carroll that seem reminiscent of Jonson: '*I passed by the garden and marked with one eye How the Owl and the Panther were sharing the pie*,' recalls a long nonsense speech in *The Vision of Delight*: '*Yet would I take the stars to be cruel If the crab and the rope-maker ever fight duel*,' etc.; and Sir Politic Would-be of *Volpone*, with his succession of ridiculous inventions, of which he likes to boast, 'Mine own device', is a forerunner of the White Knight. In the first decades of our own century, that very first-rate comic writer, Ronald Firbank, with how little direct contact one cannot tell, represents the latest de-velopment of Ben Jonson's typical methods – eviscerated personalities and monstrous motivations labelled with bizarre names – which, though it shows perhaps a certain decadence, keeps also a good deal of vigour. And James Joyce, who told his friend Frank Budgen that Ben Jonson was one of the only four writers that he had ever read completely through, seems to have had in common with Jonson some of the traits of his psychological type, and may be said to have followed his example – failing, sometimes, from faults like Jonson's – rather, perhaps, than to have exploited to better effect any special aspect of Jonson's work. Joyce, too, hoarded words and learning and attempted to impress his reader by unloading his accumulations; he, too, has his coprophilic side and his husbands who aquiesce, at the same time that they torture themselves, in the sleepings-abroad of their wives; he, too, is defiant and arrogant, self-consciously resistant to pressures, and holds himself apart and aloof.

It would be interesting, from this point of view, to compare Ben Jonson at length with Gogol as well as with Joyce. Undoubtedly Gogol is a case even more narrowly developed than Jonson of the type in question here. He, too, likes to store up words – his notebooks were full of the jargons of special trades and milieux; and he voids them in long dense sentences that agglutinate as massive paragraphs. His characters, in *Dead Souls*, are themselves almost always collectors, and they sometimes collect sheer rubbish – like Manilov, who saves all his old pipe-ashes. Gogol loves to write about eating, he has little sensual interest in women. His comedy *The Inspector General*, farcical, at once gross and inhuman, has something in common with Jonson's comedies; and, like Jonson, he is powerless to lift himself – in the unfinished later instalments of *Dead Souls* – out of the satirical comedy of roguery into a sterner and less turbid medium. The virtuous judge and the altruistic landowner of the second part of *Dead Souls* are as obviously maniacs as the misers and boors of the first part – as the senators, conspirators, and emperors of Jonson's Roman plays are just as much 'compulsive' one-track minds as the characters of his comedy of 'humours'. So Joyce, with greater genius and wider range than either Jonson or Gogol, cannot seem to function comfortably and freely except when he has given himself, as in his two most ambitious books, the latitude of a comic frame: his protagonists are comic figures, humiliated, persecuted, rueful, and their epics are systematic ironies, in which their heroic pretensions never wholly emerge from the mud. Gogol and Joyce, too, both share with Jonson his ideal of feminine sweetness and purity – seen only in wistful glimpses – that floats somewhere above and divorced from the smelly and dirty earth. With this motif Gogol succeeds least well: the lovely face fleetingly seen in the coach by Chichikov of *Dead Souls*, the maidenly pensionnaire who strikes him dumb at the ball; Jonson, a little better in the lyrics mentioned above; Joyce, with triumphant success in the vision of the wading girl that makes the climax of *A Portrait of the Artist*.

Later years did not mellow Jonson. When he visited Drummond at forty-five, with most of his best work behind him, he was still running down his contemporaries and asserting his own merits as peevishly as in the days when he had written *The Poetaster*; and at a supper given for him by his younger admirer the year before his death, he painfully embarrassed his friends by inordinately praising himself and vilifying his fellow poets. He could never afford to be generous, because he had never achieved what he wanted; and one suspects that, even in the case of such a lesser contemporary as Marston, Jonson's hateful hostility towards him had in it an element of envy of that touch of sublimity and magic which Marston was able to manage and which was quite beyond Jonson's reach. To Drummond he even grumbled about Shakespeare; and his reference to *The Tempest* in *Bartholomew Fair* betrays how much it must have irked him to see his friend, a much older man, find suddenly a new field for his genius in a form so close to that of the masque, in which Jonson had worked for years without ever striking more than an occasional spark from his pedantic made-to-order prettiness. It is therefore all the more a proof of the deep devotion he cherished for the art that they both practised that he should have put on record so roundly his high opinion of Shakespeare – and not only of Shakespeare, but also of Donne. In his elegy on Shakespeare especially, in estimating him above all their contemporaries and setting him beside the greatest of the ancients, he does justice to all that is noblest in his own aspiring nature, which had to drag so much dead weight, all that is soundest and most acute in his own cramped but virile intellect. The one thing he really loved was literature, and, having served it as well as he could, no touchiness of personal pride could keep him from honouring one who had been fitted to serve it better precisely by the qualification, among others, of possessing, as Jonson said, 'an open and free nature', so that he 'flowed with that facility that sometimes it was necessary he should be stopped'.

1948

'Mr Rolfe'

I

THE first days of my first fall at prep school were passed in complete confusion. We were always being shrieked at by bells, which uprooted us from what we were doing and compelled us to report somewhere else. We had to get there while the bell was still ringing, and I used to be swamped by the mob of boys pouring in and out of the classrooms and pushing along the corridors and porches, and finally arrive late in a panic.

One of the places in which I used to land was a room that was larger than the others and that had white classical busts above the blackboards and a dais for the master's desk. This was the room to which I went for Greek, and I realized at the first recitation that what occurred there was of a special nature. The master, who was tall and well-dressed and who loomed taller from sitting on the dais, had an aspect, an accent, and a manner unfamiliar to the point of seeming foreign. He was blond, with drooping-lidded blue eyes and a high-domed oval head, which was very inadequately thatched with strands of thin yellow hair, and he wore a yellow drooping moustache of the kind that was supposed then to be English and which reminded me of a character called Mr Batch who figured in the funny papers. His eyebrows were of the kind that arch away from one another like a pair of quotation marks and had the perpetually lifted look which conventionally indicates distress but also comports with irony, and his moustache concealed his mouth, so that his expression remained enigmatic, and you could never be sure whether he were smiling at you kindly or withering you with mock sweetness.

At any rate, as soon as he entered, he dominated the room

to the last row of seats. From the moment he sat down at his desk, rearing his neck and his back very straight and setting out his book before him with a kind of sober directness that was a part of his approach to his subject, he kept the class in a state of tension as if they were witnessing a performance in which – and all too often without knowing their lines – they themselves were to be called upon to take part.

The first characteristics of Mr Rolfe's which impressed a new boy in his class were the wittiness, pungency, and promptitude of his sarcasm and the mercilessness of his demands. He put you on the spot for your assignment as none of the other masters did; he would not allow you to slide over anything, and it seemed that he would not help you; if you failed, he made you feel by some caustic touch a criticism of your classroom personality. He evidently made tacit but definite assumptions about the classroom personalities of us all – I was supposed to be moony and inattentive which one might feel did one less than justice. He had a way of going around the class in pursuit of the answer to some question– designating us as 'First little gentleman . . . Second little gentleman', and so forth, and pointing at us with the butt of his pencil – which could put one at a distance and be paralysing. And there were also his special drawl, which could be musical and yet so mocking, and his queer but distinguished accent. I knew that he was not an Englishman, in spite of his British moustache and though he pronounced words like *bath* and *advanced* with what was called the 'broad *a*'. *Afterwards*, when it came at the end of a sentence, he pronounced *ahfterwúrds*, with the accent on the last syllable. It seemed impossible to appeal to him outside of class or to establish with him the personal relation by which boys seek to protect themselves from masters, and one got to be afraid of being snubbed. If anyone were rash enough to ask him whether Xenophon, which we were to start next term, or the verbs in -μι, which were looming as the next ordeal in the grammar, were as hard as they were rumoured to be, he would answer, glancing away: 'Oh, very difficult! almost impossible.'

I had been rather badly trained at my previous school, and I at once resented Mr Rolfe. I took to brooding outside of class over his sarcasms; and there were days when I was obsessed by his image and some brief derisive remark of which I had been the victim that morning. The Greek class both excited and scared me.

One night I went to see him in his rooms. He had invited us to come to him for help, and I had finally picked up courage to do so. He was engaged with someone else when I came in, and I shyly glanced about the room and then bent over the books on the table. The incident must have been one of those which sharply and suddenly mark the emergence of some new element into consciousness, because whenever I dream of going back to school and calling on Mr Rolfe, I never find him in his later rooms where I often went to see him, but always in these earlier ones where I could only have gone a few times and in which, when awake, I never place him. These rooms were the rooms of a bachelor but not those of a bachelor schoolmaster: in their relative elegance and luxury, they reminded me rather of the apartment inhabited by a bachelor uncle; and Mr Rolfe was sitting back on a couch and giving attention to the passages presented to him less like a master after class than like a gentleman receiving at his ease. In the bookrack, with their titles upturned, I saw volumes of Bernard Shaw, and this somewhat startled and shocked me. I had, at fourteen, not yet read Shaw; but I had heard he was a perverse cynic, who considered himself superior to other people and who liked to wound his reader's sensibilities.

Mr Rolfe, when my turn came to talk to him, answered my questions with his usual aloofness; and I went out of the room convinced that he was a disciple of Bernard Shaw, and that his brilliant performance in the classroom at the expense of us poor Fourth-Formers had something to do with the scandalous plays and the arrogant personality of which I had been hearing such disturbing accounts. I thought that I had conceived an antagonism, bitter and for ever intransigent, against Mr Rolfe and Shaw.

I began to like Greek, however, which I was only just beginning that year. The truth was that, in spite of his sarcasm, Mr Rolfe shed on everything he dealt with a peculiar imagination and charm, and that this held you even while you resented him. My feeling about Greek was becoming quite different from my feeling about Latin, which I had not been taught especially well and which seemed to me something technical like algebra, with almost no relation to literature or human speech. The Greek words as he pronounced them or wrote them on the board in his clear and beautiful hand took on an aesthetic value; and when you came to understand his attitude, the recitation turned into a kind of game, which, though taxing, had its rewards and its amusements.

I came to see that he was not really cruel. Though severe in his conception of his duty towards his students and of their duty towards their work, he was not really the sort of master who takes a joy in humiliating his class. He never failed to acknowledge good work, though he liked to express his approval in Greek; and he told me one day, in his drawl that always sounded ironic, that if I continued as I had been doing I might get to be his favourite pupil. I decided, thinking it over, that he had meant it; but this won me no indulgence or tenderness, and he would curtly correct my vagaries. It was characteristic of Mr Rolfe, who aimed to do so much more for his pupils than get them through their college examinations, that he should one day have explained to us in passing the theory of the lost *digamma*, which he described as 'a little thing like a tuning fork'; and it was characteristic of me, with my interest in literary *arcana*, that I should then have become fascinated by the letters that had been dropped out of the Greek alphabet. It was suggested

to me by Mr Rolfe that I should do better if I concentrated
on those they had retained.

And I came to understand that his rigour was really in
the interests of Greek. I have found out from later experience
that it requires a rare blend of qualities for a man or a woman
to teach Greek well: he must have a real taste for Greek
(which seems rarer than a taste for Latin), a real feeling for
its luminosity and subtlety, its nobility and *naïveté*, a lively
imaginative picture of the civilization behind it; and he must,
at the same time, be capable of insisting on the high degree of
intellectual discipline that is needed to keep the class up to
the effort demanded by the difficulties of the subject –
difficulties which do not consist merely of the more or less
automatic application of formulas one has learned, but
involve, along with accurate memory, a certain precision of
feeling, in which one can be trained by an adept but which
cannot be learned by rote. Mr Rolfe was the perfect Hel-
lenist. He made you get everything exactly right, and this
meant a good deal of drudgery. But one was also always
made to feel that there was something worth having there
behind the numbered paragraphs and paradigms of Goodwin's Greek grammar, the grim backs and fatiguing notes
of the Ginn texts 'for the use of schools' – something exhilarating in the air of the classroom, human, heroic, and
shining. The prospect of knowing this marvellous thing
lent the details excitement – and so it did the daily contest
between Mr Rolfe and you, which eventually became quite
jolly. You felt that he was not unkind, that he merely wanted
people to learn Greek, that teaching people Greek was an
exalted aim to which he had devoted his life, and that he
only became really unpleasant with students who did not
want to learn it.

I therefore began working hard to keep myself on the
right side of his severity. Besides the appetite I had acquired
for Greek, I was stimulated also by the fact that I had
grown to enjoy his wit. The truth was that I myself had a
satirical turn which I was just beginning then to learn to

exploit, and that I had never before met in the flesh a real past master of mockery. Hence my resentment, and hence my admiration. I was soon reading Bernard Shaw.

II

The Hill School in 1909 represented a combination of elements which must have made it unique among prep schools. It had been founded by the Reverend Matthew Meigs, a Presbyterian minister from Connecticut, who had settled in Pottstown, Pennsylvania, and started a small school in an old stone house on a hill. In my time it was run by John Meigs, his son, who had extraordinarily enlarged and improved it and made for it a great reputation.

John Meigs, whom we always called 'Professor', was not really, however, a schoolmaster. He had taken on his father's school and accepted it as a career with reluctance; but once he had done so, he had worked at it tremendously. He had no endowments and no wealthy patrons; and he had at first kept all the accounts, written out all the letters in longhand, and taught twenty-five hours a week as well as personally handled the discipline, the records, and the relations with parents. He had created a big school out of small beginnings – just as a boy from a Pennsylvania farm like Henry C. Frick had bought up coke-ovens and created an industry; and, in spite of his New England origins, I have always assimilated John Meigs to the Pennsylvania Dutch of that countryside of the extreme western corner of Montgomery County. A short, stocky man with a wide straight mouth and a square head that was made to seem even more cubelike by a nose flattened out like a boxer's – broken at football, I think – he resembled a successful manufacturer who had made himself something of a man of the world. He had gone to college at Lafayette instead of at Yale or Harvard; and the school had certain qualities of the back Pennsylvania of solid farmhouses and brick-streeted towns rather than of the Eastern seaboard, of Sewickley rather than Philadelphia. Professor had a certain smartness, but it was the smartness of a local man of substance, and not at all like the Episcopalian smartness that one sometimes found in the headmaster of the quite different New England schools. His hair, which was silver and parted in the middle, curled crisply at the corners of his forehead, and he liked to wear a bright red tie, and sometimes a flower in his button-hole, with a spotless white vest. As he would walk down from the platform after prayers, leading the rest of the school, stepping so firmly and yet jauntily, he was a figure that inspired confidence and in whom one could feel pride.

In the state he was a man of some consequence, quite active in local politics. He had, as one of the masters has told me since, no real interest in education whatever. But he did possess qualities which enabled him to organize a first-rate school. He had certainly a touch of the brutality characteristic of industrial Pennsylvania, but with it went the independence of the man who has built up his own busin-ess, and a downright and four-square directness in his deal-ings with students, parents, and faculty. The school was financially sound as I imagine few prep schools have been, and quite free from the tremors and depressions that reflect the inability to raise funds. Nor were there, as far as I was aware, any of those moral leaks which cause favouritism, ill-feeling, and inefficiency.

The efficiency of the Hill was perfect – as perfect as Bethlehem Steel. It was a legend at the time that no student who had been graduated from the Hill ever failed to get into college, because the drill we were given was so stiff and the tests we had to pass so difficult that entrance examina-tions became child's play; and it was true that we mostly landed in the top sections of the college courses. But this system had its disagreeable side. Every moment of our time was disposed of; our whole life was regulated by bells; and – till we reached the Sixth Form, at any rate – we had hardly an hour of leisure. The intention was beneficent, of course; but the remorseless paternalism of the Hill had something of the suffocating repressive effect of the Pennsylvania mill-town in which the company owns the workers' houses, controls their contacts with the outside world, and runs the banks, the schools, and the stores. Save for walks in the country and excursions into town, for both of which we had to get permission, we were confined to the Hill grounds, which rose like a segregated plateau in the midst of the little steel town – the narrow and cobbled streets where the greenery showed meagre in spring, the slag pits and the blast furnaces that startled new boys and kept them awake at night by blazes that would light up the whole room.

The same ideals in John Meigs, however, which had produced this iron regime, had secured for the Hill School some admirable things. He had spared no pains or expense to provide the best equipment obtainable: the staff as well as the plant were as good as they could possibly be. The buildings, the gymnasium, the tennis courts, the swimming pool, the showers, the ballfields somewhat offset the drabness of our surroundings. And the masters, to keep us up to scratch, had to be first-rate too. Yet, here, I believe, Professor must have been aiming at something beyond efficiency and may have displayed a certain creativeness, for he did get very able men who, though quite different from one another, evidently worked well together and felt a genuine interest in the school. In talking afterwards to boys from other schools, I never found the same enthusiasm for their masters that the Hill graduates had for theirs. Some of them, I came to realize, were quite above the usual prep-school level and would have adorned any university. Alfred Rolfe was one of these. It was characteristic of Meigs, with his ambition to have the best of everything, that he should have installed, to teach Greek, an accomplished New Englander in the best tradition.

For that was what Mr Rolfe was – a New Englander. And it was that about him that had seemed to me foreign.

He was moreover a special kind of New Englander: he came from Concord, Mass.; and this, as I afterwards observed, was quite distinct from being a Bostonian (and Mr Rolfe had gone to Amherst, not Harvard). He had that quality of homeliness and freshness that one finds in a Concordian like Thoreau, combined, as it was in Thoreau, with a sharp mind and a fine sensibility. The Yankee accent and rustic expressions with which he sometimes roughened his speech were a feature he knew how to make use of to set off his natural elegance, just as his very large feet and hands were somehow made to play a part in the grace with which he went about his business, and as the touches of gruffness and brusqueness that had the sea captains of New England behind them gave his urbanity a greater authority. All this side of him, in fact, was the rocklike base on which the flowers of Hellenism flourished: the sophistication of his comic sense, his exquisite literary taste, and the benignant incandescence of his mind. Alfred Rolfe has been my only personal contact with the Concord of the great period, and I feel that if I had not known him, I should never really have known what it was, and what a high civilization it represented. For there was nothing about Mr Rolfe either of the schoolmaster or of the provincial. He had in his early years studied in Germany, but he cared little for travel or cities, and now spent every school year in Pottstown and every summer in Concord; yet he seemed to enjoy, just as Emerson did, the freedom of the great social world as well as of the great world of literature. His brother, Henry Winchester Rolfe, was also a classical scholar. I later read a book of his on Petrarch and discovered that my friend Rolfe Humphries, the Latinist and poet, had been named after him.

The manners that we tended to learn at the Hill were a little on the heavy and flat side; and Mr Rolfe, for all his dignity, moved among us with a charming ease and what can only be called a kind of blitheness. He was tall but not very well built: besides large feet and hands, he had shoulders that were narrow and sloping. He stooped and thrust forward his head as he walked; and in the skirted black frock-coat and striped trousers which were *de rigueur* for Sunday chapel, he would look like some long-legged great auk as he stalked back to his rooms after service. Yet he was one of the real ornaments of the school, perhaps its principal ornament.

He was an admirable after-dinner speaker and always in demand for banquets. He cultivated the dry, solemn, drawling manner which Mark Twain had made the fashion but which became very New England in his hands. His face, when he was not in conversation, tended to lapse into a Saint Bernard sadness, and he liked to exploit this for comic effect. He was wonderful at 'morning exercises', where the reading of profane literature had been substituted for passages from the Bible. His fine voice, deep, resonant, and rich, was not the voice of a school elocutionist who likes to play-act for his students, but always remained personal and in some special way colloquial: what it was rich in were nuances of humour and perceptions of the values of style. And the rhythms of poetry to Mr Rolfe seemed something natural and dear; it was as if they represented a dreaminess which, for all his Yankee common sense, was a part of his everyday life and did not require a condition of trance. The first time that you heard him read aloud a passage of Homer in class, you knew what Homer was as poetry, and no amount of construing and syntactical analysis could blur the effect of that rhythm. We used also to read Browning's plays with him, for fun, between chapel and midday dinner on Sunday, and he would easily disentangle the speeches of such things as *A Blot on the 'Scutcheon* and get out of them their own kind of music. Sometimes at morning exercises he would read from the New England writers, and he would give them a kind of distinction which I had not known was there. In those days we had been brought up on the New Englanders, and by the time we came to read for ourselves we had decided they were childish and a bore. But Mr Rolfe could put, say, Oliver Wendell Holmes, whom I did not at that time think amusing, in an attractively different light. When he did scenes from *The Autocrat of the Breakfast-Table*, he really made you hear the people in that ideal Boston boarding-house: you felt that he had boarded there himself, and that the quality of the talk in its way had been good. His rendering of *The Wonderful One-Hoss Shay* was one of his most brilliant performances. When the deacon swore as deacons do with an 'I dew vum' or an 'I tell *yeou*', the voice of the old man would come through with a sudden dramatic realism that startled us and made us laugh.

He had certainly the sense of audience. When, in the absence of Professor and Mrs Meigs, he would preside at our meals in the big dining-room, one felt his presence even here as one did during a recitation. While he would be waiting for the boys to assemble, he would stand up with folded arms, joking with the Sixth-Formers beside him; then he would press the buzzer and say the brief grace – 'Bless, O Father, thy gifts to our use and us to thy service: for Christ's sake. Amen' – in which, many times though I heard it, the words never seemed merely a rite, but something said and felt. At the end of the meal, when it would sometimes happen that a general silence fell as we waited for the buzzer to release us, he would mutter some amusing remark which would be caught by the whole room and bring a laugh; if the buzzer stuck, as it sometimes did, he would make it a whole little comedy and would send us out quite lighthearted from the then rather close and crowded dining-room and its Pennsylvania Dutch food.

There was a moment, I remember, when Mr Rolfe had read something that impressed him about the importance of pulling in one's stomach in order to carry oneself correctly and when he would preach this to us half-humorously as he attempted to practise it himself. As I watched him one day in the dining-room, throwing back his shoulders and drawing in his chin, which was round and rather recessive, I thought of his luxurious lounging on his comfortable couch and armchair. And there was also his gesture which was so much of a betrayal of his effortful and Spartan pose: a wandering of his hand to his necktie and breast, as a woman fingers a necklace, which came from the something poetic – the something almost romantic – in him. I remembered how he had warned us once in class that it was impossible to study properly when sunk in an easy chair; and I realized that in Mr Rolfe a certain strain of the sybarite coexisted with rectitude and discipline. I recognized it thus very early because I was unmistakably myself on the sybaritic side. I incurably disliked athletics, carried myself very badly, and loved to read in bed. And at this moment I became aware, though I did not formulate the perception, that what made Mr Rolfe interesting and gave him a sort of rarity was his having reached just that point when a tough and well-tried stock first gets the freedom to smile and to play, to work at belles-lettres for their own sake.

At some point in our early stages of Greek Mr Rolfe had handed us over for a term or two to his assistant; and by the time I got back to him again, I was no longer so much afraid of him. The Greek class still imposed a certain tension, but it stimulated for those students who had literary tastes a genuine interest in Greek. Mr Rolfe worked us awfully hard, harder than any other master, but we did feel that we were getting Homer and not just boning assignments. We had to scan every line and understand every form, and we had to translate every word into an English not unworthy of the original. It was as serious to give clumsy equivalents as to miss out on a case or a mood, and would bring down on us his tartest derision. He accepted as a standard for the proper tone of a successful Homeric translation the passage by Dr Hawtrey cited by Matthew Arnold in his essay on translating Homer: 'Clearly the rest I behold of the dark-eyed sons of Achaia' – and made us commit it to memory.

With all his exacting demands, he had many entertaining devices for relieving the dryness of our drudgery. We were encouraged to think of ὀδύρομαι as 'oh, dear! oh, my!'; we were taught that when γάρ begins a sentence it is always pronounced 'yar', on the principle on which children are told that a guinea pig's eyes will fall out if you hold it up by its tail; and we were made to learn the speeches of the trial of Orontas in Xenophon and act it out in class. At the end, when Orontas was led into the tent and put to death in a mysterious manner, the boy who played him was taken out into the hall and grisly sounds were heard. Mr Rolfe shied so naturally away from the tone of the textbook and the classroom that it was difficult for him to remember the wording of the rules as they were given in the book. There is a principle of Homeric versification which was formulated by Goodwin somewhat as follows: 'The penthemimeral caesura gives the line an anapaestic movement, from which it is often recalled by the bucolic diaeresis.' We would be called upon to demonstrate this by rapping it out on our seat-arms with pencils; but Mr Rolfe, when he cited the rule, would resist the language of the grammar, by stumbling over the second part and turning the 'from which it is often recalled' into 'from which it is frequently rescued'. The whole thing got thus a faint comic flavour; and this little involuntary touch has always remained in my mind as an example of his putting in its place of the academic side of his subject.

The impulse to parody was strong in him, though he usually indulged it quite casually. When Tennyson's *Enoch Arden* was read once at morning exercises, he suggested that the end of the poem really needed another line:

> So pass'd the strong heroic soul away.
> And when they buried him the little port
> Had seldom seen a costlier funeral;
> *And Annie wore her best black bombazine.*

I was thus tremendously flattered when he complimented me on a parody of Browning which I had published in the school magazine. And later, when another Hill boy and I had invented, as freshmen at college, an imaginary figure of speech, I was surprised at the amusement it seemed to afford him when we told him about it on a visit. 'Thypsis... thypsis,' he murmured to himself at some later moment of the conversation.

In my last year of school, when I lived above him, I used to go and read in his rooms. It was one of the paradoxes of the Hill, which excelled in literary activity, that Professor, in installing his extraordinary equipment, should almost completely have neglected the library. He must have conceived of books as something to be fed us in calculated doses by the masters in the different departments. He could never have had any interest in making literature generally available, for the two or three small rooms called the library contained almost nothing up to date, and they were full of ancient textbooks and works of reference that had belonged to the Reverend Matthew Meigs and went back to the eighteenth and seventeenth centuries. There were not even good editions of the classics, and I almost put my eyes out my first year at school on a copy of *Vanity Fair* in double columns of microscopic type. (This deficiency was long ago remedied: the library, I am told, is now first-rate.) But at least half a dozen of the masters had considerable private libraries, which they encouraged us to use. And Mr Rolfe's was among the most interesting, as it was certainly much the handsomest. He went in for well-bound sets, and he kept up with contemporary literature as no other of the masters did. The new volumes of Chesterton and Shaw always appeared on his table, and I sat on his couch and read them. Sometimes he would come in, greet me briefly, put on his pince-nez, sit down in his large armchair, and silently correct his papers.

I was still shy with him: for all his humour he was one of the most remote of the masters. With his conviction of intellectual superiority and a sensitive personal pride, there was one thing that was quite impossible for him – a capacity that makes life easier for schoolmasters: he could not be a good fellow with the boys, he could not meet them on their own level. The masters who lived in the Sixth Form Flat took turns keeping order in the halls, and most of them could do it quite amiably; but it went against the grain with Mr Rolfe. When one of our bedtime roughhouses became too long and too loud, he would suddenly appear in his bathrobe like the Statue in *Don Giovanni* and freeze us to the marrow. A few cutting words would silence us and send us rather sulky to bed. His rebuke had been so evidently hostile that it made us feel hostile, too. But I who admired him so much was embarrassed by what I felt was the indecency of his having to do this kind of thing at all. I felt that he hated our seeing him in his bathrobe, that he ought never to be seen in a bathrobe; and I pictured him lying in bed, as I so loved to do at home, enjoying some book from the well-stocked bookcase which I had seen through the doorway beside his bed without being able to make out the contents. How he must have loathed and resented being distracted by our scuttlings and shrieks, and obliged to climb two flights of stairs and pit himself against ribald and breathless boys. He liked to live in his rooms like a man at his club.

One day I had a glimpse, my only glimpse, of Mr Rolfe's pre-school personality. It turned out that some cousins of mine had known him at the end of the eighties when he was studying Greek in Dresden. They had stayed at the same pension with him, and they said that he had been wonderful in those days – so charming and so funny. My mother and aunt came up one week-end, and he produced an old photograph of a group in which he and my cousins figured. They had been playing charades in the pension and had had themselves taken in their costumes. He had said sadly of my pretty dark cousin Bessie, my mother afterwards told me – for I had not been present at the conversation: 'So poor Bessie is dead!' I wondered whether he had ever been in love. He was now such a complete old bachelor that this was almost impossible to imagine. I remembered that when he was clowning in his after-dinner speeches he sometimes made fun of his homeliness.

IV

Against one element of life at the Hill School Mr Rolfe, by his very tone and presence, provided a constant correction. The Hill had an evangelical side which it required some stubbornness to stand up to. This was mainly, I have always understood, due to the influence of Mrs Meigs – always known as Mrs John – a very earnest and capable woman related to the theological Dwights of New Haven. The school had passed through a series of disasters – three fires as well as a typhoid epidemic in which a hundred students and masters had been ill; and it may be that this had had the effect of stimulating in the Meigses a desperate faith in and dependence on God. But what I was aware of at the time when I was in school was simply that we were worked on systematically by a rotation of visiting evangelists. We had to go not only to chapel, but also – under irresistible pressure – to the meeting of a school Y.M.C.A.; and we were always being called together to listen to special exhortations.

At the bottom of the scale of our speakers was the reformed debauchee and bad egg who testified to the miracle of his salvation. He always had what the stage calls a 'straight man' with him, who gave him his cue and showed him off, with an attitude that fell between that of a man with a trained ape and the 'feeder' of a team of comics. These bums who had been saved used to seem to me still very unpleasant people, who had, before seeing the light, evidently reached such a state of corruption that their new respectability looked precarious, and one listened rather apprehensively to their boasts about their present state of grace as if one feared they might go to pieces as soon as the performance was over.

277

Then there was a man who had made a speciality of preaching to boys' schools and colleges and whose line was a lachrymose and mealy-mouthed virility. He used to read us Kipling in a way that did much to disgust me with that writer, and announce that he would be accessible in a certain room the next morning and would be glad to discuss with any boy any kind of problem whatever. An imitation of 'Weeping Bob's' speeches has long been current among old Hill men and is one of the things that bind them together. 'Moys,' he used to say in his deep adhesive voice, 'I want to speak to you first of all about the use of foul and filthy language. Moys: they have a nog up in Alaska that they call the mlue-mlack nog. He is known as the mlue-mlack nog because the insine of his mouth is mlue-mlack. And I want to say to any moy who has the impulse to innulge in foul language that, if he gives way to this impulse and hamitually uses oaths and innecent expressions, the insine of his mouth – spir-it-u-ally speaking – *will mecome mlue-mlack like the mouth of the mlue-mlack nog!*'

A more sophisticated level was represented by a liberal preacher from New York. He was well-dressed in a secular way, and dynamic, free-spoken, and pear-shaped. His line was to shock and be witty, to be modern in the interests of the evangelist's God. He was also of course social-minded, and I remember a characteristic touch by which he hoped to make us feel, and to convince himself that he felt, a warm sympathy for the labouring classes: 'Coming up on the train today, I sat opposite an Italian workman. He was dressed in his work-clothes; he had been sweating; but there was nothing dirty about him except the grime of his work. I caught his breath and it smelled of garlic, but it was a good breath; it was wholesome, not foul.' And then of course there were the two-fisted missionaries who shook us down for funds to Christianize and modernize China.

At the centre of all this activity stood a kind of special Hill School myth of sin and regeneration. The legend that was handed on from one class at the Hill to another had it that

Professor in his college days had been a very fast young fellow, who was known as 'Cigarette Jack', and that Mrs John had snatched him as what used to be called a brand from the burning and had made him into the man we knew. This may very well not have been accurate, but it was what we had come to believe: it was like the miraculous conversion from which a cult or an order dates. It was the archetype of the spiritual drama which we seemed to be expected to enact. The hero of this sacred drama was an able and promising boy, well-fitted to be a leader of men, who at college succumbed to temptation: he gambled, he smoked, he drank; he went with a class of women who were not so much bad as misguided. But he was caught on the edge of the abyss and saved for the life of service. I am afraid that there was a little the impression created that you had to have taken the dip towards perdition or you could not make the plane of the élite. The Sixth Form was searched, as it were, every spring for candidates for this sacrificial role. Mrs John saw every member separately and probed into the state of his soul in a solemn heart-to-heart talk that usually took place in a room on the top floor of the Meigses' house, which was significantly called 'the Sky Parlour'. I have heard the most gruelling accounts of the scenes that sometimes occurred at these interviews; but I myself was not a good prospect, and when it came my turn to go, I found that Mrs John had forgotten the appointment. She was writing at her desk and was surprised to see me; but she made me sit down and told me gently that the literary type of boy had his temptations, too – the temptation, for example, to become so much absorbed in his intellectual interests that he neglected his relation to his fellows, and she prayed with me a moment and let me go. I walked back to my room relieved and yet feeling a little let down that I had not been considered susceptible to the more exciting kind of temptation.

There was a terrible taboo on sex, which was turned into something frightening. Though I was used, before I came to the Hill, to the adolescent folk-lore and gossip of boys of my own age, my speech and my mind had become so purged by the end of my school career that I was shocked when I heard, after leaving, that Mr Rolfe had once told the story of the man who had started in church when the Seventh Commandment was read and muttered, 'Oh, now I know where I left my umbrella!'

It was true that the boys from Hill had the reputation of slipping at college, and Mrs John was attempting to fortify them, but her influence worked, also, the other way. If a boy were not naturally serious-minded (as, I must say, a good many were – in which case they had a decided advantage over boys from most other schools), he might forget about the life of service when the restraints of Hill had been removed; but the pattern of the school myth might have been stamped on his mind so strongly that he would be plunged into despair or disorder by the first drinking party or pick-up. (This is no longer true today: the evangelism has disappeared and the paternalism been very much modified.)

I do not know what Mr Rolfe thought of all this side of Hill; I do not know even what his religious beliefs were. He might have been a liberal Congregationalist or a conventional Episcopalian. He never talked about religion, and when he presided at chapel, he read the Bible in such a way as to make it seem noble and beautiful just as he did Homer. I particularly remember his giving us the last chapter of *Ecclesiastes*, which did not interest our moralistic evangelists. When he prayed, it was never for salvation, but simply for moral stimulus to enable us to deal with our work or get along with our fellows.

v

My own Presbyterian religious training had involved a certain amount of churchgoing and had more or less familiarized me with the Bible, but I had never known what it was to feel faith as something vital; and from the moment I had begun to think about such things for myself, my reactions towards religion had been negative. Under the constant stimulation of the Hill School, however, I tried hard to keep God in my cosmos. I was unable to accept as real for myself – that is, as having serious claims on me – anything that I could not recognize as a part of my own experience, so I had to try to translate my moments of exalted or expansive feeling into terms of the religious illumination about which I was constantly hearing – just as I imagine the eighteenth-century Deists, who had drawn all the rationalistic conclusions, attempted still to provide a Deity who would be somehow the fountainhead of reason. But the fact irreducibly remained that I didn't have the revelatory experience, that I didn't even want it; that my attitude towards our repertoire of dervishes seemed inevitably to become more humorous, and that what had at first been a certain awed respect for this side of the activity of Hill began to give way to the conviction that it was all in awful taste.

One day in my Sixth Form year, when I was coming back to school on the train, I did at last have a sort of revelation, which was, however, as it were, in reverse. I always had to change in Philadelphia, and, as I usually had to wait for my train, I had got into the habit of killing time in Wanamaker's book department. There I bought one by one all the volumes of Bernard Shaw and even, when there were no more to buy – at the moment I graduated – Archibald Henderson's enormous biography. But I had not yet got to this, and on the occasion of which I speak was reading *Major Barbara*. At the end of the preface about money and religion, I came to the following words: 'At present there is not a single credible established religion in the world.' For a moment I was jolted a little; but I looked out the window at the landscape, rather muddy and sordid with winter, and had to recognize that this was true, that I knew perfectly well it was true, and that I ought to have admitted it before; and the flickering childish faith to which I had been giving artificial respiration expired then and there. I have never thought of religion since save as a delusion entertained by other people which one has to try to allow for and understand. On the train another Hill boy had sat down beside me, and I had reluctantly suspended my reading to have a little conversation with him. He was the simple and candid type. He was built stoutly and went in for football and took the Y.M.C.A. seriously. I derived an ironic pleasure from the reflection that, whereas for him our ridiculous prep-school revivalism would still have the power to plunge him into struggles, earnest labours, sleepless nights, my faith had passed quietly out on the stretch between Norristown and Phoenixville, between two passages of banal conversation in which I had descended affably to the level of my companion. I felt as I had never felt before that such people as he were barbarians.

Professor Meigs had died that autumn – the ordeal of the typhoid epidemic was thought to have weakened his heart; and Mr Rolfe took over as headmaster. The alumni gave a chapel as memorial, and we were using it by the spring of our commencement. We were to have for our last Sunday service of the year a very famous New York preacher whom we had never heard before. It was as if he were the climax and crown of our whole circus procession of evangelists. But this high point of the theological hierarchy marked for me the nadir of faith. I had heard a great deal about this man. He had long been a public figure. He had been associated with Henry Ward Beecher, and later with Theodore Roosevelt. He was one of those preachers of the turn of the century who had been trying to bring the Christianity of the churches into contact with industrial and social problems; he had published several books on the subject, and even, late in life, turned journalist. I had therefore, I think, been prepared for something a little more stimulating than the figure that appeared in the chapel. He was, to be sure, seventy-seven, but he looked even older – he was the oldest-looking person I had ever seen. He had a beard that was long and stringy and that grew out all around his face. It was the kind of undisciplined beard that we associate with Hebrew prophets, but this old man had none of the fire of the prophet. His eyes under their straggling eyebrows had a greyness almost of blindness, and even his skin was grey. His rather long bottle-ended nose had pores so enormous that you could see them plainly as he passed by the pews up the aisle, supported on either side by one of the adoring Meigs ladies and looking as limp in his long black robe as a Punch-and-Judy puppet from which the showman's hand has been removed. I remembered the scene years later when I saw the Diaghilev ballet do Stravinsky's *L'Oiseau de feu*: the figure of Kashchey the Deathless, the enchanter of the Russian fairy-tales, in his flimsy and hirsute senility, reeling back and forth across the stage as the egg that contains his life is tossed from hand to hand, and finally, when it cracks, collapsing into the arms of his faithful attendants while the captives stream out of his castle – this vision has blended in my memory with the image of that Sunday morning service.

It may be that the religious basis of the school had already been somewhat weakened by the breakdown and death of Professor and by the conduct of public ceremonies by the moderate Mr Rolfe, whose authority was mainly cultural; it may be that this spokesman of the Church at grips with social problems would have seemed a little less deliquescent if Professor had been there behind him. But the whole thing made an unpleasant impression.

The sermon itself was feeble. The subject was immortality – another link with the imperishable Kashchey, who eventually went to pieces; and this old man, who had prided himself on his modernism, announced in a quavering voice that, though we boys, with our lives still before us, might not at this time be disposed to give much serious thought to the life after death, this would come, when we got to be old, to seem 've-ery impo-ortant indeed'. This finished immortality for me – since, if your reason, I told myself, had convinced you in your years of vigour that there existed not a shred of evidence for the survival of the human soul, it was an act of weak-mindedness and cowardice to give in to this primitive myth when you had got to the end of your rope and were about to be extinguished yourself.

I argued the question with a friend of mine, a boy of much intellectual ability, who was related to Mrs Meigs and whose principles were quite in the tradition of the theology of the Dwights. Some time after our argument, he suddenly renewed it: 'Of course you know', he said, 'that even if there were no immortality, it would be fatal for the human race to take the belief in it away from people.' I had not yet heard the famous saying about how much difference it makes whether you put truth in the first or the second place; but I knew then, as I left school for college, that the code I was evolving for myself could never have much in common with the official morality of Hill.

VI

Mr Rolfe ran the school for a time, though I imagine he much preferred teaching. I continued to see him occasionally, and I found that my admiration for him held up as few schoolboy admirations do. I used at first to send him books at Christmas, and when he wrote to thank me for them, he never made the polite pretence of having enjoyed them beyond their merits. He acknowledged Compton Mackenzie's *Youth's Encounter*, about which I had written him a hyperbolic letter, with what I thought was the pointed suggestion that '$\mu\eta\delta\grave{\epsilon}\nu$ $\ddot{\alpha}\gamma\alpha\nu$ is a good motto'. I imagine that my own writings after I got out of college were not of a kind that he particularly approved. When I saw him, he used to kid me in a way that I thought rather old fogyish about the then excellent liberal weekly on which I had a job in the twenties.

The *bête noire* of his later years was progressive education. He used to compose little poems on the subject and was very amusing about it. I had a sort of idea at first that I ought to be on the other side, since my magazine supported John Dewey, but the more I read of Mr Rolfe's satire, which reached me through the Hill School alumni bulletin, the more I felt that there was something to be said for his position. Wasn't it true that, in order to train children to do anything really well, you had to break them to an exacting discipline as he had done with us in Greek? Without that you couldn't do anything with Greek – you couldn't do anything with anything. How great were the chances that a schoolboy could be counted on to choose what he needed? – my father had made me take Greek, I was too young to know anything about it – or to acquire this discipline through natural bent? Mr Rolfe may to some extent, of course, have understood and misrepresented what was proposed for progressive education; but when I came later on to see something of the teaching both in progressive institutions and in the ordinary kind, I was appalled by the slackness of the training. Where would our American railroads and ships and buildings and bridges and bathrooms be if the techniques of engineering were taught as the arts and humanities are – so that students are graduated from college, and not merely from progressive colleges, and even take M.A. degrees, without having any idea of the top human achievements in their fields, without, often, being able to express themselves in decent English?

It did not really help to point out that much of our old-fashioned teaching was uninspired. As far as inspiration went, Mr Rolfe could not teach us an irregular declension without lending its cadences poetry; and one felt that it was doubtful whether progressive education would increase the number of inspired teachers. On the other hand, it probably did tend to make people trust unduly to vague ideas and currents of feeling, to the Rousseauist supposed natural instinct to do well if left to oneself. This trust in the impulses of humanity is perhaps only a transference from the heavens to our hearts of the old idea of Providence; and whatever kind of God Mr Rolfe believed in, this God, like that of A. E. Housman, had not arranged the world so that anything could be accomplished without somebody in particular doing it and doing it with conscious effort. *You* had to find out about Homer by digging in the Greek lexicon and grammar: you couldn't find out about it by reading an outline of literature written by somebody else; and *he* had to teach you Greek: Greek wouldn't teach itself. He did not depend for this purpose on the natural rectitude of our inclinations – either his own or ours – any more than he did on the evangelistic Christ who was supposed to come to your rescue and give you a bracer of salvation, as the victims of dementia praecox are supposed to be roused to normality by the jolt of a shot of insulin.

Mr Rolfe of course thus represented both the American individualistic tradition which has cultivated the readiness to think and act for oneself without looking to God or the State as something outside oneself, and the older humanistic tradition: the belief in the nobility and beauty of what man as man has accomplished, and the reverence for literature as the record of this. I had been exposed at the Hill to this humanistic spirit at the same time as to the inspirational religion which has always remained linked in my mind with the industrial background of Pottstown; and the humanism had continued to serve me when the religion had come to seem false. The thing that glowed for me through Xenophon and Homer in those classrooms of thirty years ago has glowed for me ever since.

And at the Hill Mr Rolfe himself long survived the fading-out of that evangelism. There was a time when I tended to think of him as drying up and growing crabbed at school; but I ran into him one day at Columbia, where he was supervising examinations, and was struck by his kindliness and the attractiveness of his face, which seemed to have grown terribly sad. In the crowd of assembled teachers from a variety of schools and colleges, he still stood out as a distinguished figure who did not seem to belong to that company. An old Hill friend has written me recently of seeing him a few years ago: 'I sat next to him at luncheon. He was then eighty years old and told me that the doctors had said he was in perfect health except for low blood pressure. I told him to drink burgundy or bourbon, and he said that I seemed to speak with authority and experience. He said grace, and when I told him it was a *new* grace, he said he'd be glad to sound the buzzer again and deliver the old grace for dessert.' I wrote to Mr Rolfe when I heard that he was retiring from Hill. In answering, he explained that he still expected to take a few classes, 'but I shall have plenty of time to write, if I can think of anything to write about . . . I am sorry about Greek,' he said. 'I used to think it would last my day, but it hasn't quite done so'; and he wished me good luck in Greek.

He died last June in Concord, and it is hard to imagine him gone: I had thought of him as a permanent element, a kind of human classic, who persisted through the changes at the Hill and the wars and revolutions of the world. After all, there had always been Mr Rolfe; and suddenly, as I write this memoir, it seems to me that the stream he was following flowed out of a past that is now remote: from Emerson with his self-dependence, and *The Wonderful One-Hoss Shay* with its satire on the too-perfect Calvinist system; from the days when people went to Germany to hear Wagner and study Greek; from Matthew Arnold, from Bernard Shaw – now almost an old-fashioned classic like Arnold. And I am glad to renew my sense of Alfred Rolfe's contribution to it, as I realize that I myself have been trying to follow and feed it at a time when it has been running low. Its tradition antedates our Christian religion and has in many men's minds survived it, as one may hope it will, also, the political creeds, with their secular evangelism, that are taking the Church's place.

1942

The Historical Interpretation
of Literature*

I WANT to talk about the historical interpretation of literature – that is, about the interpretation of literature in its
social, economic, and political aspects.

To begin with, it will be worth while to say something
about the kind of criticism which seems to be furthest removed from this. There is a kind of comparative criticism
which tends to be non-historical. The essays of T. S. Eliot,
which have had such an immense influence in our time,
are, for example, fundamentally non-historical. Eliot sees,
or tries to see, the whole of literature, so far as he is ac-
quainted with it, spread out before him under the aspect of
eternity. He then compares the work of different periods
and countries, and tries to draw from it general conclusions
about what literature ought to be. He understands, of course,
that our point of view in connexion with literature changes,
and he has what seems to me a very sound conception of the
whole body of writing of the past as something to which new
works are continually being added, and which is not thereby
merely increased in bulk but modified as a whole – so that
Sophocles is no longer precisely what he was for Aristotle,
or Shakespeare what he was for Ben Jonson or for Dryden
or for Dr Johnson, on account of all the later literature that
has intervened between them and us. Yet at every point of
this continual accretion, the whole field may be surveyed, as
it were, spread out before the critic. The critic tries to see it as
God might; he calls the books to a Day of Judgement. And,
looking at things in this way, he may arrive at interesting
and valuable conclusions which could hardly be reached by
approaching them in any other way. Eliot was able to see,

* A lecture delivered at Princeton University, 23 October 1940.

for example – what I believe had never been noticed before – that the French Symbolist poetry of the nineteenth century had certain fundamental resemblances to the English poetry of the age of Donne. Another kind of critic would draw certain historical conclusions from these purely aesthetic findings, as the Russian D. S. Mirsky did; but Eliot does not draw them.

Another example of this kind of non-historical criticism, in a somewhat different way and on a somewhat different plane, is the work of the late George Saintsbury. Saintsbury was a connoisseur of wines; he wrote an entertaining book on the subject. And his attitude towards literature, too, was that of the connoisseur. He tastes the authors and tells you about the vintages; he distinguishes the qualities of the various wines. His palate was as fine as could be, and he possessed the great qualification that he knew how to take each book on its own terms without expecting it to be some other book and was thus in a position to appreciate a great variety of kinds of writing. He was a man of strong social prejudices and peculiarly intransigent political views, but, so far as it is humanly possible, he kept them out of his literary criticism. The result is one of the most agreeable and most comprehensive commentaries on literature that have ever been written in English. Most scholars who have read as much as Saintsbury do not have Saintsbury's discriminating taste. Here is a critic who has covered the whole ground like any academic historian, yet whose account of it is not merely a chronology but a record of fastidious enjoyment. Since enjoyment is the only thing he is looking for, he does not need to know the causes of things, and the historical background of literature does not interest him very much.

There is, however, another tradition of criticism which dates from the beginning of the eighteenth century. In the year 1725, the Neapolitan philosopher Vico published *La Scienza Nuova*, a revolutionary work on the philosophy of history, in which he asserted for the first time that the social world was certainly the work of man, and attempted what is, so far as I know, the first social interpretation of a work of literature. This is what Vico says about Homer: 'Homer composed the *Iliad* when Greece was young and consequently burning with sublime passions such as pride, anger, and vengeance – passions which cannot allow dissimulation and which consort with generosity; so that she then admired Achilles, the hero of force. But, grown old, he composed the *Odyssey*, at a time when the passions of Greece were already somewhat cooled by reflection, which is the mother of prudence – so that she now admired Ulysses, the hero of wisdom. Thus also, in Homer's youth, the Greek people liked cruelty, vituperation, savagery, fierceness, ferocity; whereas, when Homer was old, they were already enjoying the luxuries of Alcinoüs, the delights of Calypso, the pleasures of Circe, the songs of the sirens, and the pastimes of the suitors, who went no further in aggression and combat than laying siege to the chaste Penelope – all of which practices would appear incompatible with the spirit of the earlier time. The divine Plato is so struck by this difficulty that, in order to solve it, he tells us that Homer had foreseen in inspired vision these dissolute, sickly, and disgusting customs. But in this way he makes Homer out to have been but a foolish instructor for Greek civilization, since, however much he may condemn them, he is displaying for imitation these corrupt and decadent habits which were not to be adopted till long after the foundation of the nations of Greece, and accelerating the natural course which human events would take by spurring the Greeks on to corruption. Thus it is plain that the Homer of the *Iliad* must have preceded by many years the Homer who wrote the *Odyssey*; and it is plain that the former must belong to the north-eastern part of Greece, since he celebrates the Trojan War, which took place in his part of the country, whereas the latter belongs to the south-eastern part, since he celebrates Ulysses, who reigned there.'

You see that Vico has here explained Homer in terms

both of historical period and geographical origin. The idea that human arts and institutions were to be studied and elucidated as the products of the geographical and climatic conditions in which the people who created them lived, and of the phase of their social development through which they were passing at the moment, made great progress during the eighteenth century. There are traces of it even in Dr Johnson, that most orthodox and classical of critics – as, for example, when he accounts for certain characteristics of Shakespeare by the relative barbarity of the age in which he lived, pointing out, just as Vico had done, that 'nations, like individuals, have their infancy'. And by the eighties of the eighteenth century Herder, in his *Ideas on the Philosophy of History*, was writing of poetry that it was a kind of 'Proteus among the people, which is always changing its form in response to the languages, manners, and habits, to the temperaments and climates, nay even to the accents of different nations.' He said – what could still seem startling even so late as that – that 'language was not a divine communication, but something men had produced themselves'. In the lectures on the philosophy of history that Hegel delivered in Berlin in 1822–3 he discussed the national literatures as expressions of the societies which had produced them – societies which he conceived as great organisms continually transforming themselves under the influence of a succession of dominant ideas.

In the field of literary criticism, this historical point of view came to its first complete flower in the work of the French critic Taine, in the middle of the nineteenth century. The whole school of historian-critics to which Taine belonged – Michelet, Renan, Sainte-Beuve – had been occupied in interpreting books in terms of their historical origins. But Taine was the first of these to attempt to apply such principles systematically and on a large scale in a work devoted exclusively to literature. In the Introduction to his *History of English Literature*, published in 1863, he made his famous pronouncement that works of literature were to be understood as the upshot of three interfusing factors: *the moment, the race, and the milieu.* Taine thought he was a scientist and a mechanist, who was examining works of literature from the same point of view as the chemist's in experimenting with chemical compounds. But the difference between the critic and the chemist is that the critic cannot first combine his elements and then watch to see what they will do: he can only examine phenomena which have already taken place. The procedure that Taine actually follows is to pretend to set the stage for the experiment by describing the moment, the race, and the milieu, and then to say: 'Such a situation demands such and such a kind of writer.' He now goes on to describe the kind of writer that the situation demands, and the reader finds himself at the end confronted with Shakespeare or Milton or Byron or whoever the great figure is – who turns out to prove the accuracy of Taine's prognosis by precisely living up to this description.

There was thus a certain element of imposture in Taine; but it was the rabbits he pulled out that saved him. If he had really been the mechanist that he thought he was, his work on literature would have had little value. The truth was that Taine loved literature for its own sake – he was at his best himself a brilliant artist – and he had very strong moral convictions which give his writing emotional power. His mind, to be sure, was an analytic one, and his analysis, though terribly oversimplified, does have an explanatory value. Yet his work was what we call creative. Whatever he may say about chemical experiments, it is evident when he writes of a great writer that the moment, the race, and the milieu have combined, like the three sounds of the chord in Browning's poem about Abt Vogler, to produce not a fourth sound but a star.

To Taine's set of elements was added, dating from the middle of the century, a new element, the economic, which was introduced into the discussion of historical phenomena mainly by Marx and Engels. The non-Marxist critics themselves were at the time already taking into account the influence of the social classes. In his chapters on the Norman conquest of England, Taine shows that the difference between the literatures produced respectively by the Normans and by the Saxons was partly the difference between a ruling class, on the one hand, and a vanquished and repressed class, on the other. And Michelet, in his volume on the Regency, which was finished the same year that the *History of English Literature* appeared, studies the *Manon Lescaut* of the Abbé Prévost as a document representing the point of view of the small gentry before the French Revolution. But Marx and Engels derived the social classes from the way that people made or got their livings – from what they called the *methods of production*; and they tended to regard these economic processes as fundamental to civilization.

The Dialectical Materialism of Marx and Engels was not really so materialistic as it sounds. There was in it a large element of the Hegelian idealism that Marx and Engels thought they had got rid of. At no time did these two famous materialists take so mechanistic a view of things as Taine began by professing; and their theory of the relation of works of literature to what they called the *economic base* was a good deal less simple than Taine's theory of the moment, the race, and the milieu. They thought that art, politics, religion, philosophy, and literature belonged to what they called the *superstructure* of human activity; but they saw that the practitioners of these various professions tended also to constitute social groups, and that they were always pulling away from the kind of solidarity based on economic classes in order to establish a professional solidarity of their own. Furthermore, the activities of the superstructure could influence one another, and they could influence the economic base. It may be said of Marx and Engels in general that, contrary to the popular impression, they were tentative, confused, and modest when it came down to philosophical first principles, where a materialist like Taine was cocksure. Marx once made an attempt to explain why the poems of Homer were so good when the society that produced them was from his point of view – that is, from the point of view of its industrial development – so primitive; and this gave him a good deal of trouble. If we compare his discussion of this problem with Vico's discussion of Homer, we see that the explanation of literature in terms of a philosophy of social history is becoming, instead of simpler and easier, more difficult and more complex.

Marx and Engels were deeply imbued, moreover, with the German admiration for literature, which they had learned from the age of Goethe. It would never have occurred to either of them that *der Dichter* was not one of the noblest and most beneficent of humankind. When Engels writes about Goethe, he presents him as a man equipped for 'practical life', whose career was frustrated by the 'misery' of the historical situation in Germany in his time, and reproaches him for allowing himself to lapse into the 'cautious, smug, and narrow' philistinism of the class from which he came; but Engels regrets this, because it interfered with the development of the 'mocking, defiant, world-despising genius', '*der geniale Dichter*', '*der gewaltige Poet*', of whom Engels would not even, he says, have asked that he should have been a political liberal if Goethe had not sacrificed to his bourgeois shrinkings his truer aesthetic sense. And the great critics who were trained on Marx – Franz Mehring and Bernard Shaw – had all this reverence for the priesthood of literature. Shaw deplores the absence of political philosophy and what he regards as the middle-class snobbery in Shakespeare; but he celebrates Shakespeare's poetry and his dramatic imagination almost as enthusiastically as Swinburne does, describing even those potboiling comedies, *Twelfth Night* and *As You Like It* – the themes of which seem to him most trashy – as 'the Crown Jewels of English dramatic poetry'. Such a critic may do more for a writer by showing him as a real man dealing with a real world at a definite moment of time than the impressionist critic of Swinburne's type who flourished in the same period of the late nineteenth century. The purely impressionist critic approaches the whole of literature as an exhibit of belletristic jewels, and he can only write a rhapsodic catalogue. But when Shaw turned his spotlight on Shakespeare as a figure in the Shavian drama of history, he invested him with a new interest as no other English critic had done.

The insistence that the man of letters should play a political role, the disparagement of works of art in comparison with political action, were thus originally no part of Marxism. They only became associated with it later. This happened by way of Russia, and it was due to special tendencies in that country that date from long before the Revolution or the promulgation of Marxism itself. In Russia there have been very good reasons why the political implications of literature should particularly occupy the critics. The art of Pushkin itself, with its marvellous power of implication, had certainly been partly created by the censorship of Nicholas I, and Pushkin set the tradition for most of the great Russian writers that followed him. Every play, every poem, every story, must be a parable of which the moral is *implied*. If it were stated, the censor would suppress the book as he tried to do with Pushkin's *Bronze Horseman*, where it was merely a question of the packed implications protruding a little too plainly. Right down through the writings of Chekhov and up almost to the Revolution, the imaginative literature of Russia presents the peculiar paradox of an art that is technically objective and yet charged with social messages. In Russia under the Tsar, it was inevitable that social criticism should lead to political conclusions, because the most urgent need from the point of view of any kind of improvement was to get rid of the tsarist regime. Even the neo-Christian moralist Tolstoy, who pretended to be non-political, was to exert a subversive influence, because his independent preaching was bound to embroil him with the Church, and the Church was an integral part of the tsardom. Tolstoy's pamphlet called *What is Art?*, in which he throws overboard Shakespeare and a large part of modern literature, including his own novels, in the interest of his intransigent morality, is the example which is most familiar to us of the moralizing Russian criticism; but it was only the most sensational expression of a kind of approach which had been prevalent since Belinsky and Chernyshevsky in the early part of the century. The critics, who were usually journalists writing in exile or in a contraband press, were always tending to demand of the imaginative writers that they should dramatize bolder morals.

Even after the Revolution had destroyed the tsarist government, this state of things did not change. The old habits of censorship persisted in the new socialist society of the Soviets, which was necessarily made up of people who had been stamped by the die of despotism. We meet here the peculiar phenomenon of a series of literary groups that attempt, one after the other, to obtain official recognition or to make themselves sufficiently powerful to establish themselves as arbiters of literature. Lenin and Trotsky and Lunacharsky had the sense to oppose these attempts: the comrade-dictators of Proletcult or Lev or Rapp would certainly have been just as bad as the Count Benckendorff who made Pushkin miserable, and when the Stalin bureaucracy, after the death of Gorky, got control of this department as of everything else, they instituted a system of repression that made Benckendorff and Nicholas I look like Lorenzo de' Medici. In the meantime, Trotsky, who was Commissar of War but himself a great political writer with an interest in belles-lettres, attempted, in 1924, apropos of one of these movements, to clarify the situation. He wrote a brilliant and valuable book called *Literature and Revolution*, in which he explained the aims of the government, analysed the work of the Russian writers, and praised or rebuked the latter as they seemed to him in harmony or at odds with the former. Trotsky is intelligent, sympathetic; it is evident that he is really fond of literature and that he knows that a work of art does not fulfil its function in terms of the formulas of party propaganda. But Mayakovsky, the Soviet poet, whom Trotsky had praised with reservations, expressed himself in a famous joke when he was asked what he thought of Trotsky's book – a pun which implied that a Commissar turned critic was inevitably a Commissar still *; and what a foreigner cannot accept in Trotsky is his assumption that it is the duty of the government to take a hand in the direction of literature.

This point of view, indigenous to Russia, has been imported to other countries through the permeation of Communist influence. The Communist press and its literary followers have reflected the control of the Kremlin in all the phases through which it has passed, down to the whole-sale imprisonment of Soviet writers which has been taking place since 1935. But it has never been a part of the American system that our Republican or Democratic administration should lay down a political line for the guidance of the national literature. A recent gesture in this direction on the part of Archibald MacLeish, who seems a little carried away by his position as Librarian of Congress, was anything but cordially received by serious American writers. So long as the United States remains happily a non-totalitarian country, we can very well do without this aspect of the historical criticism of literature.

Another element of a different order has, however, since Marx's time been added to the historical study of the origins of works of literature. I mean the psychoanalysis of Freud. This appears as an extension of something which had already got well started before, which had figured even in Johnson's *Lives of the Poets*, and of which the great exponent had been Sainte-Beuve: the interpretation of works of literature in the

*Первый блин лег наркомом, *The first pancake lies like a narkom* (people's commissar) – a parody of the Russian saying, Первый блин лег комом, *The first pancake lies like a lump.*

light of the personalities behind them. But the Freudians made this interpretation more exact and more systematic. The great example of the psychoanalysis of an artist is Freud's own essay on Leonardo da Vinci; but this has little critical interest: it is an attempt to construct a case history. One of the best examples I know of the application of Freudian analysis to literature is in Van Wyck Brooks's book, *The Ordeal of Mark Twain*, in which Mr Brooks uses an incident of Mark Twain's boyhood as a key to his whole career. Mr Brooks has since repudiated the method he resorted to here, on the ground that no one but an analyst can ever know enough about a writer to make a valid psychoanalytic diagnosis. This is true, and it is true of the method that it has led to bad results where the critic has built a Freudian mechanism out of very slender evidence, and then given us what is really merely a romance exploiting the supposed working of this mechanism, in place of an actual study that sticks close to the facts and the documents of the writer's life and work. But I believe that Van Wyck Brooks really had hold of something important when he fixed upon that childhood incident of which Mark Twain gave so vivid an account to his biographer – that scene at the deathbed of his father when his mother had made him promise that he would not break her heart. If it was not one of those crucial happenings that are supposed to determine the complexes of Freud, it has certainly a typical significance in relation to Mark Twain's whole psychology. The stories that people tell about their childhood are likely to be profoundly symbolic even when they have been partly or wholly made up in the light of later experience. And the attitudes, the compulsions, the emotional 'patterns' that recur in the work of a writer are of great interest to the historical critic.

These attitudes and patterns are embedded in the community and the historical moment, and they may indicate its ideals and its diseases as the cell shows the condition of the tissue. The recent scientific experimentation in the combining of Freudian with Marxist method, and of psychoanalysis with anthropology, has had its parallel development in criticism. And there is thus another element added to our equipment for analysing literary works, and the problem grows still more complex.

The analyst, however, is of course not concerned with the comparative values of his patients any more than the surgeon is. He cannot tell you why the neurotic Dostoyevsky produces work of immense value to his fellows while another man with the same neurotic pattern would become a public menace. Freud himself emphatically states in his study of Leonardo that his method can make no attempt to account for Leonardo's genius. The problems of comparative artistic value still remain after we have given attention to the Freudian psychological factor just as they do after we have given attention to the Marxist economic factor and to the racial and geographical factors. No matter how thoroughly and searchingly we may have scrutinized works of literature from the historical and biographical points of view, we must be ready to attempt to estimate, in some such way as Saintsbury and Eliot do, the relative degrees of success attained by the products of the various periods and the various personalities. We must be able to tell good from bad, the first-rate from the second-rate. We shall not otherwise write literary criticism at all, but merely social or political history as reflected in literary texts, or psychological case histories from past eras, or, to take the historical point of view in its simplest and most academic form, merely chronologies of books that have been published.

And now how, in these matters of literary art, do we tell the good art from the bad? Norman Kemp Smith, the Kantian philosopher, whose courses I was fortunate enough to take at Princeton twenty-five years ago, used to tell us that this recognition was based primarily on an emotional reaction. For purposes of practical criticism this is a safe assumption on which to proceed. It is possible to discriminate in a variety of ways the elements that in any given department go to make a successful work of literature. Different schools have at different times demanded different things of literature: *unity, symmetry, universality, originality, vision, inspiration, strangeness, suggestiveness, improving morality, socialist realism,* etc. But you could have any set of these qualities that any school of writing has called for and still not have a good play, a good novel, a good poem, a good history. If you identify the essence of good literature with any one of these elements or with any combination of them, you simply shift the emotional reaction to the recognition of the element or elements. Or if you add to your other demands the demand that the writer must have *talent,* you simply shift this recognition to the talent. Once people find some grounds of agreement in the coincidence of their emotional reactions to books, they may be able to discuss these elements profitably; but if they do not have this basic agreement, the discussion will make no sense.

But how, you may ask, can we identify this élite who know what they are talking about? Well, it can only be said of them that they are self-appointed and self-perpetuating, and that they will compel you to accept their authority. Impostors may try to put themselves over, but these quacks will not last. The implied position of the people who know about literature (as is also the case in every other art) is simply that they know what they know, and that they are determined to impose their opinions by main force of eloquence or assertion on the people who do not know. This is not a question, of course, of professional workers in literature – such as editors, professors, and critics, who very often have no real understanding of the products with which they deal – but of readers of all kinds in all walks of life. There are moments when a first-rate writer, unrecognized or out of fashion with the official chalkers-up for the market, may find his support in the demand for his work of an appreciative cultivated public.

But what is the cause of this emotional reaction which is

the critic's divining rod? This question has long been a subject of study by the branch of philosophy called aesthetics, and it has recently been made a subject of scientific experimentation. Both these lines of inquiry are likely to be prejudiced in the eyes of the literary critic by the fact that the inquiries are sometimes conducted by persons who are obviously deficient in literary feeling or taste. Yet one should not deny the possibility that something of value might result from the speculations and explorations of men of acute minds who take as their primary data the aesthetic emotions of other men.

Almost everybody interested in literature has tried to explain to himself the nature of these emotions that register our approval of artistic works; and I of course have my own explanation.

In my view, all our intellectual activity, in whatever field it takes place, is an attempt to give a meaning to our experience – that is, to make life more practicable; for by understanding things we make it easier to survive and get around among them. The mathematician Euclid, working in a convention of abstractions, shows us relations between the distances of our unwieldy and cluttered-up environment upon which we are able to count. A drama of Sophocles also indicates relations between the various human impulses, which appear so confused and dangerous, and it brings out a certain justice of Fate – that is to say, of the way in which the interaction of these impulses is seen in the long run to work out – upon which we can also depend. The kinship, from this point of view, of the purposes of science and art appears very clearly in the case of the Greeks, because not only do both Euclid and Sophocles satisfy us by making patterns, but they make much the same kind of patterns. Euclid's *Elements* takes simple theorems and by a series of logical operations builds them up to a climax in the square on the hypotenuse. A typical drama of Sophocles develops in a similar way.

Some writers (as well as some scientists) have a different

kind of explicit message beyond the reassurance implicit in the mere feat of understanding life or of moulding the harmony of artistic form. Not content with such an achievement as that of Sophocles – who has one of his choruses tell us that it is better not to be born, but who, by representing life as noble and based on law, makes its tragedy easier to bear – such writers attempt, like Plato, to think out and recommend a procedure for turning it into something better. But other departments of literature – lyric poetry such as Sappho's, for example – have *less* philosophical content than Sophocles. A lyric gives us nothing but a pattern imposed on the expression of a feeling; but this pattern of metrical quantities and of consonants and vowels that balance has the effect of reducing the feeling, however unruly or painful it may seem when we experience it in the course of our lives, to something orderly, symmetrical, and pleasing; and it also relates this feeling to the more impressive scheme, works it into the larger texture, of the body of poetic art. The discord has been resolved, the anomaly subjected to discipline. And this control of his emotion by the poet has the effect at second-hand of making it easier for the reader to manage his own emotions. (Why certain sounds and rhythms gratify us more than others, and how they are connected with the themes and ideas that they are chosen as appropriate for conveying, are questions that may be passed on to the scientist.)

And this brings us back again to the historical point of view. The experience of mankind on the earth is always changing as man develops and has to deal with new combinations of elements; and the writer who is to be anything more than an echo of his predecessors must always find expression for something which has never yet been expressed, must master a new set of phenomena which has never yet been mastered. With each such victory of the human intellect, whether in history, in philosophy, or in poetry, we experience a deep satisfaction: we have been

of some ache of disorder, relieved of some oppressive
n of uncomprehended events.

as relief that brings the sense of power, and, with the
of power, joy, is the positive emotion which tells us
we have encountered a first-rate piece of literature.
t stay! you may at this point warn: are not people often
placed and exhilarated by literature of the trashiest kind?
hey are: crude and limited people do certainly feel some
uch emotion in connexion with work that is limited and
rude. The man who is more highly organized and has a
wider intellectual range will feel it in connexion with work
that is finer and more complex. The difference between the
emotion of the more highly organized man and the emotion
of the less highly organized one is a matter of mere gradation.
You sometimes discover books – the novels of John Stein-
beck, for example – that seem to mark precisely the border-
line between work that is definitely superior and work that is
definitely bad. When I was speaking a little while back of the
genuine connoisseurs who establish the standards of taste, I
meant, of course, the people who can distinguish Grade A
and who prefer it to the other grades.